GENERATION

OF WEALTH

GENERATION
OF WEALTH

Time-Tested Rules for Worry-Free Investing

JULIUS WESTHEIMER

bancroft
press

BALTIMORE, MD

Published by Bancroft Press
P.O. Box 65360, Baltimore, MD 21209 (800) 637-7377
www.bancroftpress.com

ISBN 0-9631246-9-2
Library of Congress Catalog Card Number 97-75067
Printed in the United States of America

First edition

1   3   5   7   9   10   8   6   4   2

Designed by Melinda Russell, Bancroft Press
Distributed to the trade by National Book Network, Lanham, MD

To Dorrit Westheimer,
my wife, who worked day and night for years
to help me get this book written and published.
Without her support, Generation of Wealth *would still be a dream.*

To the late Milton F. Westheimer,
my father, a stock broker, whose guidance was invaluable.
I wish I'd have listened to more of his superior guidance.

$\mathcal{A}$CKNOWLEDGEMENTS

Carolyn Walpert, my capable assistant for 36 years.

Mark Dyer, my loyal business partner and tower of strength for 22 years.

Morry Zolet, my creative and capable business partner for 11 years.

Brian Kroneberger, Jr., my newest partner.

(*When I refer in the text to "my partners," I mean Mark Dyer, Morry Zolet, and Brian Kroneberger, whether I mention them by name or not.*).

George Ferris, CEO, Ferris Baker Watts, whose organization has allowed me to "do my thing," including all of my outside activities.

Bruce Bortz, Bancroft Press, my publisher, who kept telling me I had something valuable to say and whom I now believe was probably right.

Evonne Smitt of Bancroft Press, who lovingly edited and shaped *Generation of Wealth* into the readable, useful book I think it is.

The late Ernestine H. Westheimer, my wife of 45 years, who lent solid encouragement every step of my brokerage and journalistic career.

My daughters Pat and Gloria, who cheered me up on "down" days and gave great ideas for this book.

Sue Ransohoff, my sister, who bucked me up when I suffered "writer's block."

"WALL $TREET WEEK WITH LOUIS RUKEYSER"

Louis Rukeyser, host, who put me on his show 27 years ago, "kept me going" these many years, honored me graciously on my 80th birthday, and offered kind words in print about this, my first book. All of that means a great deal more to me personally than I can ever say.

Rich Dubroff, Executive Producer, who helped me numerous times on the show and with this book. John Davis, Senior Producer.

George Beneman, director. Natalie Seltz ("Ms. Smyth"), who, for 27 years, has brought us on the set at show's opening, then rejoined us at the end.

Anne Truax Darlington, creator of the show, who asked me to be an original panelist, 1970.

Co-panelists who gave me helpful ideas: Frank Cappiello (who also went beyond the call of duty to provide this book a wonderful testimonial), Gail Dudack, Alan Bond, Eddie Brown, Monte Gordon, Marty Zweig, Mary Farrell, Bob Stovall. Some well-known guests with whom I've appeared on this coast-to-coast TV show: Alan Greenspan, John Templeton, Jack Kemp, Henry Kaufman.

WBAL RADIO, BALTIMORE

Alfred E. Burk, former general manager, who hired me in 1981 as financial broadcaster. Ed Kiernan, Vice President and General Manager, WBAL-AM and WIYY-FM. Jeff Beauchamp, Vice President and Station Manager, who opened the station's 50,000 watt microphones to me in 1981 and has kept a place for me ever since. Mark Miller, news director, WBAL Radio. Michael Wellbrock, executive producer.

Talk-show hosts who have been good to me: Allan Prell, Ron Smith, and Bruce Elliott. Alan Walden, morning newscaster, who offered encouragement and guidance. Dave Durian, WBAL Radio morning show anchorman. Adam Gold, producer, WBAL Radio morning show. Ryan Bogash, WBAL Radio producer, who (at 5 a.m.) helps me record my afternoon show. Aaron Harris, WBAL Radio music director and producer.

WBAL TV, CHANNEL 11, NBC IN BALTIMORE

Phil Stolz, vice-president and general manager, who always wrote me encouraging notes about my my TV broadcasting activities. Katherine Green, News Director, who has consistently supported all my appearances on Channel 11 (pre-dawn, noon, evening, and late). David Roberts, my long-time News Director, now News Director at WXIA-TV, Atlanta who pushed me forward at WBAL-TV and suggested "Tip of The Day," a popular daily feature. Carolyn McEnrue, Tony Pann, Liz O'Neill, and the other folks I share the set with regularly.

Tina Jolly, Holly Gauntt, Augusta Brennan, supportive executives at WBAL-TV. Lorna Adolph, long-time director, WBAL-TV News. Jon Petrovich, who hired me for WBAL-TV back in 1981, and is now Executive Producer of CNN Headline News.

THE BALTIMORE SUN

Gerald Merrell, Business Editor, who edits and publishes my "Ticker" column every Wednesday and Friday. His business section provides excellent coverage of local and national financial matters. Georgia Marudas, Deputy Business Editor, who unsplits my infinitives and shortens my long run-on sentences. Harold Williams, retired Sunday editor, *The Sun*, who printed some of my first articles and photographs. The late Philip Heisler, former managing editor, *The Evening Sun*, who hired me "on the spot" in 1977 to write "The Ticker" column. It's still going strong, 20 years later.

Fred Rasmussen, veteran writer and great guy, who, among other things, is writing my obituary. Gilbert Sandler, who gave me good publicity in his many op-ed articles. Eric Siegel, reporter, who encouraged me along the way. Sun publishers who apparently liked my output over the years: William F. Schmick, Jr., Donald H. Patterson, Reg Murphy, Michael Davies and Mary Junck. The folks at the Los Angeles Times syndicate, which has carried my column and allowed its appearances all over the country for years.

SPECIAL FRIENDS

Arthur J. Gutman, an involved, capable friend who provided valuable ideas for this book, and who also helped publicize it. Carla Hayden, director, Enoch Pratt Free Library, to which I've always been devoted. Ann Neumann, who helps me write about — and answer TV questions concerning — real estate, REITs, mortgages, home equity loans, etc. Michael Davis, Editor, *The Jewish Times*, who has always shown interest in my work. The late Bill Leonard, President, CBS News, who encouraged me to write a column, "Give Us This Day," for *The Daily Dartmouth* in 1936. *Baltimore Magazine*, which has profiled me with cover stories several times over the years. Johns Hopkins University, where I taught evening investment classes for 15 years. Wharton School of Finance where, with the Securities Industry Association, I taught security salesmanship for 20 years. Dan Dorfman, former columnist, *Wall Street Journal* (now with *Financial World*), who wrote about my growth stocks in the 1970's. Robert Metz, *New York Times*, who also wrote about my growth stock notions in his "Market Place" column. The editors of *Registered Representative*, who paid me the high honor of calling me, in a very kind cover profile, "America's Best Known Retail Broker." Jack Russell, Park School English teacher who taught me how to write, and who took a final look at my coast-to-coast prize-winning Wharton School essay, "Fundamentals of Securities Salesmanship."

DOCTORS & SURGEONS

These are some of the medical professionals who have kept me alive and healthy for 81 years, allowing me to actively pursue my activities: Norris Horwitz, Boris Kerzner, Joseph Salomon, Jerry Hofkin, Steve Acuff, William Baumgartner, Michael Schultz, Howard Weiss, Irv Pollack, Harold Katz, and Jeffrey Schein.

If there's anybody I left out, it was unintentional. If there's anything wrong in the ensuing pages, it's my fault and no one else's.

CONTENTS

Acknowledgements   I

Introduction: **The Generation of Wealth**   **1**
    Why Another Book?
    Generation of Wealth
    A Conservative Investor
    Giving Something Back

Chapter 1: **Investing as a Way of Life**   **9**
    Before Investing
    Procrastinating Doesn't Earn Much
    Overcoming Fear

Chapter 2: **Your Tolerance for Risk**   **19**
    Too High: The Speculative Craze of the Twenties
    Too Low: The "What if I Lose It All" Syndrome
    You Must Be Comfortable

Chapter 3: **What's a Broker?**   **31**
    Why Do I Need a Broker?
    What Do I Do As a Broker?
    Results Are What Count

Chapter 4: **Choosing a Broker**   **51**
    How To Choose?
    What Makes a Good Broker?
    The Small-Time Blues
    Investment Clubs
    When Things Go Wrong
    "Tele-brokers"

Chapter 5: **Reading the Stock Listings**　　　　75
    Stocks Without Dividends
    Stocks *With* Dividends
    The Feeling Is Mutual

Chapter 6: **The Housekeeping of Investing**　　　　87
    Leave Your Stock With the Broker
    How to Read Corporate Reports
    Proxies
    Interest Rate Fluctuations
    How Often Should You Track Your Stocks?
    Don't Discard Your Monthly Statements

Chapter 7: **Tracking the Market**　　　　101
    The Trouble with Bombardment
    The "Good Media"
    The Unreliability Factor
    The Powerful Hand of the Press
    Company-Driven Publicity
    "Info-brokers"

Chapter 8: **Mutual Funds**　　　　119
    Are Mutual Funds for You?
    Mutual Funds in Your 401(k)
    Choosing a Mutual Fund
    Bond Mutual Funds

Chapter 9: **Bonds and Fixed Income Investments**　　　　133
    Bonds are Secure
    Before You Invest with Bonds
    Choosing Bond Investments
    Which Way Interest Rates?
    Corporate Bonds
    Tax-Free Municipal Bonds
    Zero Coupon Bonds
    Cash Reserves and Money Market Accounts
    Certificates of Deposit

Real Estate Investments
Are Annuities For You?
Are Metals Precious?

Chapter 10: **Stock-picking**   **163**
Take Anecdotal Evidence with a Grain of Salt
The "Hold-Everything" Philosophy
Diversifying By Sector
Initial Public Offerings (IPOs)
Don't Get Infatuated
Don't Overlook Dow Five and Ten Theories
Pros and Cons of Investing Locally

Chapter 11: **To Be a Savvy Investor**   **189**
Spread Your Risk
Don't Over-Diversify
Stick to Fundamentals
Let Dividend Increases Be One Guide
Price/Earnings Ratio
What Does "Earnings Per Share" Mean?
One Size Doesn't Fit All
Don't Believe Everything You Read

Chapter 12: **Savings and Earnings for Your Future**   **211**
For Your Retirement
For Your Child's Future
Other People's Money
For Richer, For Poorer
As You Grow Old

Appendix: **227**

Index: **233**

The Generation of Wealth

If you're like me, you have enough problems in life without having to worry whether some foolish move will instantly wipe out your savings.

The other day, an older couple paid me the ultimate compliment. Twenty-five years ago, when they were just getting underway as investors, working for salaries and raising their family, they retained me as their broker. I gave them investment advice and handled some of their stock transactions. They did well, meeting their financial needs of the time. Several years after retiring, however, they decided to roll the dice and transfer a good chunk of their portfolio to a New York investment manager who, friends of theirs told them, had made them a lot of money.

It didn't work out so well for this couple. For three years during which the market as a whole was going up and up, their man in New York was betting the other way, concentrating on selling short, and hoping to benefit from expected drops in stock prices. Unfortunately, he bet wrong more often than he bet right, he lost money for their account, and they became quite worried and upset.

They apparently did not fully appreciate the risks he would be taking with their money.

After a very bumpy ride, this couple apparently decided that they would rather invest their money with a minimum of risk — so that, under my renewed guidance, they could generate wealth the way my father and his generation did — safely, conservatively, and without, as Dad used to say, "grabbing for the last 10 percent."

If you're like this couple — in fact, if you're like me — you have enough problems in life without having to worry whether some foolish move will instantly wipe out your investments. You want to sleep at night, knowing that your money is secure, that it will be there when you need it later. I hope that, like this couple and many of my other clients, you will find my investment approach reassuring.

I'm proud to say that this "minimize your risks" approach, explained in *Generation of Wealth*, is built around the use of professional assistance. No matter how many investment advice books you read and commit to memory, including this one, I strongly advise you to have a broker or other investment professional helping you. There is no replacement for personal contact with a broker who understands your changing wants and needs and can invest your money the way you want it invested.

WHY ANOTHER BOOK?

One day, some time ago, I woke up and said to myself, "So many people feel insecure about investing. Many procrastinate way too long. I've had a very successful career. I'm almost 80. All but ten of my adult years have been spent in the investing business. Wouldn't it be nice to leave behind what I've learned, not learned, and should have learned? Wouldn't that be a useful legacy to leave behind?" Fortunately, an experienced, sophisticated book publisher in my hometown of Baltimore immediately jumped on the idea, and here is our product.

Nobody has to tell me how many other investment advice books there are. As a broker for 35 years, and a newspaper columnist and TV/radio financial analyst for 25, I've seen them all. Practically every one of these investment book contains some of the same information and advice. But many are quite different.

In the end, it's no accident that this area of endeavor is called "personal investing." Not only is it personal to the advice-giver, but it's very personal to the advice-getter. Put another way, no investment advice fits all people simultaneously. Everyone's tolerance for risk is different. Everyone's financial circumstances are different.

In a world awash in investment information and advice, I write to leave behind what's worked for my father (himself a longtime stockbroker), his clients, my clients, and, I daresay, many of my longtime readers, viewers, and listeners.

On TV and radio, as in newspapers, millions of Americans have listened to my advice over the years. The advice is what's worked for my clients. It's what people have paid attention to.

In some cases, it's even worked well for non-clients. In 1987, I was sitting at my office desk when my phone rang. The man running the large pension fund for State of Maryland employees was calling with a thank-you. "Westy," he said, " you saved Maryland $1 billion."

"How?" I asked.

"All of us were nervous about the market — and wondered what to do. Then the state comptroller [Louis Goldstein] came into our pension board meeting and said, 'I just heard Julius Westheimer say on WBAL Radio that if you're terribly worried about your stocks, sell half of your positions.' That's what we did. One week before the October 1987 crash, we sold half of our portfolio and you saved us an absolute fortune."

In my years as an investment manager and a financial journalist, I've tried — as I have in this book — to keep it as simple as possible.

Many of my simple rules originated with my father and his brothers, who headed their own investment firms and banks. Some, like the Dow Five and the Dow Ten, are relatively new. All are for the investor who wants to sleep well at night.

GENERATION OF WEALTH

I chose the title for this book very carefully and with great pride. The word "generation" means a great deal to me, because I was born into the investing business. From the time I was a child, I was trained in it. I remember the roughest times in the stock market. I lived and worked through them. From the inside, I came to know some of the people who lost their shirts. I remember not seeing my father at home for a full two weeks when the market was crashing in 1929.

Investing is so much in my blood that I made it my second career — one I entered in the early 1960s. It was then that I set about learning the business on my own. I adapted my father's knowledge and the views of others. I hustled for business. I mastered, then taught, the techniques of selling.

I soon realized that, in personal investing, and in investor advising, there is a flip side to everything — very few concepts are absolute or unanimously accepted. I also found that, like my father, I preferred the proverbial tortoise to the notorious hare. I wanted my clients' money to grow slowly, rather than race to the finish line and be lost. I have never gotten one of Dad's repeated sayings out of my mind: "Son, trees don't grow to the sky." He meant that there is a limit to how high the market will go. It can't just keep going up and up forever.

As you'll discover, I'm old-fashioned in some of my opinions and attitudes, and *au courant* in others. I respect the marketplace a great deal. Unlike many of the whiz kids of the securities business today (forgive my prejudice!), I've lived through down markets. I have felt the investor's pain. I have personally felt the pain of loss, as advisor and as investor. It was during the market's ups and downs that I cobbled together my investing philosophy. This book is the sum total of my experiences and insights. It aims for generating wealth without taking on an unsettling amount of risk. It argues that some of the best investment strategies you can adopt trace back to my father's generation, and to my own — strategies that have proven themselves over time and several generations.

A CONSERVATIVE INVESTOR

Mention my name to most brokers and they'll tell you: "No razzle-dazzle, no gimmicks, no shortcuts — just solid, proven techniques that may even be a little boring." I happily wear my industry reputation as a conservative advisor. My longtime friend Louis Rukeyser gently needles me about it, reminding me how surprised I am that the market continues to soar.

During the last 15 years in the U.S. (1982-1997), we have witnessed a very strange and wondrous market that seems to go upward continually. My clients and I have done well during this period, but, as Dad would put it, I haven't reached for the sky. The trees don't grow that far. I have not tried for 50 percent annual returns on investment, or even 30 percent. I have been content doing as well as the market, or a little better.

To use a baseball analogy, I don't swing for the fences and try to hit home runs. I'd rather hit singles and doubles and — most of all — not strike out. And I have reached that goal practically every year. Among panelists on "Wall $treet Week With Louis Rukeyser" who put down their best investment selections at the beginning of each year, I never end up at the very top, but I'm usually within shouting distance of it.

Perhaps the market will keep right on going skyward in the years ahead. But I'm inclined to think that markets go in cycles. Although I'm happy to earn all the money the stock market has to give, I feel certain that investment times will, eventually, become rougher than they are today. Major corrections will happen. They always do. The market is predictable for its unpredictability.

It's primarily for that reason that I want investors to set up portfolios that aren't buffeted by the headlines. I want them to invest in good companies, to diversify, to invest in tax-free bonds, to have some of their investment dollars in foreign/international companies, to put some of their funds in mutual funds, and to use the Dow Five or Dow Ten approach to investing. When your money is spread out in this fashion, you are less likely to lose it.

GIVING SOMETHING BACK

More than anything else, I'd like this book to help you become a successful, confident, secure investor. That kind of investing is not only possible: It is smart. Dad always said that it was a lot better to sleep well at night than to have an extra meal during the day.

I'm grateful for my my many blessings and good fortune and want to give something back to a world that's been good to me. With humility, I offer this book as a way of sharing some of my experiences with people who may find them valuable.

So this book is very personal and very different from others you may have read. It's me. I stand before you not as an authority figure but to tell you what's worked and not worked for me. It's the distillation of all I learned about investing. It is not intended as an encyclopedic reference. Many such books are available.

Nor is it a compilation of columns or articles that I wrote and have been previously published. To make the original contribution I intended, I started this book with a terrifyingly blank page and placed every word here after asking myself one basic question: "What do I know and what have I seen that really matters and that I can well explain?"

And, rather than couch my answers in cold, stilted, formal language, I tried to be as conversational as possible, as if I were having a conversation with you the reader rather than delivering some monumental lecture to an audience of faceless figures.

I also plead guilty to repeating myself at times, but it was intentional. Some of the important concepts I talk about overlap from one chapter to the next, from one important subject to the next. Not knowing if everyone would read the book straight through, as planned, I decided that a certain amount of reiteration was necessary, especially for those who decide to read the chapters piecemeal or out of order.

Another caveat to bear in mind as you look over the book: In those instances where I used real life companies as examples, I did so merely to make a point more vivid and understandable, especially in the chapter on how to make the most of the stock listings. Unless I said so expressly, I was not recommending the purchase or sale of the companies mentioned.

I'm glad you're going along with me on this journey, heading out towards the goal we all share: the generation of wealth. To be useful is my life's work, and I leave this book behind in that spirit. Only you can say ultimately whether I've succeeded.

Julius Westheimer
Baltimore
August 1997

P.S. Life is a long series of changes we often can't anticipate. And so is investing. I'll never forget that sign in a New York City restaurant. It read: "Life is uncertain. Eat your dessert first." Please dig into *Generation of Wealth* as soon as you can.

CHAPTER ONE

Investing as a Way of Life

*Don't be a "market timer." The best time to invest
is when you have the money.*

As a broker, I deal with a crucial part of my client's life. Outside of
the obvious other things like decent health, a good marriage,
and a happy relationship with family, financial security may be
the most critical. Without financial security, life is a terrible struggle —
a monthly battle to survive, with nothing left over for simple enjoyment.

There are two kinds of expenses we incur in life. First, there are the
must-pay bills like rent, mortgage, food, medicine, and utilities. Then
there are the discretionary bills. From time to time, most of us like to
travel, eat out, and buy nice clothes. This second level of bills can never
be reached until the first level has been paid. Without a good financial
base, you may have to cut out a few discretionary things *now* so that you
can afford to incur other discretionary expenses *later.*

Investment is the best way I know to guarantee financial security.
The problem is that the vast majority of people find lots of convenient
excuses for not investing. Other things always jump to the top of their

money priority list, though they may not be truly the most important things in their lives.

Intellectually, people know they must put money aside for retirement. However, they often think they will need two or three thousand dollars just to get started, and so they wait. Coming up with two or three thousand dollars can be difficult. The fact is, though, that you don't have to wait to come into a lot of money before you begin saving for retirement. That's why I like the retirement accounts that are funded straight from weekly, bi-weekly, or monthly paychecks. They build up quickly and can be invested sooner than taxed income.

Most people invest only when money is taken out of their paychecks. If they don't see it, they can't spend it. By anticipating their own weaknesses, they do themselves a big favor. Money that goes straight from a paycheck into a retirement program escapes income tax. It doesn't even show up on the W-2 tax form for their 401(k) or 403(b). For some reason, more people seem more interested in legitimately avoiding taxes than they are in putting money into the stock market.

A lot of people say to me, "Westy, I can't max out on my 401(k). I can't put in 100 percent of what they allow." Most people who feel this way about their retirement plans think they will not be able to survive now if they invest some of their earnings for later. They may also lack the discipline to reduce expenses they've become accustomed to paying. The temptations, obviously, are quite great: Shopping malls, trips, restaurants, gift-giving at Christmas time. But I think it is better to put some of that money into investing. Over time, it's going to add up. In fact, it should grow ten and a half percent a year.

It may be a little high-handed to say this, but I often tell people, "If you can live on 100 percent of your income, you can probably live on 90 percent of it." Most people can survive quite nicely if they never see the extra ten percent. There are enough discretionary expenditures that they can say no to. Soon, they will have enough to invest. And their money will build up quickly in a 401(k) because it's not taxed.

The easiest way to be a good investor is to "max out" on your retirement contributions. Cutting as little as 10 percent of your discretionary spending usually allows you to "go to the max."

If you really cannot spare anything from your paycheck, make yourself invest when you "come into money," which happens with surprising regularity. Not many people win the lottery, but they sometimes receive substantial amounts of money — at tax-refund time or with end-of-year bonuses. Most often, people "have money" when they come into an inheritance, or when there's a lump sum distribution from a retirement program. Over the years, a lot of my clients at some point or another have been beneficiaries of an inheritance.

BEFORE INVESTING

Before you invest in the stock market, your first and primary investment must be in yourself. To build your own long-term financial security, you should have a strong education, get a good job, take supplemental courses, go to job-related conferences, and read up on your business. You have to invest in your own business and your own future, because your earning power is the most dependable investment you have. Your career is not peripheral to your welfare. It is hard, even silly, to disassociate your job from your money.

I wrote a paper once on how to get a job. I mention this here because I think it is particularly important that you use, and invest in, your most important commodity: yourself. Your own earning power is the best thing you have going for you. And finding a job is strictly sales: You are selling yourself. Don't spend too much time talking to low-end clerks. Talk to the person who has the power to hire you. Many job seekers spin their wheels and waste their time because they don't know how to get into the power structure.

It's not that hard. When you are looking for a job, you've got to do research. Find out who the boss is, either by calling the library or making friends with one of the employees. The boss is always looking for good people to feather his nest. Personnel departments typically are trying to get rid of you. If you can get to the person who has the power to

AUTHOR AT CAMP, 1929

In my teens, after school and on Saturday mornings, I would go down to 211 East Redwood Street in Baltimore where Dad's bro-kerage office was. I was what was called a board boy. In those days, there were no electronic boards. The stock quotations came from New York by telegraph into a bell shaped glass jar under which chattered a machine called the ticker. Out of that bell jar streamed a narrow yellow piece of tape called ticker tape. The tape was worthless after you had recorded on it. So, they threw ticker tape out office windows like confetti. That's why tick-er tape parades in New York were usu-ally held on Wall Street. (Of course, that is also where I got the name for my newspaper column in The Baltimore Sun, "The Ticker.")

The bell jar was in my father's smoke-filled board room, where dozens, maybe hundreds, of investors watched. The tape would be projected onto a screen called the Translux. The stock symbols and their latest quota-tion went by fairly quickly. It was my job to put the stock prices up on a huge blackboard, so investors had more time to see where their stocks stood. I wasn't the only one posting the results in chalk. My part of the board might be say, U.S. Steel (the symbol for which was and is X) to Woolworth (the symbol for which was and is Z). After my part of the board was filled, I erased the old prices to put up the new ones. At the time, there were only two ways to find out the stock prices: by watching in one of these board rooms, or by reading the newspaper — which was printed in several different edi-tions every day.

Dad would bring home the Five Star Financial, the Six Star Market Close Edition, or the Seven Star Edition so that he had the last stock quotes of the day. I did my boardwork mostly during the era of rapidly plunging stock prices. The big crash was in October 1929. I was 13 then, and remember seeing many people in tears.

Once, at the dinner table, Dad said, "Now children, we're in the midst of a terrible depression. I'd like each of you to come up with an idea of how we can save some money." One of my ideas was to cut out the home delivery of the Evening Sun, which Dad was bringing home anyway. He took up my idea, but my father wasn't poor in those dark days. Even though he lost part of his invested wealth dur-ing the crash, his brokerage firm, Westheimer and Company, was very profitable, because the trading volume was huge. He even had enough to pay me $5 a week. ❧

hire you, show him your wares, and convince him that you can put money in his till, you'll probably get a job. It's all about sales.

Take, for example, Carl Bernstein, who turned out to be one of the two reporters on the *Washington Post* who made such a tremendous reputation uncovering Watergate (the other was his investigative colleague, Bob Woodward). Long before Watergate, Bernstein wanted to get a job with the *Post.* He finally found out the home telephone number of Ben Bradlee, the newspaper's executive editor. He called that number on a Saturday morning and talked to Sally Quinn, Bradlee's wife. He said, "I'm Carl Bernstein. I must talk to Mr. Bradlee, it's absolutely urgent, because I've got something that he wants." Words to that effect. She said to him, "He's painting the roof. He can't talk to you." Bernstein, with nothing to lose, said, "Get him down off the ladder. I absolutely have to talk to him. I've got a news scoop he's got to hear." Quinn got Bradlee off the roof and Bernstein, by his pluck, was eventually hired. The rest, as they say, is history.

The story of Bernstein's hiring at the *Post,* which is at least 90 percent accurate, provides a couple of lessons. The first is that you're more likely to get a job when you're not responding to an ad. And if you go to large enough organizations like the *Post,* whether or not they're actually looking for someone at the time, they'll hire someone they really like. There's always room for one more.

Once, I wanted desperately to do business with the head of a large company here in Baltimore, and he wasn't returning my calls. I decided to greet him when he parked his car at work in the morning. So one weekday I drove out to his office parking lot, where I saw a bunch of signs reserved for the top brass. As I arrived, one fellow, whom I sort of knew, hopped out of his car. "Julius Westheimer," I introduced myself, "I've just got to see you for five minutes. I've got an opportunity that I think" — "Come on in, Westy," he interrupted. "Let's have some coffee."

Sometimes you've got to take chances like that. The head honcho's secretary is paid to protect him, not to put my calls through. You've got to use every connection and everything you can think of when you really want a job.

Tell the boss, "I promise not to take too much of your time. I'll put my watch on your desk and if I'm here more than 10 minutes, you can have it." So you offer to give him a $15 Timex. He won't take it anyway.

Another time, I wanted to sell tax-free municipal bonds to a well-known, affluent Baltimore real estate man, but was having trouble getting an appointment. I found out where his locker was at our country club and what time he played golf. One Sunday I showed up just as he was putting his golf shoes on and — with one shoe on and the other half off — he said, "OK, Westy call me tomorrow and we'll discuss your bonds." He became one of my best bond customers.

The great part about these strategies is they can't backfire, because you're absolutely nowhere anyhow. It harks back to the old days, when people got jobs just by waiting around and showing they were determined and committed, rather than sending in a resume in response to a published ad.

DON'T PUT IT OFF

When you are happy with your job and your earning potential, it's time to invest in the stock market.

I have known many people who put off deciding what to do with their money. Some placed it in a money market fund in order to delay making an investment decision. Doing nothing, I point out, is a decision also, but frequently a bad one. An error of omission, particularly in the strong stock market we've had, can be very expensive. The money you have in a money market account could be growing in the stock market, but, by not deciding on stocks, you lose that possibility.

Take the case of the fellow who inherited $360,000 from his mother. Because of a business deadline, he delayed making permanent investment decisions, putting the entire amount inherited into a money market account. If he allowed deadlines to keep coming for a year, and his money continued to make four percent in a money market account, he would earn $14,400 a year in income, whereas he could be making

$36,000 by investing the money in the stock market. His decision to forego the stock investment decision for a year would cost him almost $22,000.

Apparently, this individual was more interested in devoting his time and energy to his number one source of revenue, namely his occupation, than he was in sitting down and stewing over the investment of his money. It may just have been a delaying tactic by someone uncomfortable or unfamiliar with investing. It may have been the result of fear. Or it may have been the correct move.

The market has gone straight up to where we now are, with the Dow Jones over 8,000. A lot of people are still afraid of a crash. "Isn't the market too high now?" they ask. There's no right answer to that question. Who says we're not going to have another October 1987 collapse? In that recession, stocks lost 25 percent of their value in just a few days, and only recovered 18 months later.

OVERCOMING FEAR

Some people refuse to invest when the market is high. That might seem reasonable, although it shouldn't keep *you* from investing. Other people will not invest when the market is "too low." That is plain silly.

You should never be afraid of a low market. My father used to say, "One dollar invested on Black Friday is worth $10 invested on any other day." In other words, when the boardrooms are empty, you can make far more money than when they are filled. When stocks are put on sale involuntarily, it's a good time to invest. Louis Rukeyser once said, "Wall Street is the only place where they hang out a bargain sign and no one comes rushing." People dash out to shoe stores when there's a sale, but they dash *out* of the stock market when *stocks* are on sale.

The problem, I guess, is a lack of certainty; you don't know how much lower the sale price will go. People get scared, often at the wrong time. When the market had a shakeout like it did in mid-July of 1997, people should have been putting more money into the market, not less.

Do not avoid investing because of fear. I have said before and will say again, "Your emotions are often the best *reverse indicator* of what you should do in the stock market." Your fear during a low market is usually misplaced.

You may have a whole truckload of reasons holding you back from investing. Everyone has them. Some time ago, a mutual fund ran an advertisement listing 60 reasons given over 60 years for not investing in the stock market. Mostly these were world events or market occurrences — "bad news" headlines that kept people from investing because "it was not the right time." (*See Appendix.*) But $10,000 invested in the stock market 60 years ago, achieving only an average return, would now be worth $6,600,000. Now that is "bad news" for the people who hesitated.

My Uncle Irvin, my father's brother and a prominent stockbroker in Cincinnati, advised me, "Build a portfolio for your clients that every headline doesn't buffet." He was right. Yes, there are crises that can stagger an entire nation. But you lose much more by letting even big crises keep you from investing. It is foolish to say, "Oh, it might be a good idea someday to invest in the market," then wait for the perfect time. There is never an absolutely right time, but that doesn't mean it is the wrong time to invest.

Investing in the stock market is something you do for the long term. It secures your financial future. And, as that mutual fund advertisement suggested, it is well worth overcoming your initial fear of diving in.

CHAPTER SUMMARY:
INVESTING AS A WAY OF LIFE

1. *Without financial security, life is a terrible struggle — a monthly battle to pay the bills.*

2. *Cut out the fat in your discretionary spending and invest for your own future.*

3. *Get a good job. It's okay to use bold or radical methods.*

4. *Take the fullest advantage of the pension plans available to you at work.*

5. *The best time to invest is when you have money.*

6. *Invest in yourself and in your career before you invest in the stock market.*

7. *Don't let bad headlines keep you from investing.*

8. *"Build a portfolio that every headline won't buffet."* — *Uncle Irvin*

CHAPTER TWO

Your Tolerance for Risk

Hope is a good breakfast
but a poor supper.

It is important that you know, right from the start, your own risk tolerance as an investor. First, you'll be able to say what kind of stocks you're willing to try. Second, you'll be able to tell your broker how much you're willing to gain or lose, over what period of time. It is a good idea to test your own tolerance for risk on a small scale at an early point in your investing life. Some people, like me, are able to put their money into an investment, know that it's there, and then basically forget about it, or at least not check it every day. I think that is the best policy.

Risk tolerance is so important because it determines how you allocate your assets — that is, how much money you put into the various building blocks of investing. As I'll discuss in detail later, there are basically three such building blocks. The first are bonds, which is what you put your "safe money" into. The second are stocks that regularly pay you income, such as utilities. And the third are growth stocks, which include the Dow Five and growth mutual funds. These are the stocks that grow in value over time. How much you put into these three investment categories is determined by your financial needs and goals — which, in turn, determine your risk tolerance.

No matter what their risk tolerance is, everyone needs to know what investing is all about, and what the risks and potential gains are. I often hear people say: "I don't know the first thing about stocks and bonds. I just retired and I have X dollars in my 401(k). I'd like to roll that into a self-directed IRA and have you guys manage it. I don't understand anything about this investing business." They're asking me to step in completely as both their financial advisor and manager, and to decide everything for them. That's not a good idea.

I often say, "Nobody cares as much about your money as you do." And it's true. It's your responsibility to make sure that the shape of your portfolio is right, and, even more important, that it's adjusted as your needs change. It's fine to put your confidence in a broker you know, and it *is* the broker's responsibility to keep an eye on your portfolio. But the final responsibility is your own.

Once I've determined their financial goals and structured their portfolio, I ask my clients if they feel comfortable with the allocation. If they don't, I make adjustments. In fact, investors at all times should let their advisors know how they feel about what's going on with their investments. There are far too many investment choices you can make to sit with choices you don't like or don't understand.

One way to keep track of your investments is to spend some time with your broker's reports. This is your financial blood pressure, the equivalent of your annual medical report. When I'm at the receiving end of that report, I love to see a good result. However, if I get a bad report, at least I know where I stand and can adjust if I want to. It is very important that you have at least some idea of your investments, even if you trust the broker who is handling them. And even the very good brokers still make a mistake once in a while. So you have to be aware of what is happening with your money.

Some people get into an investment with so little information that they haven't the remotest idea what it is. The broker, not having a real feel for the client's needs and wants (possibly because the client didn't even know his needs or wants), may have recommended something that was a terrible match and therefore a bad deal.

When using a broker, make him or her fully aware of your financial situation. Review with the broker your income from all sources, your debts (including a mortgage), all savings, CDs, investments and retirement accounts. Also let your broker know about potential expenses, like college, or potential windfalls, like a large inheritance.

The investment professional is required to "know you, the client." Only in this way can the broker put together the correct mix of investments for you. Only in this way can you determine if your risk tolerance is being met or exceeded.

TOO HIGH: THE SPECULATIVE CRAZE OF THE TWENTIES

In the late 1920s, everyone — from working class to middle class to the rich — was speculating in the stock market. My father always retold the story of the famous speculator and successful investor Joseph P. Kennedy. Dad quoted Kennedy as saying, just before the 1929 crash, "When my shoeshine boy tells me what stock to buy, I sell out." In those days, every taxi driver and elevator operator, male and female, was investing in the stock market. It was a speculative craze. Kennedy apparently sold out just in time and saved his sizeable fortune.

People could invest then on what was called 10 percent margin. Stated another way: With one dollar, you could buy $10 worth of stock. You would owe the broker the rest of the money, and hope your stock would go up enough to pay him back. As a result, in the Twenties, people could become — and did become — speculators or investors with very little money of their own. That was an instance when the general public's risk tolerance went way too high. Today, you have to put up at least $5 in cash for every $10 in stock you buy, so there is far less speculation.

As the stock market crumbled in 1929, brokers would call their customers at night asking them to "supply more margin." In other words, as the stock values of their customers dropped, the brokers needed more collateral, more cash to match the money they owed. These were tough calls to place, and I had to help my Dad make some of them. I called households who were already hurting badly from the stock crash. I'll never forget. I had to ask clients for more money, which most of them didn't have.

Both the system and the people were vulnerable back then. For example, a broker bought $100 in stock for a client who put up only $10. The broker lent the client $90. When the stock dropped, and was worth only $90, the client might have to sell the stock and give the broker the $90 he received, leaving him with nothing. If the stock dropped down to $80, the broker would make a margin call to ask for the extra $10 that the client owed the broker but was not held in stock. If the client had to sell at $80, this meant that he had not only lost all of his $10 investment, but also had to pay an extra $10 to make up for the money owed to the broker. The client actually lost 200 percent of his money. And if he decided to hold on to his money, pay the broker $10, and hope the stock would come back in price to make up the difference, he could lose even more. Finally, if the stock dropped to nothing, the client still owed the broker $90, and would actually have to pay him $90. This means the investor eventually lost $100 ($100 = $90 owed to the broker + $10 lost in the stock), or 1000 percent of his original investment.

During the Roaring Twenties, just before the Depression, everybody was speculating, much as they still do at the racetrack today. You might read about the horses' records and put two bucks or a hundred on one of them, but you don't really have any evidence about who or what will win. Investing is a more complex operation — digging into a company, visiting it, talking to management, examining a company's competitors, finding out the succession if the president dies. Speculating is a half-baked way of playing in the stock market: putting a few bucks down and hoping it'll work out. As I'm fond of pointing out, "Hope is a good breakfast, but a poor supper." You can get by on hope only for a short time before you must pay the consequences.

As investors, one of the riskiest things of all is to use what I call curbstone or backyard barbecue advice. This is advice that comes from a friend, neighbor, or just a man or woman on the street, but it should not be trusted, even if the person giving you the advice means well.

Let's say a man comes up to you and says, "I have a hot tip for you. I'm close to the management of XYZ Co. I know the president. I suggest that you buy a hundred shares of XYZ Co. It's now selling for $10 a share." Okay, you take his advice. He's well-meaning and you buy the stock at $10 a share. It goes up to $15 or $16 or $17. You say to yourself, "I've made myself a tidy little profit."

At this point, something goes wrong at the XYZ Co. The cashier has embezzled millions of dollars. The president has blown out his brains. The company's chief product has become obsolete. For a dozen reasons, the company's fortunes start to ebb.

Unfortunately, when this happens, the man who gave you the well-meaning tip — he wanted to see you make money — forgets how many people he gave the tip to. He doesn't remember to call you or even give the matter a second thought. He's probably suffering badly himself. Now, all of a sudden, the stock that you bought at $10 and saw go up to $17 is worth $4.

Curbstone advice is very different from professional investment advice. If a broker follows a stock, he will call his investors and tell them when something goes wrong at XYZ Co. "They lost their patent. I think we ought to sell the thing." It may be profit or it may be loss, but at least the investors aren't forgotten.

With backyard barbecue or curbstone tips, it's not the tipster's responsibility to follow up. He might have passed along his tip to hundreds of other people — perhaps as long as five years before. The tipster might even be dead by the time things go awry at XYZ Co.

And the fact is, the tipster might not have known anything to begin with. Most presidents of most companies tell everybody that things are "going great," even when they're not. It's called the "bullish bias." The original tipster may even have known the company inside and out, and have been tracking it carefully for his own investment purposes. But he was never paid to have another investor's best interests at heart.

If you are lucky, one of a hundred stocks recommended to you in a friendly exchange of information will work out. If you want to follow up on the tips you get, have professional investment managers research them. Brokers typically don't know much more about many stocks than the investor does, since they each follow only a limited stable of stocks, somewhere between 30-50. But, brokers have access to huge research departments that can figure out whether the information is valid. They can track a stock so that the investor won't be left in the cold if something goes wrong later.

I am not immune to the passions and emotions that feed a high risk tolerance. Once, after getting some dinner-table advice on what the next Xerox would be, I invested in a company called University Computing. I fell into the mold of the average greedy person. I looked at a report or two but I didn't research the company very much beyond that. I had strong reason to think computing itself was going to be a technology important to the economy. But my instinct was premature. And further, I didn't realize that there were a thousand computing companies out there competing with mine. I lost every nickel I personally invested in University. I don't do that anymore and I certainly wouldn't do that with my clients' money.

When I encounter clients who are not investors but gamblers, I tell them point blank that I don't think I can handle them. I'm not their type of broker. I don't like to lose money, and when you gamble, you generally do lose in the long run. It's like the lottery. I used to put a few bucks on it every week, but got tired of it because I never won.

Another kind of speculator, at least in my opinion, is the so-called day trader, who will do a lot of buying and selling of stocks in a short time. This kind of trader wants to capitalize on slight ups and downs in the market. I refer those folks to people in our office who are good day traders. I am not interested in the slight ups and downs of stocks. I would rather build a portfolio for the long run.

There are other things in the stock market that I avoid. Put and call options are other, even more complicated forms of investing. A call is an option to buy a stock at a given price at a given time. A put is an option to *sell* at a given price and time. They can be used for short-term trading (to increase yields on stocks), or as a hedge for a portfolio, or for income. They *can* be used in non-speculative ways. But I have never placed a single put or call during my entire career. Some investors and brokers deal a great deal with them, attracted as they sometimes are to a combination of high-risk and high payoff potential. I generally advise people to stay away from puts and calls unless they fully understand the nature of the investment.

Once, about ten or eleven years ago, I had a very embarrassing experience. In the early part of a "Wall $treet Week" show, the host, Louis Rukeyser, asked me a completely unrehearsed question about options. Instead of saying I didn't know the answer, as I should have, I answered badly, and the more I answered, the deeper I dug my grave. A huge sack of mail came in to "Wall $treet Week With Louis Rukeyser" asking why they let an idiot like me on the show. And the truth is I just didn't know. It reminded me yet again: In investing, stay away from what you don't understand.

Selling short is something else I tell people to stay away from. My dad once told me, "Son, never sell a stock short. When you sell a stock short, you are gambling." By selling a stock short, you are betting that a stock's price will go down so you can rebuy it at a lower price. You sell stock you don't actually own because, in effect, you've borrowed it from your broker. When the stock goes down, you replace it by buying in at a lower price. The difference between the price at which you sold the stock short and the lower price at which you buy it back is your profit.

However, all things may not go as planned, so when you sell short, you subject yourself to unlimited liability. If the stock, instead of going down, goes up and up and up, you owe all that money when you "cover" your liability, and there is no limit to the amount of money you can lose. If you buy a stock "long," which is the normal way, the most you can possibly lose is the original amount you invested.

Over the years, I've found that you usually can't make a buck on bad financial news even if you want to. In most cases, Wall Street already knows the bad news. The Wall Street analysts have been to the company that seems to be in trouble. They have talked to the executives and also to the foremen, who have seen orders slow down and have an inkling as to why they have. The analysts know how to analyze the information, and they also know about that company's competition, which you the investor usually don't. So if you're sitting at a bar or a backyard barbecue and hear somebody authoritatively predict that a company is headed for a bad quarter, bear this in mind: The stock may have already taken its dip and not go down any further. Any bad news about that stock is generally known far in advance by the Wall Street professionals whose job it is to know. The unsophisticated investor has no idea how little he really knows.

TOO LOW: THE "WHAT IF I LOSE IT ALL" SYNDROME

At the other end of the risk tolerance spectrum are those who don't invest at all because they fear a large loss, or total disappearance, of their investment dollars. They take an apocalyptic view of the world. I don't think any reasonable person thinks stock investments generally will lose *all* their value, although the Dow Jones Average dropped from 381 in September 1929 to 41 in July 1932 — a 90 percent drop in less than three years. It took a full 25 years for the market to regain its pre-crash level.

Understandably, a lot of people are particularly risk-averse when getting into an area that they don't know. But this business of investing can be complicated or simple, depending on how you want to approach it. There are a lot of nuances, but the basic principles are not so complicated. With an endless stream of books, radio, columns and TV, practically everybody can understand how to be an investor if they want to be one. If you are afraid of investing simply because you don't understand the stock market, now is the right time to learn.

But even when they know something about investing, people who are really averse to risk look at the stock market, see a roulette wheel, and imagine themselves "gambling." Remembering the crash of '29 or '87, they catastrophize everything. When they see a market that's "too high now," they say to themselves, "My goodness, it's going to crack something terrible." When it does crack, they stay out of the market because "it might fall further."

A few years ago, a man came to my partners and me with roughly a million dollars he had received from a legal settlement. He was a very tense guy, about 50, who had had heart problems. He stressed over and over again that all his settlement monies were then in the bank and if he was to bring us his million bucks to invest, we were not to take any risks with it, and we were not to lose any money. Yet, he said he wanted a higher return than what he was getting from the bank.

We could have advised him to put all his money into short-term government bonds. Instead, we recommended a diversified portfolio of bonds and stocks. And we told him that there was always some short-term risk to investing. He agreed to go ahead. The year we handled this man's account, the market, after many years of going up, was either flat or down a little bit. And, rather than taking a more patient view of things, he watched his investments every day. After sensing some dissatisfaction in his telephone calls, we invited him in for a conference. His report showed that the million dollars he had brought us had edged down to $950,000, roughly a 5 percent decline.

We tried to explain why this had happened, especially the general market downswing. A few months later, he took the account away from us and moved it elsewhere. He said he was angry and unhappy, that we had done what he told us not to do — lost some money (on paper). That was not really the case. Even though his portfolio was off a little, his income was up, because some of his stocks had increased their dividends. My experience with this investor reinforced an idea I can't emphasize enough. Do you really want your investments to generate income in the short term? Or do you want your investments to grow so that they can generate more income later? These are the most important questions to ask and answer. And once you've figured out your target, keep a focus on it.

This particular investor, in my opinion, was ill-suited to be in the stock market. He should have kept his money in the bank. He personifies the old adage, "If you can't afford to lose any money, if only on paper, you don't want to go into Wall Street, because you can lose money in Wall Street." This particular client was distressed over a generally positive experience. He would have committed suicide if he had been investing in the market in 1973-74, or in the fall of 1987.

In my experience, only a small percentage of people shouldn't be investing in the market. Most people with a mature outlook on life realize that short term the market can be very emotional, that stock prices can be driven by forces unrelated to the earnings of the companies involved.

To those people who regard investing as gambling, I say: "If stocks frighten you, if you can't eat or sleep because of them, stay out of the stock market. Above all else, you must be comfortable with your investments, and if they don't include stocks, you probably won't miss a meal because of it."

YOU MUST BE COMFORTABLE

I heard recently of a small, non-profit human services organization which suddenly received a lot of stock from a woman who had happily used its services, put the organization in her will, and died at the age of 91. The group's head, an older woman, asked the donor's trust department to sell the inherited stock and invest the money for the organization. Almost from the beginning, most of this large legacy was put into a money market account and government bonds.

That became a matter of controversy. During a group budget meeting, $100 and $200 appropriations were being intensely discussed when a younger board member said, "If we just reallocate our portfolio in a way that would take prudent advantage of the rise in the stock market, this whole discussion would be irrelevant. We'd be talking about taking in $20,000 to $30,000 more a year than we are now."

The group's head was very defensive, noting that her biggest worry was that somehow or other this huge amount of money would disappear, and it was her job as trustee to keep this from happening. The younger member said that, if that were to happen, Armageddon would first have to take place, and that was very unlikely in the modern world. To him, the group's investing carried an excessive streak of conservatism.

In fact, neither the older woman nor the younger member was wrong. Between the two, there's a middle ground of risk tolerance. The older woman had a point. If we unexpectedly run into a very bad set of economic and social circumstances — a revolution, an atomic accident, a wave of inflation, a series of riots, or something to send the stock market down dramatically — the group's stock market portfolio could drop 50 or 60 percent. I'm not saying any or all of these things will happen. I am saying that there's no law that they can't. It happened in 1973-74, when a combination of horrible events related to the oil embargo sent the market down painfully.

At the time, I had more than half of my money in three so-called one-decision stocks: Polaroid, Texas Instruments, and Xcrox, and they each dropped 75 or 80 percent. I was a financial and emotional wreck. It taught me an important lesson. Very bad things can happen. However, there is a middle ground where you diversify and trust the stock market, because your chances for making money there are far greater than anywhere else.

CHAPTER SUMMARY:
YOUR TOLERANCE FOR RISK

1. *Most people don't know their tolerance for risk. It is good to figure this out early, so you can help your broker serve you.*

2. *The money you invest is your own. It is your responsibility to know where and how it is invested.*

3. *Test your tolerance over time. If it doesn't sound right or you don't understand it, don't do it.*

4. *Don't jump into the market on the basis of curbstone advice.*

5. *Don't stay out of the market because of fear.*

6. *Prefer the middle ground of risk: Invest in the stock market for the long term. But above all else, be comfortable with your investments.*

CHAPTER THREE

What's a Broker?

If you wanted to build a house, you wouldn't do it yourself.
You would go to a professional.

When investing money, I think everyone needs professional guidance. The investment of money, in my opinion, is a sophisticated task that requires professional skills and assistance. People who go to professionals do better than people who invest alone.

A stockbroker, first and foremost, should be able to help assess what the client's needs and goals are. The assessment process is very much a joint effort. The broker should be asking such questions as: How old are you? How is your health? Do you own your home? How much debt do you have? What is your net worth? How much do you have in stocks, bonds, savings, retirement assets, etc.? In fact, the first thing I tell my prospective clients prior to a meeting is to complete a profile that I mail to them. The client needs to be responsive and open, disclosing everything pertinent to his financial picture.

Once I have a complete financial picture of the client, I have a much better sense of his goals and timetable. If the client and I continue to have an open, trusting relationship — and trust is the single most important ingredient to a successful client/broker relationship — I will be much better equipped to keep the client on track with his or her investment goals. When an estate planning issue arises, I will be in a much better position to pass it on to his or her attorney. When a tax problem arises, I'll be much better positioned to bring in his or her accountant. A good broker needs to be able to work with a client's entire financial team to achieve his or her investment objectives.

Another mark of a good broker is someone who provides you with good service through all the changes in your life. The broker is trained to take the emotion out of the decision-making process and to keep you tuned into what your investments are doing and why.

That's not to say that some people don't do well investing entirely on their own, either through mutual funds or individual stocks. Louis Fox of Fox Chevrolet was an extremely successful individual investor. He knew what he was doing, and he had charts sent to him all over the world so he would always be able to track his stocks, wherever he was. He was a customer of mine briefly, but I couldn't keep up with him. Later, he donated all his profits to charity.

Lots of people have been successful recently as individual investors in the stock market. But, in the last 15 years, they had to be pretty dumb not to do well. Some individual investors have done well in spite of themselves. As we all know, a rising tide lifts all boats. In a dropping market, making money is not so easy.

My recommendation is to go to a broker and open an account when you begin to invest, and even to have a broker's help if you previously have been investing alone. There are a lot of brokers out there who will take a relatively small account these days. As I often say: If you had a toothache, you wouldn't pull your own tooth. You'd make an appointment with your dentist. If you wanted a new house, you wouldn't plan or construct it yourself. You would go to a professional architect or builder (or both). That is just what you should do when investing your money. Go to a professional.

When people are sick, they have many places they can go — to a doctor, to an emergency room, to a clinic, or to a hospital. When people have financial problems, they usually can't think of a single, central place they can go to find out where they can solve their financial problems or put their money. Or if they do, they're afraid of being sold investments that aren't best for them.

If you follow my advice, I'm quite sure you can find a financial professional to provide you objective advice based on your own needs and goals.

WHY DO I NEED A BROKER?

Brokers *are* professionals. They know the stock market, understand stocks and other forms of investment, and they do their best to understand and help their clients. They are not infallible, of course, but they know their jobs — much more than a person who tries to invest alone. All professionals make mistakes, but usually fewer and less consequential ones than an amateur.

I sometimes think of this in baseball terms. In baseball, the best players do not hit the ball every time at bat. But the best of the hitters know the strike zone and don't swing at terrible pitches. Very inexperienced and frightened hitters, on the other hand, might swing at anything that comes along, whether it's eight feet over their heads or headed toward the dugout. It's the same with investing. There's usually a wide gap between the experienced professional and the unseasoned amateur.

The management of money, in my view, demands a professional skill that many people, quite frankly, do not have on their own. The average person today might think he or she does have that skill, because of all the do-it-yourself media advice available on investing. But, in my opinion, all of that put together is not as good as going to someone deeply involved in money management 24 hours a day, who knows from experience what opportunities to take advantage of and what pitfalls and potholes to avoid. I feel very strongly about this. Brokers have more experience than anyone who picks up a newspaper or hears a television report. They can evaluate the information that comes to the individual investor, distill it, work it, and knead it, thus giving the investor the whole picture. And it doesn't cost anything to get the broker's recommendation. Whether *you* select the stock entirely on your own or ask the full service broker for some input, the commission is the same.

In the old days, it was much simpler to be an investor. There was not nearly as much advice offered then as there is now. People didn't have to wade through a volume of inconsistent reports and conflicting advice to know what to do. There were no investment television shows then. (In fact, there were no transistor radios to take to the beach.) What we needed then, and what we got, was information rather than advice. Today, would-be investors hear advice from so many different voices they can't help but be confused.

In the old days, because advice and information were not so readily available to the general public, everyone invested with brokers, to whom it *was* available. Today, as a result of the Internet and other communications technology, everyone is bombarded with both information and advice about the stock market. A lot of people, armed with this information, have decided to leave their brokers and go it alone. A very good friend of mine, and a client of mine for many years, called me last year and told me he was going to invest himself from then on. He wanted to go to his computer, track his investments there, and do his own trading. He had retired and had a lot more time to watch his money than when he was working.

Another guy I know, a retired federal employee, wanted me to look at his portfolio. It was very impressive — he had personally shaped and organized the entire list — and it was appreciating beautifully. But investing had become his abiding interest, and he was willing to commit himself fully to it. I can understand wanting to be on your own, but I don't recommend it.

As I've suggested, I don't think all this information and general advice is necessarily a good thing. The best thing to do when investing is to use brokers, rather than investing alone with the help and advice of the media. Brokers still have access to so much more information than the layman does, just through the brokerage firm's own research department. And some brokers read prodigiously.

In the old days, brokering was not nearly as technical as it is now. My father was the kind of broker who went by intuition, by the seat of his pants, and he did well. Brokering was an art back then, rather than the science it is today. My uncle Henry, who worked as a broker with my father, sold everything he and his clients owned in September of 1929. He had seen automobile sales slumping in Detroit and foresaw the great market crash that would come the next month. Now, brokering is more sophisticated. Everyone not only talks about the economy, but thinks he knows what will happen next. Investment advisors talk until they are blue in the face. The overflow of information means everything has to be studied, analyzed, and compared with all the information available to us.

Being a broker is not easy. It demands real professionalism to tear a company's balance sheet apart, make a detailed study of the firm's historical profit and loss statements, and analyze the management. These are things the general public cannot do. You may have enjoyed your stay at a vacation hotel — the towels were soft, the pools were filled, and everyone was having fun. But a judgment on whether to buy the hotel stock cannot be made in that sort of vacuum. You have to know about Motel Six, Motel Eight, and Days Inn to see how your favorite hotel company compares to the competition. And then, after you have all those facts, you have to reach the right conclusion. This is not a simple business, this picking of stocks. But it is the broker's business and the best reason I know to make the broker part of the investing process.

If the professionalism of brokers is not enough for you, consider going to investment counseling firms, where you will pay a premium for services (say one percent of the account's value each year). Every bank has an investment counseling arm. A broker, by contrast, lives mainly by transaction commissions. If you are willing to spend the extra money, investment counseling firms can be useful, but, for most people, brokerage firms have always been enough.

TO BE A BROKER

In my early years as a stock broker, I needed all the exposure I could get. One way of getting it then in Baltimore was to become very active in charities. That's where I mixed with people who had money to invest, and early on I got into the orbit of the Associated Jewish Charities. It cost me a great deal of money, because when you are moving up the ladder within the Associated, you have to set an example. I became fund raising campaign chairman for two years, and after that I became president of the Associated for two years.

When I was the head of the Big Gifts division of the Associated in 1973-74, and on my way to becoming campaign chairman, it was the year of the Yom Kippur War, when we virtually insisted that everybody double their contributions. And I, having given $16,000 the year before, which I could afford, immediately found myself on the hook for $32,000, which I could not afford. This was when I was fairly new in the business. But I made the contribution anyhow, because I had to. I stayed at a fairly high level for a while, and then I gradually whittled it down. But at my start in the brokerage business, I needed exposure, and I needed exposure to some affluent people — I couldn't make a living nickel and diming it.

Today, the character of my business has changed completely. When I went into the brokering business, the only people I knew were the people I had grown up with. They were born and raised in Baltimore: in most cases, Northwest Baltimore. Now, 90 percent of my business comes from retirees of big corporations — BGE, Allied Signal, Westinghouse, Procter & Gamble, USF&G, and Bell Atlantic.

Over the years, some clients took their portfolios to investment counseling firms and I lost that business. My partners recommended that, in addition to handling personal portfolios, we seek big blocs of retirement monies. To get "self-directed IRA rollovers," we gave seminars to people who were retiring. Retirement money is what we deal with mostly in our group now. ♣

WHAT I DO AS BROKER

Over the years, I've enjoyed working with a lot of clients. The best are those who bring me a substantial amount of money (it doesn't have to be a million dollars), and who let me know in the initial or second interview what they want, how they like to be handled, and what their total financial picture is. My partners have developed a client questionnaire that establishes for us a client profile. We send this questionnaire to people who want to come see us. When it comes back in the mail, we study it carefully, and then schedule an appointment. By the time the interview takes place, we know a good deal about would-be clients: their age, their savings, their income, their retirement picture, their list of stocks and bonds, their children or dependents, their debts, their mortgage, their insurance.

Before we take people into our office for the first time *as* clients, before we'll really talk to them, we very carefully review the questionaire responses. Before we can say they have invested too much or too little in a particular stock, we must know who they are and where their financial blind spots are.

Then, when we meet with them, we go over the questionnaire, pointing to specific responses. The questionnaire is really a portrait of what they are worth. We tell them what we would change or what we think they have neglected. If clients do not have insurance, for example, and are of working age and have dependents, we'll tell them they need insurance. Or, if they have too much insurance, we'll tell them to cancel some of what they have. After analyzing that questionnaire, we build them a portfolio.

At some of these first interviews, I feel a lot like a doctor whose patient has come in for the first time. Usually, they're coming to me for one of four reasons: they aren't sure what's in their portfolio; they think something is wrong with their portfolios; they just want to improve their portfolios; or they're just starting out as investors. So as the broker/doctor, I want to first find out what, if anything, is hurting them financially before I spell out the correct treatment.

For some clients, the prescription is *not* to hop into the stock market at all. If a couple comes to me with $20,000 in a savings account earning three percent interest, which is pretty much nothing, I usually have them pay off their debts first. Instead of putting their savings into stocks, I'll tell them to use their money to make additional payments on a mortgage or on their credit card loans, because the sooner they finish paying those bills, the more money they will have saved. And those savings are certain. There are no guaranteed results in the stock market.

Sometimes people come to me because their parents have died prematurely, and left them, the surviving children, a large sum of money they don't know what to do with. If you are thrust into such a situation, the best thing is to go to a person who knows what he or she is talking about. Our initial focus with such clients is usually on diversification. People in high tax brackets sometimes come in with lots of government bonds, which is a big mistake, because those bonds are federally taxable. Clients often don't know how to purchase tax-free bonds, which in the old days, were generally thought of as purchased only by the rich.

Some parents leave their children a lot of good, diversified stock. In that case, I might advise the children to hold onto most of the stocks they already have, while usually offering at least a few suggestions on making portfolio improvements.

Some couples will come in and say, "We want to pass our money on to our children." (That's the case more often than not.) Others will tell us, "We want to die on the same day our money runs out. We've educated our kids. They're on their own financially. We want to enjoy life now." So, from different sorts of clients, we encounter diametrically opposite goals.

Whatever goal they establish is fine with us, but the clients need to be forthcoming and assertive about it. We don't want people to sit there and say, "Here I am," because then we don't know what to do with and for them.

You might think that some people would be reluctant to lay out their whole financial world to us, that they would judge themselves a financial failure when showing us what they've accumulated by that point in their lives. But I have never seen a client show any such embarrassment. If a client is a little reluctant to talk about their existing assets and liabilities (which most people are not), we say, "Look, when you go to a doctor, you don't tell him only about what hurts. You give him your whole physical picture, your whole history." What's most common among prospective clients is uncertainty. They rarely are sure of their financial picture or investments.

Some of our new clients have already worked with other brokers before. We may ask about these experiences: what was good and what was bad. Dad used to say, "Son, never disparage your competition. Just sell your own merchandise." I try to stick to the topic of investing — not the professionals who once helped them do it — though I don't mind criticizing big mistakes that show up on their portfolios, like low quality junk bonds or speculative stocks — especially if the new clients happen to be elderly.

Occasionally, we encounter clients who are quite advanced in years and who aren't "all there" mentally. But those folks usually come in with a spouse or relative, so we're able to chop plenty of wood during our discussions.

When I first meet with clients, I generally advise them to move out of stocks that I don't follow closely. I also nix stocks that seem speculative to me, whose purchase might have been triggered by a whim or a curbstone tip. I look dimly on companies that don't pay any income. But I don't drop a stock just because I might not know it well. In addition, it can be fairly useful to hold onto a good stock that's had its problems. I bought one company after its crash, and I made a fair amount of profit after it partly recovered, but the investment, I thought at the time, was semi-risky (arguably, the stock price could have gone to zero).

Lots of people have biases against a certain stock, which I have to deal with when working with their portfolios. One client once instructed me never to buy a share of General Motors, even though it was in the Dow Five and perfect for her portfolio. She had had a couple of GM cars that turned out to be lemons, and GM didn't help her out of her misery. She would invest in anything except that company, she told me.

Some clients will not buy Philip Morris because of the tobacco connection, even though it is one of the largest food companies in the world. If you have this kind of bias, my best advice is to try to make sure the bias is rational. Would you really refuse to buy RJR Nabisco when it makes so many good snack foods? To soften the blow when their tobacco products are eventually regulated to death, practically every one-time tobacco company has diversified. Investing in the stock market is not about loyalty; it is about your money. You must decide whether your political beliefs will supercede your desire for financial security.

From an interview, we can usually tell pretty well whether or not a client will be a pain in the neck. As I said earlier, I see the broker-client relationship as similar to the one between a doctor and patient. When a doctor prescribes something for me (the patient), I don't pin the doctor down to find out why he likes pink pills instead of green ones. I believe that if a doctor prescribes pink pills for me, he knows what he's doing, and if he doesn't, I have the wrong doctor. As a patient, I just want the doctor to relieve my problem. I realize that doctors do make mistakes. For that reason, I usually ask them a few questions here and there.

As a broker, I'm happy to talk about why I like a particular investment, but I don't like to be pinned down on why I like this stock relative to a whole bunch of others. Providing that kind of explanation can be very time consuming. I prefer the client who asks questions about a specific investment, lets me answer, and feels more confident as a result of my answers. Our best clients have enough confidence in us to give us discretion to make their investment moves — within the parameters of what we talk about during the interviews.

I like to bring clients back at least once a year to go over their updated portfolio, to show them where they started and where they are now. A new customer recently came in with a big block of Allied Signal stock and was a little reluctant to part with it, so we said to him, "If you had no Allied Signal stock today, would you go out and buy 3,000 shares of it?" The guy said no, so we moved along fine from there.

One of the great rewards of brokering is when a client's investments do well. It's always a pleasure to look at such a client's list. It's especially gratifying prior to a client's annual visit, which we know will go well.

A stockbroker's main obligation to his firm is not to generate commissions, but to bring in assets and to serve clients while meeting the highest ethical standards. The firm wants more assets brought under control, believing that, when the right things are done for clients, sufficient broker commissions will result.

When I talk security salesmanship, I urge brokers to make a persuasive case to clients for the stock they're selling, but to also point out that there is a risk of loss. There is nothing wrong with making a case for buying the stock because, after all, the broker feels in his own heart that the stock he's proposing is better for the customer than keeping his money in the bank. That's one of the essentials of salesmanship.

However, that having been said, brokers always must sell with integrity. They shouldn't oversell. They shouldn't be deceitful. They don't want to use phrases to unsophisticated customers like, "Oh, you can't lose money on this." Or, "Everybody's buying this stock." Or, "Airlines are booming today." They don't want to use such phrases because people can indeed lose money.

It doesn't matter at all how often your broker takes you to lunch, and it doesn't matter how often your broker plays golf with you or sends you holiday presents. It's nice if those things happen but they must happen in conjunction with the most important thing of all — good results. In investing, as in sports, winning isn't everything. It's the only thing. That's why people come to me. They don't want a fancy lunch or an Orioles ticket. Those are nothing more than fringe benefits. The bottom line is that I must do well for my client — that is, help achieve his financial goals. If I do, the chances are 99 out of 100 I'm going to keep that client. It also means that the client will spread the word about me: that I'm doing well for them. They might even send me new people with money to invest.

RESULTS ARE WHAT COUNT

Now, how do you know if your broker is serving your interests? One way is whether they deliver good, old-fashioned service. When they come to us initially, we tell clients that, at the end of every month, they'll receive the brokerage house's month-end statement. These statements are nothing special. Every brokerage house sends them out. My assistant, Carolyn Walpert, spends a good deal of time on the phone un-confusing clients who've received their statements.

But in addition to that, we supply our clients a personalized portfolio evaluation, which we grind out monthly, semi-annually, or annually on our computers. This list of their investments shows the following: the number of shares they own, the name of the company, the cost in dollars, the present market price, the present market value (which is the number of shares multiplied by the present market price), and the income earned during the year. We in effect present them with a snapshot of where they stand at the moment versus how they stood when they started the year. In the last 15 years, most of these annual snapshots have looked good because the Dow Jones Average in the last 15 years has gone up staggering amounts.

Many clients derive satisfaction just seeing their investments presented in an orderly fashion by our monthly and annual statements. For many, investing means big files and masses of papers, out of which they can't make much sense. They're deluged with so many materials that they can't sort them out or distill them down to figure out what they really have. Our monthly statements enable them to keep track of their investments, to evaluate them, to have a good sense of what they really have.

We have some very methodical clients who handle this tracking job for themselves. More client-initiated tracking takes place in a rising market than a declining one. Investors every week will pull out the business section of their Sunday newspaper and figure out exactly how much they're worth. It makes them feel good.

In general, though, most investors can't and won't keep track of their investments no matter what the market is doing. That's one of the reasons there should be a meeting every year between client and broker, face to face. At that meeting, you as client should know not only where you were when you started, and where you are now, but also where you are going in the future. Such annual meetings are especially necessary because your financial situation may have changed during the year. Maybe you have a family now, or you've gotten married, or have moved. Or, maybe the broker has new ideas. The broker may not have looked over your portfolio lately, but the fact that there's a meeting on the horizon makes him dig it out of his files, put it on his desk, and spend time evaluating it.

In my experience, not every client comes to these annual meetings. Million-dollar clients frequently attend, and it works out well for both us and them. One, it welds the clients to us. They know that we care enough to invite them in. We can show them that some things have changed and that it's a good time to sell a particular investment. A lot of our business is on the basis of referrals. The better we work with existing clients, the more likely we are to bring in additional business. One client will say to a friend, "My broker called us up and had us in." The friend will say, "My God, I haven't seen my broker in two years."

One of my jobs as a broker is to keep client files on tickler, so I can remember to call clients after some time elapses and bring them in. When they come in, they don't usually say, "Oops, I just discovered $250,000 I had invested somewhere else. Let's put it into the portfolio." But some of them have received an inheritance since I last spoke with or met them, and don't know what to do with the new money. We picked up a large client recently who insisted that we see him every three months. We said we would and we will, though the client will probably tire of the frequency. It's too often.

In investing, as in sports, excuses mean nothing. The newspapers may say that outfielder Bobby Bonilla dropped a fly ball yesterday because the sun was in his eyes. Maybe so, but he did drop it, and it was an error, which led to a run. In the investing business, it's the same way. Brokers are going to commit errors, but they should do everything they can to keep them small. And even when making errors, they should, overall, be meeting your financial goals.

As brokers, we have to be careful about suggesting that a client has made a mistake in judgment. Many years ago, back in the days when I was selling clients day by day, I might tell a client, "You're being emotional about this decision. Your emotions are getting the better of you." And as soon as I'd do that, the client would think I was criticizing him personally rather than what he or she was doing. Investors can indeed make mistakes by being emotional, but we brokers must be careful about saying that to them.

Although, in my firm, the Westheimer Group operates both as traditional brokers and as money managers, we don't charge a management fee, like investment counseling firms do. We make money strictly as stockbrokers. We are members of the New York Stock Exchange and we get paid whenever we handle a transaction. If there's no transaction, we don't get paid.

Naturally, clients often ask, "If you're paid only for transactions, don't you have a tendency to churn the account and do a lot of tickets?" Our answer is: "Once we have put your portfolio in shape, we don't have to do much buying and selling. We gather assets, and by gathering assets we know at the end of the year that we will generate a certain amount of business, particularly if the assets keep increasing and we're on the ball."

Over the years, I've found that most customers don't want us to give them a great amount of information to support a recommended investment decision. If we're not careful, we can easily oversell our pitch. That doesn't mean that the broker shouldn't know a lot. The broker has to. But as soon as we start overwhelming the client with too many reasons to do a transaction, the client gets swamped and stops listening. I usually give three reasons for an investment and then I ask, "Would you like to buy 500 shares?" I'm not asking for a discussion. I'm asking for a decision, an order.

If clients have a question, they'll ask it at that point. My objective is to get the order because I feel deep down that by making the sale, I am employing that client's money better than the client would on his own, and better than a competitor could. I'm convinced, in my own mind, that I'm doing the client a favor. So it doesn't bother me at all to do a trial close, which is asking for the order midway through my presentation. If the client says, "Yes, fine, write the order," I'll move on to something else. This is not cheating the client. If he wants to know more, I'll answer more questions, but I'll try to do so quickly, because I'm certain that I'm acting in his interests and not wasting his time or mine.

The trial close technique frequently works. A lot of it is attributable to the starting premise. The client knows I'm using a salesman's technique, but understands above all that I am trying to do things in his interest. If that isn't the underlying assumption, it's easy to rebuff me as "some guy employing just another sales pitch."

Three reasons to buy or sell a stock are usually enough for most clients. They don't want to hear any more. They have other things to do. If we tell them it's a good stock, give them three reasons why, and they have confidence in us, they'll buy or sell it as we suggest. But today the best results that we have are with accounts where we have discretion and we're able to move quickly. Half the time the clients are out when we call. Or, if they call back, clients have to "think it over." "Thinking it over" is another way of turning us down.

For the first ten or 15 years I was at Ferris Baker Watts, I worked every Saturday morning. My cubicle was adjacent to that of an older broker, W. Lloyd Fisher, who was the firm's number one salesman. I overheard some of his crackerjack sales techniques. One of them made a lasting impression on me, and I still use it. He would say over the telephone to a client, "There are some new Triple A Baltimore County bonds out this morning yielding seven percent. No federal tax, no state tax. I see you have a $10,000 balance in your money market account. Why don't we just move that money over and get you $10,000 of these?"

If clients said, as they sometimes would, "We'd like to think it over," Lloyd would say, "Let me do this just to protect you. Let me put you down for this $10,000, and, if for any reason over the weekend you don't want them, call me and tell me on Monday and you're not obligated." Nobody ever called to cancel. If he had approached things the other way, nobody would ever have called him back on Monday to buy the bonds. This might be a little pushy, but I consider it perfectly ethical.

I take the position that what I'm recommending to my client is better than what he or she now has, and I don't feel reluctant at all to push a little bit to close the sale. After all, a sale isn't a sale until you close it. It's just conversation. And having a conversation doesn't help either client or broker. If Mr. and Mrs. Gotrocks are now earning four percent on $10,000, and I sincerely believe they should instead have that money invested in seven percent tax-free bonds, which is equivalent to 10 percent taxable (or triple what they have been getting), I'll push for it. If I don't, they're not likely to do it. Investor inertia will take over. Inertia, as we know, is a physical object's tendency to stand still unless somebody or something moves it. And conversely, a moving object continues moving unless somebody or something stops it. Both rules of science apply to investing. The average investor with $10,000 in a money market fund usually feels good enough about it. It's up to me to prod the alternative move. Without my push, clients don't get what they *could* get. And I don't make any money, either.

Suppose I'm sitting at home with my nephew when his broker calls him to recommend putting his money into something that will do a lot better for him. Both from an investment and a tax standpoint, I ask my nephew a few questions about the broker. "Has your broker been good to you over the years? Do you have confidence in him?" If the answer to both questions is "yes," I'll advise my nephew to go ahead and follow the broker's advice.

Because I believe in the importance and usefulness of being a broker, I don't mind having friends as my clients. The advantage is, I know the client's core personality going in. I don't have to learn too much about them. When you call on new people, they always lay down their parameters. And so do your friends, because even though you've known them socially, you don't know them from a business point of view. There can be some surprises.

One of my best friends turned into one of my clients, and after I placed a few orders for him, he called up and said, "I don't like the executions I'm getting from you. I want you to put limited orders on my trades." A limited order is an order that gets executed at the price dictated by the buyer. So he would say to me, "Buy me Merck if and only if it hits 45 or goes below that." Up until then, I would order our trading department to "buy me a hundred Merck." But this particular client would look in the paper the next morning and see that I had paid 46 for his stock, though it had closed at 45 and three quarters. He'd wonder why I hadn't bought it more cheaply. My conclusion was, this guy was trying to get the last nickel out of every transaction. I had never known that about him until he became a client.

And there are others like him. Two of my best friends were extraordinarily wealthy people who made good investment decisions, but insisted on better executions. "Don't just let the market dictate. Tell your trader to buy me a hundred shares of Merck. Play with it, look at it, watch it, buy at the last sale, buy it if the last sale is 45 and a half. Don't pay 45 and three-quarters." I might say to them, "Well, what happens if I play around with it and it goes up to 46 and you miss the sale?" They'd say, "Why don't you sit there and watch it? Do the best you can. I expect that of you. That's why I'm giving you my business."

Some of these folks had somewhat unrealistic expectations of me as a broker. They thought the only thing I had to do was trade for them, or that doing their kind of super-tight executions was easy. It wasn't. I used to hand the tickets to the trader, who would just go ahead and handle them at market prices. Period. Ninety-nine out of 100 clients would agree to that sort of arrangement, but a couple of my affluent social friends — and maybe this is one reason why they became affluent — wanted their orders executed at no more than the last sale. They didn't want to see that they paid a quarter of a point more for a stock than the price at which it closed. Over the years, as we got to know each other better in the investment setting, such requirements tended to evaporate or disappear.

When it comes to executing transactions, I as a broker handle them quite differently depending on what kind of a market we are in. If it is a skittish and not continually escalating market, which was the case before 1981, I might insist on tight executions. There would be a greater need for them. But if clients who gave me these instructions thought that, in a rising Dow, they were "missing the market" by limiting their buy price to 45-and-a-half, sooner or later they would call me and say, "Just go ahead and buy at the market. I don't want to miss it." This was especially the case if they saw the stock going up.

Brokers are professionals who are trained and experienced in managing money. In my opinion, they are the best route to investing in the stock market. Going it alone can still be profitable, especially in a bull market. But I find the experience and information of professional brokers unmatched by the average layman, and the emotional distance of a broker a major benefit. That is why I recommend that everyone invest with the assistance and counsel of a broker.

CHAPTER SUMMARY:
WHAT'S A BROKER?

1. *Brokers are professionals who can usually analyze stock choices far better than the average investor can. They also make less emotional decisions than the investor might. It is always good to have the objective distance of a professional when dealing with your money.*

2. *When prospective clients come to me, I like to know the whole financial picture, including their future plans. Telling your broker what you want is essential to getting it.*

3. *As a broker, I don't want to be pinned down on every reason why I like one stock over another. The ideal client is one who asks questions about a specific recommendation, lets me answer, and feels more confident as a result of my answers.*

4. *Unsophisticated investors can often be pressured by brokers who assure them a guaranteed gain. I urge brokers to make a persuasive case for the stock they're selling, but to also point out that there is a risk of loss.*

5. *There is always risk in the stock market. However, I believe in my product. When I am selling a stock to a client, I always feel that it is in that client's best interest to follow my advice.*

6. *I like to have a meeting with my clients at least once a year to discuss results.*

CHAPTER FOUR

Choosing a Broker

Which broker you choose is really crucial,
especially if you are going to delegate discretion to that broker.

HOW TO CHOOSE

When I decided some years ago to seek an advisor for several family trusts, I told some friends, "I don't want the full responsibility of managing my own trusts. Who handles your trust accounts?" They told me they used Scott Marah, whom I called on the phone at Warburg Pincus's investment counseling offices in New York. I asked if I could come up and talk to him. I took the trust portfolio with me, and I asked him to look it over. He told me that if he was managing my account, he would get rid of some of this stock, and add some of another. It was a little scary and very hard to let go, but I did it. Without shopping much farther, I asked him to manage the trust for me. Scott is a lot younger than I am, and younger money managers may be more inclined to make more changes to a portfolio than older ones. At the age of 40, he was just at the right age to take advantage of the bull market, and he put my family trusts in some things I'd never heard of, which I would never have done on my own. And it has worked out very well, with excellent results.

I don't manage people's accounts by myself now. My partners help me. If I did it alone, I'd be much less aggressive, much more inclined to leave things in a portfolio just the way they are. My partners make more changes because they know the newer industries. I don't know much about high tech. But Scott Marsh, like my partners, knows Intel and Microsoft. They know the health care field, which I don't know very well at all. That's why I had him handle the trusts. He can do better with this trusteed money than I can myself.

Every quarter, I call Scott up and ask him if we have too much of one thing or too little of another. I know the market pretty well and so I often ask him if we should sell one thing or buy another. He doesn't seem to mind me calling. (I like it sometimes when clients call me occasionally to talk about their account.) And sometimes I get ideas from him, which he doesn't mind at all. I use my own professional judgment, but we all borrow from somebody, whether it's *Standard and Poor's* or *Forbes* or *Barron's* or *The Wall Street Journal.*

Which broker you choose is really crucial, especially if you are going to delegate discretion to that broker. When looking for a broker, here's what I recommend:

If you know people who are successful investors and respect their judgment, ask them to suggest a broker's name. If you don't, contact the branch managers of several well-known brokerage firms, telling them what you're looking for.

When you meet the brokers they suggest, ask lots of questions. For example:

- What do you specialize in?

- How much money do you have under management?

- Do you require a minimum amount of money to take on a new client and, if so, what is it?

- What stocks do you like now and why?

- What investments do you like for conservative growth, aggressive growth, and income?

- How do you make your choices? Do you use fundamental or technical analysis?

- What research do you use?

- How long have you been in the business? What is your background?

- What books about investing have you read lately?

- What periodicals do you read regularly?

- Can you furnish me any client references?

- What do you expect of me as the client?

- How often can I expect you to contact me?

- Do you prefer discretionary or non-discretionary accounts?

- How often will I receive statements from you?

You may not have to ask all these questions, but there certainly are many here you can choose from.

When you ask your friends about their broker, the most important thing you need to know is what the client wanted the broker to do, and how the broker performed relative to those goals. If the broker has not delivered good financial results to your friends or family, keep hunting. In investing, as with education, eighty percent of a professional's grade is based on how he or she does "on the examinations." The other twenty percent of the broker's grade depends on bedside manner. You don't want to choose a broker just because he is friendly, but you might not want one who can't or won't relate to you.

I recommend going to an experienced broker in a brokerage firm to whom you can relate personally. If the broker your friends and family recommend appeals to you, you should probably choose that person. But some brokers, especially experienced brokers, are high-handed and won't manage an account unless the client does exactly what the broker says, and some investors won't like that attitude. Other brokers won't take on clients who have too little money to invest. When a broker is new, he or she will take on anyone, even with $10,000 or $20,000 to invest. The seasoned broker, who is used to dealing with $500,000 accounts, won't. He will recommend you to someone else in the firm. So even though you might want the most experienced broker, you may end up with someone having less experience.

As I said, you the client must relate well to the broker you are working with. If the broker your friends recommend does not fit your personality, go to an experienced broker at the firm who does. If you can't find anyone at that firm whom you like, look up brokerage firms in the yellow pages. Tell the sales manager of each firm who you are and what you're looking for, and have him recommend some brokers to talk to. When the time comes for a decision, listen to what your little inner voice tells you to do.

As a broker, I try to relate to clients young and old, rich or poor — to people from both sides of the track. I try to be honest and patient, to take my time with people and listen to their stories, even if they are not the biggest investors. Often the investor with relatively little money needs much more help than the person with a lot of money. The person with a lot of money is going to be okay with or without my advice, but the person with little money really needs my help. And I do try to help.

I also try to be open to the clients' needs. If a person came to me with a portfolio that I was unhappy with, but refused to change it, I would still take on the account, but I would tell the new client that he was responsible for the securities I didn't like. A broker can only be responsible for the investments he recommends and follows closely. If I could change the client's mind over the years to do something else with his portfolio, that would be great. If not, I would continue handling the account, with that same caveat understood. The "know-your-customer rule" says that a broker should know everything about a customer before any investments are made. I try to know a customer's needs, wants, and fears, which vary widely from person to person. For instance, age makes a major difference in risk tolerance. Before starting, a broker must "know the customer." He shouldn't sell each customer the same stock because each customer is different.

When you go to a broker for an initial meeting, you must tell the broker everything about your financial picture, including your needs, wants, and fears. You should not ask the broker how he or she has done with previous clients, how much their clients average per year over time. Under NASD rules, brokers can't quote percentages in the context of performance records, and with good reason: We all could show our clients and prospects the good results. We could show them the figures we wanted to show. If you let me pick the starting point, I could show you any performance record I wanted. Though it would be convenient to judge a broker against how the market as a whole has performed, most brokers can't honestly answer the question because their clients' needs and risk tolerance levels can be so different.

(It's different for large institutions which are shopping for investment *managers* (emphasis on managers, not brokers). These institutions can require audited performance figures from prospective money managers.)

In fact, even if the broker's authenticated performance record was available to you, you don't necessarily want someone with the best short-term record: the law of averages will probably bring the return down. As when searching for a mutual fund, which I'll discuss later, the best kind of record is one that shows long-term quality despite occasional slumps. The only real way to choose a broker is to go on your best judgment and give your decision a reasonable time to work out.

The broker will tell you what he would do with your portfolio if he were managing it. If you feel compatible with the broker, you may choose him, or you may shop around a little more for another broker. If you're uncomfortable or unsure, ask your tax advisor, lawyer, or someone familiar with the investment business.

Another way to choose a broker is by the amount of personal contact you can expect. I think brokers should interact with other people. My uncle Irvin Westheimer, who was a highly successful stockbroker in Cincinnati and my Dad's younger brother, said, "Julius, heads of state get out of their comfortable chairs, leave their palaces and White Houses and travel halfway around the world to see other heads of state and other people. Stockbrokers should do the same thing." I built my business on personal contact, by going to people's offices and homes rather than operating by the telephone. I like working with people I know well. I also like working with my good friends. Knowing them well enables me to serve them better.

However, I don't like managing family investments entirely by myself. More than financial aspects are involved; there are also the emotional aspects. I manage my wife's investments, with help from my partners Mark Dyer and Morry Zolet. Doing it myself was very hard and I didn't like doing it. But it was by managing her investments that we met, so I suppose I shouldn't complain. I managed her account for ten years before we were married.

I would not reject family members as clients. I would never reject a potential client because of the relationship, and brokers will never turn down an account at the outset. But on very, very rare occasions, I will think about rejecting a client two or three years down the road, when, to me, the account becomes more trouble than it's worth, like when the client is constantly screaming at my assistants, "He never calls me back, I can never get through to him. I'll bet he never looks at my account." Fortunately, my partners are more placid than I am, and know how to get along with clients who become difficult for me.

WHAT MAKES A GOOD BROKER?

If after a full stock market cycle of several years, you the client aren't getting the same investment results that your friends of similar financial circumstances are getting, you have good reason to think about switching brokers. Ask: "How am I doing relative to my goals?" This is always the key question to ask because, since retaining your broker, you may have changed your goals, yet failed to communicate them to the broker. Judging the broker on the basis of some secret new goal is not fair, either to yourself or to your broker.

I also emphasize "a full stock market cycle." Anybody can look good in one year with a meteoric stock or a meteoric group of stocks. But what so often happens is that after a meteoric year, the next year the stock goes out of favor and dips.

The temptation to switch brokers can be considerable. Unfortunately, investors can be all too competitive. Don't let comparing notes with a friend turn you away from a good broker. Most people (and especially most people's friends) talk only about their investing successes, and rarely about their failures. For example, a client of mine may get a report from me that says he's increased the total value of his portfolio by 14 percent, which fits his needs just fine. He goes to dinner with friends of his who rave about their stock broker. Their stock is up 26 percent, they tell him, or they're in a mutual fund making 30 percent.

Now that he's comparing notes, the client is suddenly no longer as happy with me as he once was. "Fourteen percent is pretty good," he says to himself — it certainly is better than standing still — "but it is hardly 26 percent." If you have a good, open, and trusting relationship with your broker, and things seem to be orderly and successful, don't leave him. That other people are doing better than you in the market is rarely a good reason to change brokers. Their investment goals may be quite different from your own.

In our initial presentation to prospective clients, we try to get the client to have realistic expectations about performance. We say that, generally, we attempt to perform as well as the markets, or better than the markets, over time. If we say we think we can average an eight or nine percent increase a year for them, their normal response is that somebody else can do better. They see ads that promise better results. Or, they say, "The market was up 34 percent last year. Why do I need your nine or ten percent?" At this point, we explain a couple of things to them. One is, we don't think the last few years on the market are representative, that we think eventually stocks will gravitate to their historic norm of 11 percent annual increase in total return —that's growth plus income — good markets and bad. We know that there are some 34 percent "up years," but we also know that there are some 25 percent "down years." We try to lowball any figures we give prospects so they won't be disappointed, and some of them leave unimpressed, thinking they can do better elsewhere. However, most of them respect reliable estimates rather than pie-in-the-sky ones.

Many investors stay with brokers who are charming and wonderful and yet may not be particularly adept at what they're doing. Some brokers have a way of sugar-coating their results. That doesn't mean they're dishonest or unethical, but if a stock has performed only fairly during a year, they'll say, "Give it a chance. If it drops and you still like the company, let's buy more." Clients have a tendency to get attached to their brokers, just like patients do to their doctors. I don't know many people who say, "I hate my doctor. He's been lousy for me." Most of us like our doctors and praise them — perhaps because we're probably looking for father figures. Besides, we want our professionals to do well for us. We want to be reassured. And we don't want to change unless we have to. Meet and talk with your broker from time to time. If at the end of a full stock market cycle, your results are terrible, warn the broker that you're unhappy. If the results remain disappointing, change brokers. But I'd give a broker at least that amount of time. Most people expect instant gratification from an investment. But most investments don't begin to blossom for at least six months or a year, and it takes at least a few years for the market to run through its usual up-and-down cycle.

When you get a statement from your broker, there's nothing wrong with looking at each individual stock on it. I sometimes do. It makes me feel good to know where my money is. But what you really ought to concentrate on when evaluating the broker is the total, overall performance relative to your financial goals. Give the guy time to equal or outperform the Dow. If the Dow is going up and you can measure up to the Dow, you're doing just fine. However, in a doggy market, you want your portfolio to drop less in value than the market drops. Therefore, you've got to have some stars on your list. You've got to have a few Johnson & Johnsons and Hewlett-Packards. If you have triples and home runs like those, you can also have lots of singles — stocks that are doing OK but not going through the roof. If you're an investor with a portfolio of 20-30 stocks, you would be doing well — and I as your broker would probably be happy — if only a few of your investments are strike-outs. If I rid them from your portfolio, and you end up with mostly doubles or triples, both of us will be delighted.

But, again, you must allow the broker a certain amount of time. If you look at your portfolio after six months, most likely you don't want to draw any conclusions.

Over my career, I have lost a few clients due to "under-performance." Every year, some clients will show up, see their updated portfolios, and say in effect, "This isn't really as good as the market has done, is it?" And even though a broker can talk his way out of some of that, if he under-performs long enough, he's going to lose certain clients. He's not going to lose the widows and orphans who rely on him for conscientious advice, who know he's human, who are primarily interested in income to replace their husband's or father's lost earnings. But he is going to lose clients who track their portfolios on a computer and discover his performance hasn't measured up to the popular averages. After a year or so, they will drift away. One guy approached us three years ago and we gave him an hour or two of advice. I pursued him. And lo and behold, he brought his account to us from a local bank. After two years, he called me. "Westy, I hope you won't take this personally" — how else can you take it? Whenever anyone starts that way, you know you're dead already — "but I'm going to move my account to another money manager."

Another guy came to us a few years ago with a million-dollar settlement from a malpractice case — a botched heart operation. He was in two or three times. We finally got him. In every conversation with us thereafter, he reminded us, "The main thing is, I don't want to lose any money. You guys understand this?" We assured him we did. After a year or so, a housing stock we recommended to him went from 9 to 6. He could not get that out of his craw. I think his overall performance was fair to good, especially relative to his overall goals, but he kept bringing up that "housing stock fiasco." Finally, he took his account to a competitor. The one reason he gave us on exiting was, "I told you guys I didn't want to lose money and you put me in something where I lost. It's your fault, because it was your recommendation, and I'm leaving you." He did and we haven't heard from him since.

I think he was wrong to get so upset over one stock out of 30, even though it clearly was a dog. His decision was very short-sighted. But he obsessed over little things like that. He just couldn't stand it. If he hadn't pulled the account away, we'd have gotten rid of that one under-performing stock. He would have taken a tax loss and moved onto something else. Scott Marsh, who manages some family trusts at Warburg Pincus, is a professional at recognizing losers. When he loses confidence in a company, he generally sells the stock promptly and puts the money to better use. And if the sold stock somehow doubles or triples after that, so be it. The replacement he finds generally equals or surpasses the performance of the one he has eliminated.

In some senses, we brokers are like the general manager of a professional baseball team. We put together a team of 25 players, including a couple of superstars who're paid a lot of money, some real solid performers who get paid a lot less, and some journeymen whose salaries are a bit more than the minimum. All 25 are trying to play together as a team. In managing the team, as in managing the account, the biggest question is whether we take the short term, piecemeal approach or the long-term, overall approach. Are we playing for this year or are we building for the future?

As brokers, we tend towards the latter. When people first come to see us, one thing we always say is, "We don't aim for the fences. We don't try to hit home runs. We try to hit a lot of singles, a lot of doubles, and most importantly, we try not to strike out." The client with the horrible housing stock ended our relationship just before the big boom in the market in 1995. Had he not left us then, we would have made him a ton of money. It was a bad call on his part in response to a single bad call on *our* part.

If I were on the customer's side of the table, I would give the broker considerable discretion. He's the specialist. He's the person who's supposed to know what he's doing, and, if he recommends that I buy or sell an airline stock, I wouldn't question him about every propeller or landing gear or accident rate. I might ask a few general questions, but it's more important to evaluate the broker's performance as a whole relative to your stated goals. You're not going to hit a home run every time you're at bat. Inevitably, you're going to strike out a few times. It's just unavoidable.

I once defined "bad luck in the market" as hitting a home run in your first outing as an investor. In a way, that's what happened to me. I hit an early home run with Xerox, then kept looking for more and more Xeroxes until I finally found what I thought was one. In a hotel room in Chicago, some guys I considered very savvy told me that next year, the "Xerox of the market" would be University Computing. As it turned out, I lost every nickel on the investment for two reasons. I actually was listening to amateurs and not professionals. And I was tripped up by greed — I was going to have another Xerox. Along came University Computing. "Sounds great," I said.

The emotion between fear and greed is the one that most people should use when making investment decisions. I don't know if it has a name. It's not necessarily being coolly dispassionate, or completely rational. But it *is* being as unemotional as possible as much of the time as possible. This isn't easy because we're all ruled by fear, greed and dozens of other emotions. I have said before and will say again, "Your own emotions are the best 'reverse indicator' of what you should be doing in the market."

And, if you ever waver, remember: You always have at least one objective way to determine your success. Your long-term results, at minimum, should outrun the inflation rate. You have to do reasonably well versus the rising cost of living, which at the moment is quite low (about three percent a year). To be successful in the stock market, pay attention to this true measure, rather than the more fallible emotions of fear and

BREAKING NEW GROUND *Ferris Baker Watts is the investment firm where I now work. In fact, except for my time as a teenager, it's the brokerage firm where I've worked my entire career. In 1961, I broke new ground by becoming the firm's first Jewish broker. John Motz, a banker, had said, "The firm wants to open its doors to northwest Baltimore. It hasn't been able to do that. I'm going to arrange for you to talk to a couple of their executives." John set up a meeting between me and a couple of Baker Watts senior partners. One afternoon over drinks at the Merchant's Club, I told the partners who I was and what I did. These older men were of my father's generation. They knew him and knew of his brokerage firm on Redwood Street, a half block from Baker Watts. So, in a way, I wasn't an unknown.*

I told them of my background and my experience. I wasn't an obscure figure. At the department store, where I was president, I was always receiving some publicity. I ran Gutman ads with my name signed at the bottom: "Julius

Westheimer, President." I had also just been elected president of the Suburban Club. Suburban, one of the pre-eminent country clubs in the area, was full of very well-to-do members. Baker Watts knew that would be a good thing for it and me.

So they hired me. Lloyd Fisher said, "Westy, there's your desk. We'll pay you $12,000 a year or your commissions, whichever is greater [I was making $40,000 at the family store] and if you work out as well as we expect, we'll make you a partner in five years." (They made me one in three.) Never in my years at Ferris Baker Watts have I seen or felt even the slightest hint of anti-Semitism. Understandably, I would get quite innocuous questions like, "What do we say to you on Christmas?" And: "How do we get to that delicatessen in Pikesville that makes such great corned beef sandwiches?" Mostly, they wanted to know about my part of town — northwest Baltimore.

After joining Baker Watts, I spent every free Saturday morning and afternoon working, even though the market wasn't open. I spent much of my Saturday time at the Enoch Pratt Free Library, to which I remain devoted today.

Going into a new business is ➼

greed. Admittedly, it's not easy staying unemotional about your portfolio because investing, almost by its very nature, instills insecurity. That's why people should turn their accounts over to professionals. Brokers tend not to operate on the basis of emotions, or at least they operate a lot less on emotions than clients.

One of the marks of a good broker-client relationship is regular communication. We return all of our calls ourselves, every day. To a client, regular communication is a big plus, or should be. We live today in a "press one, press two, press three" world. Most people detest that. When our phone rings, I, my assistant Carolyn Walpert, or my partners Mark Dyer and Morry Zolet pick it up and answer. If clients have a question about a missed dividend, they're not automatically connected with some office out in Kansas City that keeps track of such records. It's right in our building and we do it for them.

Face to face communication can be extremely important, especially at the beginning, when we are trying to get a full picture of the client's goals. My partner Morry and I traveled recently all the way from downtown Baltimore to Taneytown, MD, in northern Maryland, on a referral. An elderly couple of farmers had said, "We'll do business with you only if you bring Julius Westheimer along. We've got to have him here in our house." On our fact-finding mission, Morry and I spent the whole morning out there, and we came back not only with valuable flavor about the

---

very hard, and it was for me. An old-timer from the department store, Leonard Eisenberg, came to see me and made me feel much better. He had dealt with Baker Watts even before I knew there was such a firm. He asked, "How you doing, Julius?" I said, "Well, I'm having a fairly hard time getting started." He said, "Remember the old saying: 'All beginnings are hard.'" I have never forgotten that. All beginnings are *hard, whether it's a job, a marriage, investing, or writing a book. You don't know the rules, and you're dealing with new people, ideas, places, and activities.*

I quickly discovered I was a good salesman. Of course, my heritage helped me. My name was well-known.

My father's was well-known. So when I went to people, I had a calling card as good as the name Baker Watts, a prestigious firm not as big as another Baltimore firm. In business since 1900, Baker Watts was also a longtime member of the New York Stock Exchange. Once I arrived there, I used every facility available to me. From the day I went there until now, I was one of the leading producers in my firm. It's no secret that in the last couple of years I haven't worked as hard. Still, I'm among the tops. Going into a brokerage was a complete transition from the retail business that I hated and did badly in. Fortunately, I discovered that I was good at being a broker. ♣

couple's way of life, but with a million-dollar account for our firm. (Of course, it doesn't always work out that way. Mark Dyer and I once flew to Kansas City to show interest in a potential client, but we struck out.)

When you are dealing with a broker, be reasonable in your expectations. Most people who buy a stock expect immediate gratification, particularly if a salesperson has painted a glowing picture of a company and the near-emergency nature of your investment decision: "You can't wait around on this. You've got to get in on the ground floor." Because of the pitches they receive, and despite the true amount of uncertainty involved, some investors develop unfair, overly high expectations for a stock and, in turn, great impatience with their brokers. They are led to think that something big will happen very quickly with that stock, while, in reality, most investments take at least six months to a year to materialize. Rarely does it happen overnight. One of the main ingredients of investor success is patience. In fact, it may take a while just to develop the portfolio and put it into the shape that you really want it to be. You don't do it instantly.

In my experience, most of the problems between broker and client surface with the novice or the unsophisticated customer. If you're a sophisticated investor and I'm the broker, I assume you know certain things, that certain things don't need to be said. There's a little more leeway allowed. The unsophisticated investor is more likely to be confused than an experienced investor, because a sophisticated investor will ask certain very penetrating questions: "What are the company's earnings this year? What is its dividend history? Have you ever talked to company managers?" An unsophisticated investor might completely take a salesman's pie-in-the-sky word for it, like "This stock can only go up." "These discount airlines are all the thing these days." "The company was very strong on the market this morning." "You'd better get in on it now." The salesman is trying to hit the hot buttons with pitches like those.

One important word of advice to potential customers or prospects: There are no emergencies in our business. There is no reason to be rushed into anything. Never. Any broker who tries to push you into signing on the dotted line right away should be viewed with a healthy degree of skepticism and suspicion. You might want to think it over. You might want to talk to other people about the investment. You should never allow yourself to be rushed into buying something.

It's worth adding that a good broker is discreet. I read once that more careers are ruined by loose talk than any other single cause. And I think brokers can absolutely kill themselves if they ever let on at a cocktail party, or anywhere else, that a client had him handle a specific transaction. I know how to keep my mouth shut. I don't even tell one brother how the other brother invests. Sometimes siblings are the most competitive. I learned my lesson early. I once told a brother that another brother took some particular action as an investor, and it backfired on me. From the outside, families may seem close, but when it comes to money, they often are not. One little expression says it all, "If a man can see both sides of a question, you know damn well his money's not tied up in it."

It once came back to me, from a group of people at a social event, that a certain very well-to-do and prominent investor "dealt with Julius Westheimer at Ferris Baker Watts, not because he's so damn smart, but because he knows how to keep his mouth shut." People are very, very guarded and private about their financial affairs. Even if they are wonderfully successful, the last person they want to broadcast their financial successes is me, the broker. If they want to brag, that's okay, but it's not my place to do it. I prefer to say nothing at all about a client. After identifying a client, the next thing I might say is, "He bought a thousand shares of this and that." Clients want me to keep my mouth shut, and that is one thing I can do without too much trouble.

I don't even tell my wife who I go to see in a day, because as soon as I start telling her, it's no longer a secret. Then I have to worry. "Did I let it slip out that I went to see so-and-so the other night?" By being quiet, I know I am safe.

THE SMALL-TIME BLUES

Good stockbrokers should never neglect the so-called small investor.

Even though this client might not have much money to invest now, stockbrokers never know when a person could inherit money, win money, or make money. I have example after example. Here's a letter that I planned to use for a radio broadcast: "Dear Julius, How right you are saying a broker should not turn away anyone with a small amount to invest. I started working at age 55 and since my husband and I didn't need the money, I decided I wanted to learn how to invest. I made an appointment with a broker and had only $500 to invest for a starter. The broker didn't even call or get in touch with me after our meeting. I guess $500 wasn't worth his time. I'm now 59 and have about $50,000 to invest, which is earning interest only in a savings account. Needless to say, I have very little confidence in the stockbroker I originally called."

The woman had the right instincts in the beginning. But, instead of investing in the market, she just put the money in a savings account, apparently because a broker didn't give her the time of day. That he ignored her is horrendous. Yet, some small investors do get treated that way sometimes by some brokers. Now, she has 50 grand, which isn't a bad account for a broker. If a client invests $50,000, and pays the usual 2 to 3 percent commission, the stockbroker earns between $1,000 and $1,500 gross. That's a good day's business. Do that every day for 300 days and you have a good year.

The fact that a broker didn't call her back after their initial meeting was lamentable, but it did not justify her simply saying, "Well, now I'm not going to invest in the market with anybody." I understand well that people can put only a certain amount of emotional energy into getting started as investors, and that if the wind is knocked out of their sails at the beginning, they might just go away. Obviously, this woman was flattened and disheartened by her experience. The broker she met ignored her because all she had was "500 lousy bucks." At that point, though, she was probably the perfect mutual fund investor, but didn't know it. She hasn't done badly in the meantime. If she now has 50 grand, she's obviously earning a good part-time salary, all of which she can put into investing.

Brokers shouldn't turn anyone away. They never know what's in back of a person's "small money." Conversely, if you are turned away by a broker, don't let this turn you off to investing altogether. There are some lousy brokers out there, just as there are in any large profession (about a half million in the U.S.), but they're not a sufficient reason to avoid investing.

However, keep in mind that taking on new customers is not always the easiest thing for a broker to do, regardless of the size of your account. Most successful brokers have at least several hundred customers. Brokers can keep track of and control Client #143's transactions correctly because a good chunk of their clients are basically in the same stable of stocks. But still, it requires a great deal of ability to make the proper, timely adjustments for clients with different financial goals.

INVESTMENT CLUBS

If you are a small investor with too little time and confidence to invest alone, and not enough money for a mutual fund, consider investing through an investment club. Whether you work through a mutual fund or an investment club depends, to some extent, on how much money you have. If all you have is a relatively limited amount of money, like fifty bucks a month, you might want to go the investment club route.

Investment clubs are good for a number of financial, educational, and social reasons. You get together, you get your feet wet as an investor, you swap ideas, you meet new people, you meet a new stockbroker. (Who knows? You might be unhappy with your present stockbroker and decide to transfer your personal account to the club's.)

Back when I was advising a lot of investment clubs, club members were mostly wives of professional men and businessmen. A lot of these investment clubs were really assemblages of friends. Most of the club members had their own or their families' investments separate and apart from the investment club's.

If you're a member of an investment club that studies different stocks and then invests in them, there's no rule that says that you shouldn't make the same investment for your own personal account, whether in larger numbers or not. If the club has bought a stock like Merck because of its solid fundamentals, as explained by the club's broker or the club member who's researching Merck, there's absolutely nothing wrong with being personally enamored of Merck and buying it on the side for yourself. In fact, it's rather a good idea to let the deliberations and decisions of the investment club be a dry run of sorts for what you do as an individual. The club has researched the stock, and a broker may have been there to guide the club's decisions. What you don't want to do is have Merck both in the club and in your private portfolio to such a point that it's more than 20-25 percent of your total holdings. Then you have to be careful.

You might think that whenever you bring 15 people together at an investment club meeting, and confront them with all the possible decisions, the likelihood of consensus would be remote, that in a short time the members would be at each other's throats. But, as the old saying goes, "In the barroom, as the hour gets late and closing nears, everybody starts to look a bit better." If, in the investment club, it gets to be around ten o'clock, members typically move quickly toward a decision. If an investment club, month after month, can't make a decision, members will stop coming. There'd be no reason for the club to exist.

In fact, members will drop in and out of clubs. In a good market, they can't wait to put their money in. In a lousy market, they don't want to do any investing, which, of course, is just the reverse of what they should be doing.

The publication of the book "The Beardstown Ladies' Common-Sense Investment Guide" may have triggered it, but hundreds of thousands of people are joining investment clubs these days. It makes sense historically — investment clubs generally flourish in booming stock markets. People would be better off, though, if they organized, belonged to, and participated in these clubs during depressed markets. But they don't. People are not machines, and when they see the market going up and everyone making money, they get together. Virtually any club that's been formed in the last 15 years has done quite well because the market started out fantastically and has never stopped.

Participation in investment clubs is beneficial for a couple of other reasons. One is automatic investment. It's something like dollar-cost averaging. Your money goes to work every month automatically. If you're a member of a club, you put in 25, 50, or 100 bucks a month. If the club has 15 members, it may be investing $750 a month. And if the average share of stock costs $40, that's about 20 shares purchased by the club each month.

Clubs invest as a whole. The purpose of the meetings is to determine how to invest. One person will give a report on a stock and a broker may be present for two reasons: one is to help with that decision and the other is to get business. I used to advise a large number of investment clubs. There's a social element to them. People don't join just to make money. It's a common activity, something to chit-chat about. They want to get together and talk about their businesses and families.

Investment clubs often make better decisions than individuals, probably because more people are involved and the broker is there at every meeting. As a result of this, clubs generally do well. More people does mean more money, which means that the club has more to work with. So if something goes up even a small amount, they have more shares and they end up doing better.

There's nothing wrong with not buying at every meeting of an investment club. Every meeting doesn't have to generate an order, especially if the club feels that they don't know enough about a stock, or the timing isn't right. On the other hand, one of the ways to make money in the stock market is to always be in it, not on the sidelines watching. One of the objectives of investment clubs is action. Members can say to their friends the next day, "We met last night. We bought Stock X." Not, "We met last night and we didn't do anything." Investment clubs enable people with limited amounts of money to do something positive — invest. On their own, they couldn't or wouldn't, partly because they don't have enough money. A club is really 15 people operating as one, almost with the same amount of money one person would hope to invest on a monthly basis.

By the same token, club members need not decide on a *new* investment each month. Increasing the club's position in a particular company is sometimes a good strategy to take. Members can say, "Look, the stock we bought six months ago is doing nicely. Let's buy some more shares of that."

Expanding present holdings, especially of a good stock, builds up a club's position to where a gain will produce a meaningful profit. Even if the stock doubles or triples, the club gains little in dollars if it has only a few shares. There's nothing wrong, either, with adding to a previous holding when the stock price has gone down. Most people like to add when the stock is going up. But dollar-cost-averaging — putting aside a set amount of money for a particularly attractive stock every month or every six months — is a terrific way to invest.

In sum, an investment club can be a suitable replacement for individual investing if that's all you can do. You are, in effect, creating your own little mutual fund.

WHEN THINGS GO WRONG

It always seems to happen. Whatever stock you've just sold immediately goes up and whatever stock you've just bought immediately goes down. It makes sense. We all have a tendency to buy stocks that are moving up in the market. We all have a tendency to sell stocks that turn doggy all of a sudden. Next to our stocks' listings in the newspaper, we all like to see plus signs. By buying a stock, we think we're going to share in future pluses. Sometimes, at the start, we overpay a little for a stock. These things sometimes equalize themselves.

But a broker can be too aggressive sometimes. If your broker has somehow persuaded you to buy a stock that drops to practically nothing, you may have recourse against the broker. Usually, when people call me on TV to tell me horror stories, they say something like, "I bought a thousand shares of the company at $20 a share from a broker who told me, 'It's a good company, it's a good stock, buy it.'" I say to them,

"Complain directly to the broker, and if that doesn't satisfy you, go over his head. Call and make an appointment with the manager of the office from which you bought the stock. Don't go back through the sales-person again."

A broker is not allowed to make up a client's loss out of his own pocket. But, if the broker painted a pie-in-the-sky picture and looked at the investment only through rose-colored glasses, some disciplinary action might be taken against him, and you may be able to recover some of what you invested. Let's say the broker intentionally misrepresented the potential for the stock, which obviously is a difficult thing to show. (More often than not, if there's an ethical breach, it's a case of broker negligence — or unintentionally bad behavior.) What can a manager of that particular brokerage do for you? Are you going to feel better if he says, "I'll talk to that broker and make sure he never does that again"? Probably not.

The brokerage firm will sometimes offer to settle with you. The individual broker can't refund commissions or make up losses. In fact, brokers are trained on this very subject. If the broker agreed to make good the loss, he or she may be doing so to make sure the complaint never reaches the boss. It's regarded as hush money and is not permitted. But the broker is the firm's paid employee, and if the matter were ever litigated and negligence found, the firm could be held liable. So the firm may have a policy where, if it believes that the broker did misrepresent the purchase, it can make a settlement with you, the customer.

If the matter isn't settled, an "arbitration panel" can hear the dispute and decide to award money to the client. If it does not, the client still has access to the courts.

"TELE-BROKERS"

Some securities salespeople actually look for you. You might get "cold calls" from people you think are brokers and who don't know you from Adam, but try to sell you some securities anyway. I would not touch those calls with a 99 foot pole. Some are from boiler shops in New York, which operate out of brightly lit offices in large warehouses. They exist by having hundreds of telemarketers make hundreds of cold calls a day, and they know what all salesmen know: If they make enough calls, the law of averages or the numbers game will eventually work for them. If they make calls 18 hours a day without eating or sleeping, they can make a good living.

All cold callers are not dishonest. But you should never do business with brokers you haven't met. If, at the beginning of their call, they do not mention a name you know, you can assume that they got your name from a magazine you subscribe to or a directory you're listed in. Especially if you hear voices in the background, you know you are being spoken to from a warehouse floor. These are not your friends and should not be trusted. You are not obligated to do any more than tell them, "Thank you very much, I have a stock-broker. Goodbye." You should not trust anything they say unless they put their offers in writing. Most of these callers are strictly telemarketers, not brokers.

If, however, the caller mentions a local brokerage firm whose name you recognize, like Alex. Brown, Dean Witter, Legg Mason or Ferris Baker Watts, or if they mention a name of a good friend who might have referred them to you, listen to what they say. I was once a young broker who had to make calls like that. If the caller sounds good to you, go to his or her office to meet. New brokers often have to get started by making cold calls. Their names aren't known and they don't have any clients yet. If you meet them in person at a brokerage firm and are happy with them, take them on as your broker.

CHAPTER SUMMARY:
CHOOSING A BROKER

1. *Which broker you choose is really crucial, especially if you are going to delegate discretion to that broker. You should be able to relate personally to the broker and feel assured of results that match your expressed needs and goals.*

2. *When looking for a broker, call up some friends or family and ask who they use. Ask whether they would recommend their broker to you.*

3. *A good broker is one who meets your financial needs and goals. One sign of a good broker-client relationship is regular communication, either annually or semiannually. A good broker is also discreet about the clients he sees. But perfection cannot be expected of even an excellent broker. We are human and occasionally make mistakes.*

4. *Some stockbrokers will not deal with clients who have very small amounts of money. I abhor this practice and, fortunately, lots of brokers will take very small accounts. But if you don't have enough money to invest on your own, consider joining an investment club.*

5. *If you have been destroyed by a major investment that a stockbroker painted as risk-free, go to the broker's boss. You may have grounds for legal action or at least reimbursement.*

6. *Do not buy securities from anyone you haven't met who tries to sell to you on the telephone. If the broker sounds reputable, make an appointment and meet him to make sure he is legitimate.*

CHAPTER *FIVE*

Reading the Stock Listings

*If you want to learn about any particular stock,
the stock listings in the paper contain a wealth of information.*

Each day most major American newspapers publish stock results according to the exchanges on which companies trade: the New York, the American, and the NASDAQ over-the-counter market. Interspersed are various summaries, often in the form of charts, that can tell you, at a glance, which stocks were most active the day before, which ones went up the most, and which ones went down the most in both dollars and percentage terms.

To most investors, that information is fairly useless. It's rare that any one person owns all of those stocks. The only thing they have in common is that they all did something spectacular on the same day. Nor do these summary listings tell you why these stocks went up or down. But other information in these listings can teach you a great deal about a stock if you read it the right way.

STOCKS WITHOUT DIVIDENDS

Let's take one of the big stocks of our day — Microsoft. It's listed on the NASDAQ over-the-counter exchange (the one that advertises itself as the stock exchange for the "next 100 years"). I took a look at Microsoft early in 1997. Even before you get to where the stock closed the day before is a column marked ticker: "tkr symbol." It shows that Microsoft's ticker symbol is *MSFT*. That's of importance if you want to spot it on the CNBC tape that runs during market trading hours, or find it quickly on various other databases.

The first thing my 1997 listing shows, on the left of the stock's name, is its 52-week high, which, in the case of Microsoft, was 158, and the 52-week low, which was 80. In order to make something of that, you have to move across the listing a little bit to see where the stock is now. Back in early 1997, Microsoft had closed the day before at $157 a share. So it was bumping up within a point of its 12-month high. That was also its all-time high. In a single year, it had almost doubled, which is an extraordinary gain.

When I am looking up a stock, the next thing I want to see is the price/earnings ratio: In the case of Microsoft that day, it was 44 times earnings. That was huge, too (compared to its norm of 25 times earnings).

Clearly, Microsoft was no cheap stock, but on the other hand, it could be cheap compared to where it might be the same time next year. I would rather buy a fast-growing company stock near its high than a lackluster growing company near its low. If I was going to buy Microsoft, the fact that it's close to its all-time high wouldn't stop me, because I might think it's going to go higher, and apparently a lot of people do, too, because it's gone way up in 1997.

The next column is DIV, or dividends. In Microsoft's case, that space was blank because Microsoft doesn't pay a dividend. Right next to dividend was the column marked Yield, which would be the percent of yield if Microsoft paid a dividend, which it doesn't, so this space was blank, too. A stock that doesn't pay a dividend has its good points and its bad. The fact that a stock doesn't pay a dividend may mean — as it does in Microsoft's case — that the company directors and executives, rather than pay company profits to the stockholders in the form of dividends, retain those earnings for future expansion. In Microsoft's case, that may be the wiser course. That way they've got money to buy other companies if they want, to open a new plant, to buy new equipment, to hire new people, to start new products.

On the bad side, nobody will ever buy that stock for income because it doesn't provide any. Since there is no dividend to rely on, there's nothing to support its price in a bad market — that is, encourage its stock's purchase. The fact that Microsoft has not paid a dividend to date and is not paying a dividend now does not mean that if its stock price were collapsing for some reason, the company wouldn't suddenly decide to pay a dividend, however miniscule. You don't see that happen often, but it does on occasion.

Dividends do provide a price support for some stocks, like utilities. In a terrible market, Baltimore Gas and Electric, which pays a six percent annual dividend, probably won't drop to $10 a share from about $25 a show. If it did, it would be paying a 20 percent yield because its current dividend is about two bucks a share. A stock that pays a dividend has a kind of price floor — one that offers some support against additional price drops. People who need extra income will buy a stock that's yielding ten percent. Let's say Baltimore Gas & Electric's stock price drops to $20 a share. At that point, BG&E would be yielding 10 percent. There's sort of a floor there. If they think the dividend is secure, a lot of people will go ahead and buy the stock even though the price has dropped.

Some companies that pay dividends don't need to retain their earnings to expand. In the past, for example, utilities didn't need much of that money. They didn't do a great deal of research, or develop a great many new products. They would raise their dividends from time to time to keep current shareholders happy and to encourage new shareholders. Nowadays, however, more and more utilities are gobbling other utilities up. That may mean a new tendency toward retaining earnings in order to have the cash to buy other utilities. Though it recently sought a

WEDDING PICTURE

I was born on September 6, 1916, one of three children, but my parents lost a son the year I was born. As a young child during the Depression, I was rarely deprived of my basic needs. I remember some hungry nights, because one of my punishments was being sent to bed without supper. But there was always plenty of food around our house. I was sometimes bothered by the limited amount of emotional support I received from my parents, who were almost two generations older than I was. My father, who was 44 when I was born, was old enough to be my grandfather, actually, and I was raised in a very rigid, strict Germanic household.

My father was a broker. At night, after seeing the market falling so rapidly, my father was quite unhappy. Dad (on extreme left of the photo above) didn't come home for two full weeks during the big crash. He had me work with him after supper, and I helped send out what are called margin calls. We sent the calls by postcard, and we

also called people by phone who not only couldn't pay their margins, but had lost all their money in the stock market. I learned a great deal of the business at the grass roots when I was very young. I spent my summers at my Dad's firm, too. I was kind of in training for becoming a broker.

My family never had any trouble supporting itself. We lived in comfortable surroundings on Slade Avenue in Baltimore. Dad had custom-made suits before people had suits custom-made, and he had a chauffeur. I had a nurse and my sister had a nurse, too. In really awful times for most of the country, I was raised with a silver spoon in my mouth.

When I was very young, my father often came home from work at night and said, "Son, stock exchange trading today reached a million shares, and that's the break-even point for brokers. That means that all brokerage firms made money today." This was very good news for my family. In effect, if the exchange did a million shares, the rule of thumb was that all brokerage houses, of which there were comparatively few, would make enough commission to show a profit. Today, the average trading on the New York Stock Exchange is nearly half a billion shares, or 500 times as much. I guess we're way past breaking even now, although I am sure there are a lot more brokers and brokerages today than then. ♣

merger, BG&E has raised its dividend nine out of the last ten years, but it has not really raised it very much. It may be retaining more money so it can acquire smaller or larger utilities.

So, to come back to Microsoft, this is not a stock for people nearing the point where they have to live off their dividend income —not, of course, unless a person is willing to chip off the principal of a growing stock to live on. Most people don't like to do that, but I do. Most of my own stocks don't pay much in dividends. So periodically, when I want the money, I sell off shares. I was raised during the Depression, when you didn't even think of doing anything like that. But I'm old enough to realize that principal is one pocket and dividends are another, but they're both pockets in the same suit. So I don't care. (Furthermore, living off of the growth of principal is a little bit better for you tax-wise because you only pay capital gains tax, whereas income is taxed at a higher rate.)

From looking at the stock listings, you might conclude that Microsoft is a world-beater. You might surmise, "It's going up beyond the current 158. Maybe it will go to 200 and split." And it has split two-for-one. This means the price of the stock is divided in half and each stockholder gets twice the number of shares. When they split the price of the stock, they split everything. The P/E (price-earnings ratio) doesn't change because they split the earnings the same day they split the stock. If the stock paid a dividend, that would also drop in the same ratio.

When you look carefully at it, a stock split doesn't give you any more value. All it gives you is more paper. It's as if I give you a ten-dollar bill and you give me two fives in exchange. I have more paper but I don't have more value. However, the fact that a stock splits is generally good news. People like a lot of shares. When, for example, I suggest a stock selling at $60 a share, lots of folks will say, "That's too high. I want a five-dollar stock."

And, for some reason I've never completely understood, the history of split stocks shows that lower-priced stocks tend to advance more in percentage terms than high-priced stocks do. Evidently, more people can buy hundred-share lots, which pushes the price up.

By combining the stock listings in your local newspaper with those in *Barron's*, you the investor can get even more guidance and information. For example, the Baltimore *Sun* shows a stock's high and low this year, as well as its last price. *Barron's* has more column entries, like this week's high and low. For Microsoft on the 1997 day I checked, this was somewhat revealing. The week's high was 158, the week's low was 148, and the close was 157. If you put The Baltimore *Sun* and *Barron's* information together, you saw a stock that had gone straight up from 148 to 157 — and that's a lot in a week.

There are a number of other column headings in the stock listings: Fifty-two week high, name of the stock, ticker symbol, dividend, yield, and P/E (meaning Price/Earning Ratio). Microsoft's P/E ratio is 44 times earnings, which is very high. Price/earning ratio is a relationship, and the fact that Microsoft is selling at 44 times earnings means that Microsoft's stock is selling at 44 times Microsoft's earnings per share. In other words, they're earning around $4 a share and selling for $157 per share. You divide 44 into whatever the stock price is, and that gives you the earnings per share. Even though they're not distributing any of these earnings, and they're plowing them right back into the company, that is a big difference. Four dollars a share of earnings is not particularly high, but the ratio depends on how many shares are outstanding, and that varies widely from company to company.

Over the years, I've found that in the short-term, markets can be very emotional, but in the long-term, markets relate pretty much to the earnings of the companies involved, plus extraneous factors like interest rates. For instance, when there's a surge in interest rates like we experienced during the Jimmy Carter years — when certificates of deposit were yielding 20 and 21 percent — people are going to dump their stocks, no matter how great the earnings are. They will buy CDs and bonds because it would take a much longer time for stocks to earn that rate of return. But interest rate fluctuations like that typically don't last very long.

Though a stock price relates to the earnings of a company over the long haul, there are exceptions. For example, a company like Coca-Cola may have very good earnings, but in the last several years, the price of its stock has gone up faster than its earnings. This means that its price/earnings ratio has moved out of "normal channels." When I last checked, Coca-Cola stock was selling at 30 times its earnings, when the norm was about 22. Because people like the stock, they are willing to pay a high price/earnings ratio for the company's strong rate of growth. They're even willing to pay "inflated prices" because they see the growth rate continuing.

What is important is that a stock price that equates to 44 times earnings is high, when the average stock today is selling at about 22 times earnings (which is historically rather high itself). So Microsoft would be selling at twice the market P/E. That's high. But there's nothing wrong with buying a stock with an exorbitantly high P/E if the earnings growth is rapid enough to justify that high P/E. Stock analysts have various formulas for determining how fast the company has to be growing to justify this or that P/E. A P/E should be compared to the company's historical P/E, not necessarily the P/E of the market.

In the stock listings, there's usually a column marked "VOL," or volume. That is the number of shares, usually in hundreds of thousands or millions, that the stock traded the day before. In Microsoft's case, when I checked in early 1997, the volume the day before had been 10,720, which, because it's shown in hundreds of shares, means almost 1.1 million shares were traded. The volume on NASDAQ is huge. Half a billion shares are traded on its exchange every day. One million shares traded in Microsoft is not quite a drop in the bucket.

The volume of shares traded becomes of special significance when a stock goes up "on huge volume." That means there's a lot more demand than supply. Generally that's interpreted as something good — that thousands more people bought it than sold it, thereby pushing the price up. If a stock moves up on low volume, it generally isn't interpreted as enthusiastically.

It's hard to know from most stock listings how many shares a company has outstanding — that is, how many Microsoft shares actually exist. To find that out, you get a report from *Standard and Poor's*,

Moody's, or Value Line. That information typically doesn't appear in a newspaper or a financial magazine because nobody, except an analyst, knows what to do with it.

The next column to examine is weekly volume and weekly change. This 1997 listing showed Microsoft up six and three -eighths points for the week. That's a lot. But you can't do much extrapolating from that number. You get yourself into trouble if you say, "Look, in one week the stock went up three percent all told, and if it keeps going up at that rate for 52 weeks, why, I'll be a billionaire." Obviously, the weekly increase is a good sign for the stock's movement. But an analyst would better know what to do with that information than the average person. Most people would like to buy a stock that's up six points for the week because they prefer stocks that are going up over those that are going down. Unfortunately, this is generally the wrong thing to do.

STOCKS *WITH* DIVIDENDS

Now, for a stock that, unlike Microsoft, pays a dividend, let's look at an early 1997 listing for AT&T, the most widely known stock, and the most widely held stock, in the world — in most cases because of its dividend history. (Somebody who really wants to dig back in time, to know what its dividends have been for the last ten years, would want to consult *Moody's Handbook of Common Stocks,* a four-volume-a-year work.).

When I checked in early 1997, AT&T's high for the year had been 49, the low 33 and it had closed the day before at 37. It was paying a dividend of $1.32. Its yield was 3.6. It was selling for 37 times earnings.

Of course, analysts can play around with price/earnings ratios. Are they "trailing earnings" (from the last twelve months), or future earnings? If you want to get a low P/E, you use future earnings, since you estimate that those earnings will be higher. Therefore, the ratio will be lower. Typically, though,when they show P/E, they're using trailing earnings, that is, those from the last 12 months.

AT&T's trading volume was listed as 20,520, or about 2 million shares traded — volume again was shown in hundreds. AT&T's net change for the week was minus a quarter. *Barron's* also gives you the earnings, dividends, the record date, and the payment date. They really go into this deeply. Their listing even shows an actual day for dividend payment.

Let's suppose that AT&T is going to pay a dividend on November 30, and I find out a week ahead of time because I read *Barron's.* It is not silly to buy the stock after the payment dividend date. It doesn't matter. The day on which stockholders get their dividend, the stock automatically drops in price the same amount. It's called the ex-dividend date. In other words, you can't buy a stock the day before a dividend is paid and get the dividend for free. Your stock will drop automatically. I wouldn't worry too much about this. The amount of money one way or the other isn't going to be that much, and you're not buying the stock just for that dividend anyhow.

THE FEELING IS MUTUAL

Let's take another example of a market report in a daily newspaper — this time of a mutual fund. Suppose you own shares in a Montgomery Growth Fund, a member of a San-Francisco-based mutual fund family. To find out information about that, you'd look under mutual funds. Every day except Saturday, the Baltimore *Sun* prints the weekly changes of mutual funds. Most newspapers publish listings grouped by fund families. Looking down the list, as I did early in 1997, I saw that the week's close for Montgomery Growth was $21.26, down .07. I noticed that Montgomery Growth has the initials "N.L." beside it, which means it's a no-load fund. In a no-load fund, the net asset value is what governs the cost of the fund. A load fund means you pay a commission. The difference between the bid and price asked in the paper is the amount you pay in commission.

If you own a mutual fund like Montgomery Growth, you should not be following the price of your shares every day. It often seems to me that people who own individual stocks know the price of their stock on a daily basis, while those who own mutual funds tend to focus not on the share price at all but on the mutual fund's total value or appreciation in value. In fact, they may have little idea of the share price, because the mutual fund is nothing more than the price of all the stocks in the fund divided by the number of shares in the fund. But mutual fund investors don't usually keep track of the exact numbers. Some mutual fund investors look only at the fund's quarterly statement, which shows how much the fund has gone up in the quarter, how much it has gone up in the last year, and maybe how much it's gone up in the last three years.

Barron's gives you a ton of data about mutual funds, much more than the daily papers. For example, it carries a 52-week high and 52-week low column for mutual funds. When I looked early in 1997, the high for the year for Montgomery Growth Fund was $21.30, the low was $16.38. It closed the day before at $21.26, so it, like Microsoft, was bumping up against its high for the year. Up to that point, it had had a good year: it had gone from 16 something to 21 something. That's not bad — about a 25 percent increase so far in 1997. The year-to-date return was 23.1 percent. That's the appreciation of the fund plus the dividends.

Some mutual funds pay dividends as well, but we don't really buy mutual funds for dividends. Timing is important in a mutual fund only around the end of November. You don't want to buy a mutual fund right before it declares its year-end capital gain dividend because then you'd be paying tax on a dividend you never got.

The other mutual fund listings of interest to an investor are: nine-week high and low, close, and net asset value. The listings also show week's change and percent return over one week, year to date, and three years. As of 1997, Montgomery Growth Fund was about three years old. Its three-year return had been 104 percent. That's adding together all of its increases over the three years. To me, Montgomery Growth Fund seemed to be a real winner. It didn't pay much income, but that's because it's a growth fund.

To determine whether I'd want to buy Montgomery Growth, I'd also want to see its annual report. Someone who's familiar with mutual funds can dig a lot of stuff out of an annual report, especially of a mutual fund: the current fund managers, how long they have been there, their prior record, what kind of stocks the fund invests in. This report can also reveal the various earnings records of the companies involved.

But a 104 percent return over three years means an average annual increase of almost 35 percent. In 1995, the market overall was up 34 percent. In 1996, it was up about 27 percent. The year before that, it went up not at all — it was a standoff. So the fact that Montgomery has done that well over three years means it's outperforming the market, nearly by double. That's a good and useful statistic to have.

Most newspapers regularly publish explanations on how to read their particular stock listings, and I recommend that investors spend some time with them. If I only read one thing, I look at where the stock closed yesterday, because I know basically where it's been and what it cost me. All most people really care about is the net change from yesterday or last week, because then they usually know how much money they have made to that point. There's far more to extract from these tiny lines of print.

CHAPTER SUMMARY:
READING THE STOCK LISTINGS

1. *The best way to get simple, clear-cut information without all the extra commentary is to read and make sense of the stock listings. Most newspapers have explanations on how to read their particular stock listings.*

2. *The first thing to check when looking up a stock in the newspaper is its 52-week high and low. If you compare those numbers with where it is now, you can see where it has been over the year. I would rather buy a fast-growing company near its high than a lackluster growing company near its low.*

3. *Next, you want to check whether a stock pays a dividend. Without a dividend, no one will ever buy that stock for income. However, this might mean that the company is retaining profits for new developments, which can be a good sign.*

4. *A stock that does pay a dividend is a little different. It might be valuable for income, although dividend rates are very low right now. There is no advantage to buying stock just before the dividend is paid.*

5. *Next you will see the Price/Earnings Ratio. Even if the price is very high, some people might continue to buy an inflated stock if it continues to generate big earnings. A broker can help explain this. (See Chapter 11 for more on P/E Ratio and other significant figures.)*

6. *Most newspapers list mutual funds by fund families. A load fund means you pay a commission for the mutual fund; a no-load fund charges no commission for buying or selling.*

7. *Barron's gives you much more data about mutual funds than the daily papers. It carries a 52-week high and low column for mutual funds as well as individual stocks, and it also includes the nine-week high and low, close, net asset value, week's change and percent return over one week, year to date, and three years. Getting a sense of the stock's price history can be quite helpful.*

Chapter Six

The Housekeeping
of Investing

*The humdrum housekeeping details of being an investor are often
overlooked, but they're important, and shouldn't be ignored.*

When you buy stock, who holds the certificate? What do you actually get? Where should you put it? What should you do to make sure you don't lose it? What do you do when you want to sell it? These may sound like picayune questions, but they are just some of the nitty-gritty areas of investing where someone's experience, like mine, is probably helpful.

LEAVE YOUR STOCK WITH THE BROKER

Let's walk through the process, starting with Step One: You decide you want to buy a stock. You call me up and say, "Westy, buy me 40 shares of Microsoft."

In the old days, after we'd had this conversation, I the broker would execute the order to buy, and in three or four weeks my brokerage office

JULIUS MILTON WESTHEIMER
5 Slade Ave., Baltimore, Md.
Park School; Soccer (3, 4);
Basketball (3, 4); Lacrosse (2,
3, 4); P. S. Board (3); Bus.
Mgr. School Paper (4); Dramatics (2, 3, 4); Dramatics As-
sembly Comm. (3, 4); Chairman (4).
312 Hitchcock

STUDENT DAYS

In my high school years at Park School in Baltimore, I generally didn't work very hard and, as a result, had rather poor grades. Teachers would invariably tell me, "You've got it in you, but you're not applying yourself." I didn't much listen. I pitched pennies and generally fooled around. If Madame Lash hadn't certified me for French, I would have had to take college boards, and I don't think I would have been admitted to college. So when I asked my father if I could go into his business after college, he said, "Son, I'm not sure you're capable of getting out of your chair and going up to some guy to sell him a hundred shares of stock." From what he had seen of my lackluster high school performance, he was right to have had such a dim view of my future.

It wasn't until after a very rough six months at Dartmouth College that things began to change. I turned diligent and, in what was a complete reversal of attitude from high school, I began to buckle down and work. I spent endless hours in the library. Not only did I decide to get a Phi Beta Kappa key, but I was single-minded in pursuing it. I even succeeded at some extracurricular activities. I was made one of the editors of the Daily Dartmouth, and became a columnist. All of this was to convince my parents or myself or my girlfriend that I was no dummy. By the way, I did get that Phi Beta Kappa key. I graduated magna cum laude: a complete turnaround from my Park School years. ❧

would send you a certificate that says, "You're the owner of 40 shares of the common stock of Microsoft." After that, you the investor would troop the certificate over to your safe deposit box and lock it up.

Ninety-five percent of investors today leave their stocks with a brokerage firm in what's called street name. Street name is short for "Wall Street," and it means that no certificate actually is printed with the buyer's name on it. But some great computer in the sky (or up in New York) registers the fact that you're now the proud owner of 40 shares of Microsoft. From that point on, your monthly brokerage statement will show that you are "long" 40 shares of Microsoft. In other words, you own them.

In the case of bearer bonds, which have no one's name on them, there used to be even more of a reason to have them given to and maintained by your broker. But there are very few bearer bonds left today, and by the time this book comes out, there probably won't be any at all. Almost all bonds are now registered bonds. They have your name on them as the owner. Also done away with, thankfully, is the very time-consuming and cumbersome process of clipping coupons from bonds.

And that's not all. Within five to ten years, I suspect there will be no more actual stock or bond certificates. Everything will be book entry. Not only will there be less possibility of theft and disappearance of stock certificates, but much less back-and-forth, signing on the back of the certificates, things like that. Everything will be automated, including the payment of dividends.

It's no big wonder that leaving stock in the hands of a broker is now the norm. There are distinct advantages over having a certificate printed with your name on it. For one thing, the quarterly dividend check, which could be lost in the mail and has to be deposited, is automatically credited to your account at the brokerage firm. Most people tell their brokers to periodically send them a certain amount of money from their credit balance, with the rest staying in their brokerage account. The broker uses direct deposit, so the money goes straight into the client's checking account. That avoids the potential problems and inconveniences of losing checks and having to go through the whole deposit process.

Another great advantage in leaving your stocks with a broker is that, when you sell the stock, you don't have to worry about locating and surrendering the certificate. You don't have to drive to the bank, open the safe deposit box, bring the certificate out to the car, worry that you're going to be held up, mail the certificate to the broker, wonder if it's going to arrive on time, and perhaps conclude you have to deliver it in person to the broker.

Mr. Murphy (of "Murphy's Law" infamy) can visit a great many steps along the way. Suppose, for example, that you the investor remove stock certificates from your safe deposit box in order to take them to your broker for sale. As you walk down the street with your stack of stock certificates, someone puts a gun to your ribs and says, "I want everything you've got." You, of course, want to save your life, so you follow the thief's directions, surrendering to him the certificates. A smart thief, with some difficulty, can forge your name on the back, take the certificates to some unwary broker, and request that he "sell them for me and send me the cash." The unsuspecting broker might well do his bidding.

Certificate questions pop up even without hypothesizing a theft. Clients can't find stock certificates with great regularity. They're forever calling my secretary and asking, "How do I get my Baltimore Gas and Electric stock replaced? I've lost it." My secretary, who, like me, has had 35 years experience in the business, knows that the clients probably did not lose the certificate, that that certificate is somewhere. It's either in the bottom bureau drawer, in an envelope from the company, or in a safe deposit box buried under a pile of pages. Ninety-nine times out of 100, the stock certificate turns up.

My advice is to avoid all this unnecessary complication and worry. Leave your stock with your broker. Every brokerage account is now insured up to $500,000 by SIPC, an acronym for Securities Investor Protective Corporation, a quasi-government agency. In addition to that, some brokerage firms have very large blanket policies, per account, to protect the client against embezzlement. If I (the broker) pick up $300,000 worth of tax-free bonds from Mrs. Gotrocks's safe deposit box and head off with them, she need not worry.

Most brokerage firms also "bond" their brokers. In our firm, we're bonded up to $300,000. And, as a client, your securities are segregated by computer from the other assets of the other clients of the broker.

There's another, more practical advantage to leaving your stocks with a broker. If your broker keeps your stocks, he has an instantaneous record of what you own. On an informal record in a file somewhere else, he may know that you bought 100 shares of BG&E from him and stuck the certificates in a safe deposit box. But if all those same stocks' certificates are at a broker and appear on a customer's statement every month, the broker can look at a duplicate copy periodically and exercise better control over the client's account. I keep a continuing file myself so that I can look back and analyze what you, the investor, have done. It's there for my reference and yours. If the client calls and says, "You bought me a hundred shares of BG&E and I notice that it's gone up three points in the last couple of weeks," I have something handy to refer to during the conversation.

Letting the broker be the custodian of your stocks and bonds is good from the broker's point of view for yet another important reason. If he wants you, the client, to sell something, he can say: "It's perfectly painless. The stock is here. If it's OK with you, we'll go ahead." If we're in the middle of a February blizzard, and you the client can't possibly get to the safety deposit box to retrieve your certificates, you'll be quite inclined to forget completely about the recommended transaction, even if it is in your best interest.

Most brokerage accounts today remain "non-discretionary" (you the investor make all the final decisions), though there are advantages to having accounts set up otherwise. My partners and I decided some time ago that, if clients are willing to entrust us with control (and discretion) over their accounts' operation, it works out better for them (many people want their brokers to make all the final decisions) and us. We can make the changes that we consider appropriate, and don't have to call the client every morning and say, "I think we should sell a hundred shares of Intel and buy 100 shares of Hewlett-Packard." That's really cumbersome. You the client might be on vacation, or just out, and when you call back, I may not be there to talk to you.

I should emphasize here that, if you give your broker discretion, it's even more important to stay in touch with him. If your financial circumstances or goals change, the broker should be among the first to find out directly from you.

Let's suppose that you, the client, had a discretionary account with me. I went ahead and handled the above stock swap — in effect, I sold 100 shares of one technology company (Intel) and bought 100 of another (Hewlett-Packard). I would send you a confirmation in the mail the day after the purchase. It would say, "On such and such a date, you sold 100 Intel and you bought 100 Hewlett Packard and the data on that should correspond with the data on your month-end statement." That way there are no surprises. You're kept abreast of activity in your account. And if you're out of town at the time, you get the transaction notices when you come home.

One more advantage of leaving your stock with a broker: You get only one 1099 tax form at the end of the year instead of a couple dozen. So it simplifies your tax preparation. At Ferris Baker Watts, you get one 1099 each year showing your income from dividends and bond interest. You give that to your accountant and that's it.

So clearly, when clients ask me, "Should I keep this certificate or should you?" I don't hesitate to say, "Let me keep the actual stocks. Let my firm be the custodian." Then, if the client calls and says, "I don't know when I bought those 100 shares," I, the broker, can find either hard copy or a computer record pretty quickly.

HOW TO READ CORPORATE REPORTS

Even though I the broker hold the stock certificate for you, the company sends its annual reports directly to you the registered shareholder. If you own stock in 20-25 companies, you'll get enough quarterly and annual reports to fill a giant drawer. You can't keep up with that volume. Nor do you want to. Most investors just scan these company reports. Few study the numbers printed in them.

Don't worry. Most annual reports are partly public relations documents. At McCormick & Co., a large Baltimore-based firm that I like, the public relations department uses the company annual report to tell you how great its spices are. (The company even "scents" these reports.) It's true that they have to include detailed financial figures in the back of their report, but the so-called average person may not be able to decipher them. An analyst can. Investors should still read the front part of the annual report, so they can know what their companies are doing, but leave most of the decision making process to the broker.

Sometimes these annual reports provide important information. They may speak of a "disappointing year," or one when a division was sold off and the company had to take a large write-off against earnings. Or they may give you a head's-up that the next several quarters should be better for the company. Or they may say that they're changing their business in some fundamental way. The president's report, which usually appears at the front of the annual report, should be read for just this sort of information, with other company claims taken with a grain of salt.

It's partly because these reports go largely unread that many companies are cutting down on them, or at least making them less elaborate or flamboyant than they used to be. It's much like putting on a TV news broadcast that you know no one will watch, except that these company reports are legally required.

Let's say I run a small to mid-sized public corporation that issues stock. For me, the annual reports are a very expensive proposition. I've got to pay people to write them, lay them out, print them, and mail them out. I go to all this expense and trouble mostly because it's a legal obligation, and partly because I see the report as a selling tool. People may read my annual report and say, "What a wonderful company. I'll buy more stock."

In this day and age, it seems to me that, if you want to find out about the state of a company's finances, you could quite easily go to the company's web site. In the comfort of your own home, you could locate the corporate numbers, download them, print them out, and analyze them without the corporation incurring the great expense of printing and mailing the reports. Yet, companies still must print and mail these reports because a lot of investors, especially older ones, don't know how to find the information on a web site (or even know what a web site is). But that will undoubtedly change in the years ahead.

I have rarely read annual reports that made me say, "Hmm, I'd better do this or that." The reports seem to have just as little an effect on my clients. Rarely do they ever phone me to say, "I noticed blah blah in the annual report." People receive a great amount of junk mail these days, most of which they don't bother to open, much less read.

Occasionally, I might hear this from a client: "I read the annual report. The company started out in the insurance business and now it's doing car rentals. Should we keep it?"

PROXIES

On the other hand, I do try to take note of proxy votes. Shareholders get proxy requests all the time. "Will you allow us to vote for you in your physical absence on various corporate matters?" Many people toss the proxy requests out, saying, "How in the world would I know what slate of officers ought to be reelected for another term? And besides, my vote compared to a mutual fund's three trillion is absolutely meaningless. I'm wasting my time and postage." But, as both investor and broker, I take a different tack. I generally sign and return proxies for the stock I own in my own name.

I almost always vote *with*, not *against*, management. I figure the company's top managers know what they're doing. If not, I don't want to hold the stock. Casting my proxy vote, I realize, generally accomplishes little. Management controls the vast number of stock shares anyhow. But I just check off my proxy in the appropriate place and send it in so I don't get a phone call back, usually during dinner, asking me why I hadn't returned it yet.

The average investor, I believe, usually should support management. Management apparently knows what it's doing or else the company wouldn't be profitable. If the company isn't profitable, you don't want to own the stock.

There's one other reason to return proxies. If I don't vote on who ought to control the company, an outside slate could get onto the board of directors, take the company in a different direction, and wreck my investment. It's much like some presidential elections, when you read newspaper stories about people saying their vote doesn't count. Next to these are stories about political races decided by three votes or six — or where a change of one vote per precinct all over the country would have changed the whole outcome. You never know.

INTEREST RATE UPS AND DOWNS

One thing to be aware of as an investor is that when interest rates are high, the market usually sinks a bit. When we have another rate increase — and such fluctuations are inevitable — it won't be the end of the world. Today's market is on strong and solid long-term pinning. Unemployment is down, production is up. If interest rates have to be hiked a little to hold off inflation during an economic boom, we should accept that. Inflation isn't good for the investor or the broker or anyone else.

Still, the ups and downs of interest rates can have a very negative effect on some stocks. When, for example, interest rates go up, public utility stocks do badly for two reasons. Number one, utilities are big borrowers of money, so high interest rates hurt them. But even more important, when interest rates go up, money goes where it's treated best. It flows into the investments which pay the highest interest rates — CDs, bonds, and things like that — and abandons utility stocks, which are generally yielding lower rates of return. Conversely, when interest rates come down, utility stocks move up, because utility stocks pay a fairly high rate of return.

After an interest rate increase during the spring of 1997, a few of my clients called in panic. I told them, "In a market like this, stick to fundamentals, which is presumably what we have been doing all along anyway." In other words, do nothing different. Don't listen to a lot of curbstone gossip. Don't follow the crowd — because the crowd is generally wrong. Don't panic. Don't sell good stocks in a bad market. Proceed in an orderly fashion.

But the public is very media-conscious today. Every time Alan Greenspan sneezes, Wall Street catches a cold. You don't ignore Greenspan. As the head of the U.S. Federal Reserve system, he has his finger on the nation's interest rates, and if he thinks the market is too euphoric and the economy overheated, he can, through his various processes, raise interest rates, which in turn affects short-term borrowing costs. That can upset a couple of things. If businesses need to borrow more money, it costs them more in interest costs, and that can hold the economy back. If interest rates shoot up, Jane Doe, instead of buying a stock that yields two percent, will buy a bond that yields more.

We must stick to the basics. In the latest big drop in the market, in the spring of 1997, a lot of people and institutions responded in a reasonably rational way, which was rather encouraging. There was no wholesale dumping of stocks. There was no general panic. On some days, the market did drop 100 points, but investors weren't as worried as they had been in the past. In 1994, when the Dow was around 3,000, a market drop of 100 points was a lot — 3 percent. Today, with the Dow slightly over 8,000, a drop of a hundred points on any single day is a mere 1 percent drop in value. It doesn't signal the end of the world, though it's good copy for guys like me on radio and television. To again put things in perspective, "Stick with the fundamentals. Stay with quality. Don't let every news bulletin upset your long-range planning."

HOW OFTEN SHOULD YOU TRACK YOUR STOCKS?

I think it's a mistake to track your stocks every week. It may give you something to call your broker about, but checking once every three months is plenty. There's no advantage in tracking a stock's price each day, either. It doesn't make you a better decision-maker. A two-month, or three-month, or six-month chart may be helpful, particularly toward year-end when you the investor are balancing gains against losses. But during the year, the stock's price isn't quite as important. It's true that if a stock you own doubles or triples, you may want to sell half of it just to salt away the profit, particularly if it's a retirement account where there are no capital gains taxes to be paid. But what counts is what's happening to the company fundamentally.

As brokers, we watch our clients' portfolios. But I don't blame clients for watching themselves. It's their hard-earned money. And it's fun to watch when the market is going up. The clients who track investments from time to time — not every day — generally make the best decisions. Watching too carefully and too often can backfire.

An example: Suppose you were tabulating your portfolio value every Sunday. A stock you bought at 40 went up a little, quickly reached 50, and then, over a four week period, went down to 30. Over a month's time, it had fluctuated 20 points, which is a lot.

Most investors who detected that movement would say, "It's in a free-fall, a meltdown. I can see the pattern. It keeps going down sharply. Let's get rid of this thing." But bear this in mind: When people see a stock going down, they always call their broker and say, "Shall we sell it?" They rarely call to ask, "Should we buy more?" which generally turns out to be the better question. If the fundamentals of the company are good and the stock is dropping, you generally don't want to sell it. Most likely it's dropping because it's being hit by an emotional wave of selling, and such waves and drops can continue. If stocks do drop that much, I don't fault clients for calling their brokers, to get from us a solid reason why we're doing nothing (that's also a decision), why we're buying more stock, or why we're selling some or all of what we have.

I'm able to deal better with you as a client if you are tracking your portfolio periodically and reacting. But if you're going to keep track of your investments fairly often, do it whichever way the market is moving — up or down. As I've observed all too often, investors tend to keep track more often in a rising market, and when a lot of people are keeping track frequently, it's usually a sign that the market's going to tumble — most people look at their stocks *only* on the way up. In 1995, the market went up 34 percent; in 1996, it rose 27 percent. In 1997, it has continued to climb sharply in a phenomenon I haven't seen before. The Dow went through the 6,000 barrier in 1996. That it has gone up to where it is in July 1997 (more than 8,000) is quite amazing though, as I'll explain later, understandable.

DON'T DISCARD YOUR MONTHLY STATEMENTS

I advise my clients to review the monthly statements from my brokerage firm soon after receiving them. Our firm's statement prices the client's investments. It will say at the top: "Today's value, $278,000. Last month's value, $263,000." The investor should look at that and, if it looks like there are more minuses than pluses, talk to the broker about it.

You, too, should also pay close attention to your monthly statement. Every month, study it and compare the list of stocks you think you own — on a list you yourself compile — with those listed on the broker's statement. If you get a monthly statement from a brokerage that shows a stock you didn't think, or didn't remember, you owned, a rare mistake may have occurred. Call your broker so he'll check to be sure no computer has unintentionally moved some of your holdings to someone else's account because of a social security number that's close to yours. Once every five years, a client will call me up and say, "Why does my statement show me with this stock? I don't remember buying it." And he turns out to be right.

That's a big improvement over the old pencil and paper days. When I was a kid, my father came home one night and said to me, "I bought some shares of stock that weren't listed on my brokerage statement, and my own firm prepared the statement!" As it happened, Dad's stock was put unintentionally in the name of Milton Wertheimer, instead of *his* name, Milton Westheimer. In his book entry, a clerk had inadvertently changed one letter in the stock owner's last name. Those were the days of bow and arrow, flint and steel. But I have seen modern, super-fast computers make a few similar mistakes in my day, too. Human beings can enter wrong data on a computer, just as they could wrongly read and write somebody's last name in the old horse-and-buggy days.

With the advent of computers, modems, and pagers, we may soon see a time when, if you have an account with a brokerage, you won't have to wait till the end of the month to get a statement. You'll be able to plug into a data base and find out right this minute, while you're thinking about it, what you have, where your stock is, and what it's worth. Some people with computers already enter their stocks on a software program and update and price their portfolios every day, every hour. It's lunacy, but they do it. It's something for them to do. It fills their day.

One person I know has a sizable brokerage account, and every morning dials a certain number, where an automated voice says, "As of eight o'clock on the morning of whatever today is, your account is worth X million and so many hundred thousand dollars." The brokerage, no doubt using a software program of one kind or another, automatically determines the account's total value, after which a voice synthesizer "reads" the client those numbers. For investors, some forms of high technology may not turn out to be so wonderful.

CHAPTER SUMMARY:
THE HOUSEKEEPING OF INVESTING

1. *Leave your stock and bond certificates with your broker. It allows you and the broker to make changes to the account when necessary, and it also eliminates the danger of losing your certificates.*

2. *Annual and semiannual reports are part of the legal obligations required when a company sells its stock. They are partly public relations materials. Many people don't read them and, if they do, are usually not influenced by them. However, the financial numbers in the back can be informative, at least for professional analysts. If you read the report, you may find items of use, such as the president's report, but take some of that with a grain of salt.*

3. *Don't worry too much about rising interest rates. They sometimes make the market come down a little, but in the long run they can be good news. Interest rates are raised to halt inflation in a good economy, and everyone benefits from a good economy.*

4. *When interest rates are high, stick to the fundamentals, like the company's earnings. If they are all right, the stock will usually come back in price.*

5. *If you want to track your stocks regularly, follow them during up periods and down ones, and don't let your emotions control your buying and selling.*

6. *To make the best decisions, track your investments periodically, like every couple of months.*

7. *Read your monthly statement from the brokerage firm with care. If you see more minuses than pluses, ask to meet with your broker. If the stocks you see don't match up with the ones you thought you owned, call to make sure there was not a computer error.*

CHAPTER SEVEN

Tracking the Market

*Only your doctor can evaluate the medical and health news
you've read, then apply it to your situation.
The same is true of brokers, financial news, and investors.*

oday, there's such a growing, even overwhelming surplus of
investment information that you could easily make it your
full-time occupation just to keep track of what's being written,
and that's not even talking about what's on the Internet. I know;
I've probably read more publications that have to do with investing
and personal finance than practically anyone I know. I have even
written about a few of them myself. For years, my newspaper column
was practically a reader's guide to the personal investment information
published elsewhere.

Each week, dozens of newspaper columns and TV programs about
investing bombard the public with more information than they will ever
need. And of course, there is now a proliferation of all-news 24-hour-a-
day networks on television, from the new Fox News Channel, to the
Financial News network, which is an offshoot of CNN, to MSNBC. All
of these networks have programs on financial subjects. I regularly watch

CNBC, which runs stock prices across the bottom of its screen, and which, in my opinion, puts some very credible people on the air.

THE TROUBLE WITH BOMBARDMENT

A lot of people, especially novice investors, welcome this bombardment. We're a self-help population. We always figure that, if there's information out there, we'll grab it, and we'll use it well. But, unfortunately, there is a downside to all this available information. Sometimes, broad-casters are merely dispensing the rough equivalent of curbstone advice, yet we believe them because they are on television. They may advise purchase or consideration of a certain stock, but they have no fiduciary obligation to come back later to say they've changed their mind. That would be burdensome, maybe even impossible, for the broadcasters — and it would be boring for the viewers.

I think there is a lesson from the old days, when there weren't four hundred experts giving conflicting advice each week. I find it helpful to strip away all the extraneous material with which we presently are bom-barded — all the advice and market-analysis tools — and stick to fun-damentals, like old-time investors did in the past.

Investors should stick to the central issues in stock worth. Ask these questions: What does the company earn? What dividends does it pay? What share of the market does it have? How strong and aggressive is its management? Is it relatively competition-free or competition-resistant?

My advice is: If, in your reading, watching, or listening, some stock gets your attention, talk to your broker about it. The broker is going to know a lot more than what's in the news, and much more than you, even with the torrent of information you may receive. Let the broker do some additional research and evaluation for you.

Suppose one day you were suffering from a terrible pain in your shoulder, and you read in the paper that such pains are generally because of pulled muscles. If you took Extra-Strength Tylenol, the arti-cle said, the pain would go away. You know immediately you must be careful about taking this advice, that before acting on it, you should have your doctor determine precisely where your own shoulder pain comes from. It might be related to your shoulder, but then again it could have something to do with your heart, which would make it an altogether more serious matter. Only your doctor can evaluate the medical and health news you've read, then apply it to your situation. I think the same thing is true of financial news and brokers. If you have faith in your broker — and if you don't, you shouldn't be using him—the broker can and should evaluate the worth of your ideas and information.

For example, you might read that Bristol-Myers-Squibb is coming out this quarter with "superior earnings." But there is so much you still don't know. The earnings are superior — compared to what? Are they better or worse than last year's? Did a big, one-time profit from the sale of a division or a subsidiary make the company's earnings look especially good? As some wag once put it, "A little knowledge can be a dangerous thing."

THE "GOOD MEDIA"

There are a lot of financial books, shows, and periodicals that I find very useful to investors. There are some excellent books on personal investing that I think we're still going to want to read years from now. *The Intelligent Investor*, by Benjamin Graham, tops that category, partly because its contents are so easy to remember. I also frequently cite *One Up on Wall Street* by Peter Lynch, because it's so accessible to the average investor. And I always recommend an old favorite: John Kenneth Galbraith's *The Great Crash of '29*. It stuns me to realize that three out of every four mutual fund managers today were not alive when the big one hit Wall Street in October 1929.

There are also some excellent television shows that are very useful for watching and interpreting the stock market. "Money Line with Lou Dobbs," is quite good (it's on CNBC). "The Nightly Business Report" on PBS is excellent. "Wall $treet Week With Louis Rukeyser" is the best of

FOR MY THIRD CAREER

I became a print journalist quite a few years ago and somewhat by chance. In 1969, I asked Jesse Glasgow, then the financial editor of The Baltimore Sun, if I could write something for him. He replied, "Sure, but I don't pay for articles." I said, "I couldn't care less." Next, I got into the Wall Street Journal. I saw Dan Dorfman's name every day on his column, "Heard on the Street." I called him one day, told him who I was, and asked if I could see him in New York. He said, "What do you want to see me about?" And I said, "I have an idea for your column." All I did was ask for the appointment. I met with Dorfman, told him my idea about the need to focus on growth stocks in the investing world. He quizzed me, quizzed me, and quizzed me more, all while taking copious notes. He asked me to send him something. Lo and behold, I picked up the Journal one day and there it was, a piece all about me and my growth stock ideas. After that, Dorfman wrote a number of columns about my investing ideas and so did Bob Metz of the New York Times.

When my freelance writing finally trailed off in 1977, I started to write regularly for The Baltimore Sun. Doing the "Ticker" column was great publicity for me and my business. So had been writing columns about investing in the Wall Street Journal or having my name pop up in other papers. I didn't do all this media work planning to become a financial journalist — I was trying to get publicity for my business.

"Wall $treet Week With Louis Rukeyser" started on Nov. 19, 1970. A year or so before, Anne Darlington, the creator of the show, asked me if I would be interested in participating. She had seen some of my stuff in print. I declined because I thought it was going to be just another local show, seen by few. It was a major mistake on my part. In 1971, when I realized what a howling success it would be, I auditioned for the show and was accepted for it. The show has been the centerpiece of my career and I have been on it as a panelist ever since (photo above is from the show's early days).

Later, Channel 2 in Baltimore asked me if I would do a weekly segment on the Sunday night 11 o'clock TV news. I agreed, and did that for five years. Then, in 1980, I moved to Channel 11, where I gave financial information a local angle and reported often on Baltimore stocks. My stuff was the only game in town. I have happily remained with WBAL-TV ever since. ❦

them all. (Obviously, I have a pretty personal attachment to that show, but I do consider it a gem.)

"Wall $treet Week With Louis Rukeyser," a prize-winning, coast-to-coast TV show aired on PBS stations, gives you a multi-part look at your money. Part One is the opening, when Louis provides an astute and witty analysis of the financial and economic news of the week. Then, carefully selected panelists from the financial world respond to Louis' (or viewers') questions and also comment about the stock market. Following that, the host, with support from the show's excellent graphic designers, educates viewers on a topic related to the program's special guest. The show's final segment finds Louis — then the panelists — asking the guest about his or her special field.

From a viewer of "Wall $treet Week With Louis Rukeyser" viewer, I had a question recently that really stumped me. A guy asked, "Are there any stocks I can buy that relate to funerals and funeral homes?" Unfortunately, I made a little light of the topic, and I shouldn't have, because it's a booming industry. The next Monday I went right to our research department and got the names of three or four publicly traded stocks from that area, and immediately supplied them to the producer.

When it comes to regular and constant coverage of financial news, I think CNBC is particularly good. Every minute the market is open, it shows you the Dow Jones Average and the NASDAQ Average, and every second you can see the whole stock tape if you feel like following it. And even though you may be interested in only a half a dozen stocks, if they're heavily traded, you will see them run across the screen. They also have good commentary, much better than they used to have. Bill Griffeth, one of their anchors, has written a best-selling book which is quite helpful. He's excellent.

There are many wonderful financial periodicals out there. I can't discuss them all, but I do say that the average investor should never be without *Barron's National Business and Financial Weekly* or the *Wall Street Journal*. These two periodicals cover everything. That's why I put both at the top of my list of essential periodicals to read. *Barron's*, which is my favorite, and the *Wall Street Journal*, are both published by Dow

Jones & Company. Every Saturday morning, even before I go on radio or TV (and I go on very early, at 7:30 A.M.), I find a newsstand that's open and I buy *Barron's*. At $3, it is a treasure house of information. It recently expanded into two sections: the main news and a statistical section in the back called Market Watch.

Barron's not only has all of the weekly stock quotations, but its Market Watch has extensive data on price/earnings ratios, dividend yields, and something called the stock-bond yield gap, which shows the difference between stock yields and bond yields. The wider this gap gets, the higher yield you are getting from bonds and the less yield you are getting from stocks. When that gap gets too wide, it can be a death knell for stocks, despite the fact that, over the years, stocks have been a better hedge against inflation than bonds. People will turn their backs on very low-yielding stocks and put their money into higher-yielding bonds, CDs, and other similar investment devices. *Barron's* massages the data so an investor, broker, or financial journalist can analyze things. In addition to that, it has very good articles. And if you get it Saturday morning, you have the whole weekend to go through it before the market opens on Monday.

The *Wall Street Journal* also has been very valuable to me over the years, particularly the third section called "Money and Investing." The first section is good. It carries editorials, op-ed pieces, and foreign and domestic news. The second section contains softer news and features. When I was younger, I always went first to the "Money and Investing" section for its good columns, good statistics, and aggressive market analyses. I still pay a lot of attention to The *Journal's* "Heard on the Street" column, which typically takes a news development as a news hook to write about a particular stock. Dan Dorfman first popularized that column. It's designed to get readers interested. But I must admit that excellent as it is, five days a week, I don't read the *Journal* that much anymore. I can't. I don't have the time. I'm sure there are shortcuts for reading the *Journal*, but there shouldn't be.

Money and *Kiplinger's Personal Finance* are two financial periodicals that I like. Both are monthlies and both are aimed at the average investor. In fact, both these magazines are especially useful *because* they talk to the "small investor," though I hate to even use that term. What people invest is never small to them. But these publications talk to people with one to five thousand dollars to invest at a time. They often run stories about real families and what they do with their money. One family is living in poverty, while another is doing well. They explore the reasons for the difference. Those successes and failures are something we can all relate to. Even the failures sometimes make us feel better. If investors have time, they ought to read the *Wall Street Journal*, *Barron's*, *Kiplinger's*, and *Money* cover to cover.

There's just one thing I don't like about *Money* and *Kiplinger's*. Although their content is excellent, some covers go too far to tempt people to buy or read the publications. I deplore such cover headlines as: "How I turned $10 into $12 million in 12 weeks." Or "Sell Your Stocks Now!" Or "Ten Winning Stocks You Must Buy!" They're employing hype to hike newsstand sales and to grab readers' attention. What bothers me the most is the certainty that some of these headlines want to convey. If they were to be fully truthful, the last of the headlines would read more like, "Ten Possible Winners You Should Consider." Obviously, "Ten Winning Stocks" will sell more magazines than "Ten Possible Winners," but doesn't sound as exciting. We the consumers are to blame in some ways. We're willing to buy these magazines off the rack. If we encounter an accurate headline, we're likely to label it "mealy-mouthed." We don't really want that much honesty. More and more, we are lured by the proverbial pot of gold at the end of the rainbow.

I read *Forbes* mostly for its back-of-the-book columnists. It's a good bi-weekly magazine that does an awful lot of profiling of companies. *Fortune* is like *Forbes*, but not nearly as down-to-earth as *Money* and *Kiplinger's*. Neither *Forbes* nor *Fortune* talks to the thousand-dollar investor.

With their reading, I usually advise brokers to stay off the beaten track a bit. Better they should be reading something unusual, something different, like the *Economist* or the *Harvard Business Review*. I think there is a liability in reading only what everybody else reads. As a salesman, of course, you want to be better than everybody else. You want to be different, individual, unique. You want to have more information that the average Joe.

It certainly doesn't hurt investors (or brokers) to read the *Harvard Business Review* periodically or on a regular basis. For example, deregulation is having a huge effect on the public utility industry. *The Wall Street Journal* and the *New York Times* and the Baltimore *Sun* business sections have covered this development, but some of the trade magazines have delved more deeply, separating out the low-cost utilities (which are the ones you should be buying) from the high-cost ones.

You get more details about utility stocks and the utility industry, for example, in a utility trade journal or a *Harvard Business Review* than you might from a short feature in a mainstream financial publication. That's also a strong argument for reading *Black Enterprise*, which is a fabulous magazine which always carries very good financial articles. I subscribe to it myself. It's slanted directly to African-Americans, but I get a lot out of its money columns.

Almost every major city now has a separate newspaper or magazine that covers just local business. In Baltimore, we have the *Baltimore Business Journal*, which is part of a large national chain. These periodicals are good for what they are. They cover the local scene in some depth, so they are of special value if you concentrate on local companies. I do offer one caveat: Though it's also true of all other sources of financial information, the quality of the reporting is not good enough to use as the sole basis for an investment decision.

Financial newsletters are another huge industry. They were, in fact, how newsletters themselves came to become such a big business in the U.S. and elsewhere in the world. I've seen many of them. One that's particularly good is *Hulbert's Financial Digest*. *Hulbert's* is a monthly review of all the financial newsletters. One of its best regular features is its determination of which financial newsletters have picked the most top performing stocks over five-year, eight-year, ten-year, and fifteen-year periods. They list the newsletters that have been the best over certain periods, and they give you the percent of increase they've achieved with their stock picks.

I look very closely at the five and ten year analysis, so I know which newsletters to subscribe to. *Hulbert's*, alas, doesn't put in addresses and contact information for some of these better-performing newsletters, so I get a lot of calls that I don't know how to answer: "You said in your column that the top-performing newsletter was something called the *Prudent Speculator.*" (That's actually a real newsletter and a good one.) "How do I get in touch with them?" They have to look it up on their own.

When it comes to subscribing to newsletters, go with one that's had a good five- and ten-year record. In one year, they can all look good. In fact, as a lifelong baseball fan and longtime broker, I have observed that stock picking can resemble a short baseball series. Any team can beat any other in a five game series, but over 162 games, the better team will usually prevail.

In addition, after reading a single newsletter for a fair amount of time, it may start to seem old and rehashed — without its original freshness. You say to yourself, "Is it me, or have I read this before? Give me something new." If you subscribe to these newsletters, I suggest moving around after a few years. Sooner or later, unless we're careful, we all start to repeat ourselves.

Practically every financial newsletter publishes expert predictions on what the market will do. These so-called experts generally make predictions for a short time frame. They are pretty much saying, "In this next couple of weeks and months, this is what I see the market doing." These predictions are published because the outside reader demand is for short-term, instant gratification, and such predictions sell newsletters, but they are generally of little value. Even if people got their predictions from the most accurate of the newsletters, they'd not be worth much. Above all, don't act merely on newsletter advice. As with everything else, let it be your starting point, not your ending point.

The New York Times, like many other general publications, has substantially improved its business coverage recently. Every Sunday, the *Times* has an excellent "Money and Business" section with lots of good, readable articles. Quite a few of them are written by women and cover personal investing topics of interest to both men and women. Particularly helpful are their real-life examples of what people are doing and should be doing with their money and investments. In this respect, the *Times* business section resembles *Money Magazine*. Both have brought investing down to a much more accessible level.

Women's magazines have made a concerted effort recently to run more financial articles. When I'm looking for offbeat copy for my column, I'll go to the supermarket and buy *Woman's Day* or *Working Woman* or *Cosmopolitan* and I often find something interesting, useful, and unexpected.

Why this proliferation of informational sources? Quite simply, business and investing are hot topics now. Young families are working two jobs just to make ends meet. Practically every worker can put money into a retirement program of one kind or another. There has been a great proliferation of 401(k)s. IRAs were introduced ten years ago, and are being souped up. All branches of the media have realized the popularity of *Money Magazine,* and are trying to emulate it. It's only a slight exaggeration to say that, in the old days, the stock market was just for rich people. Now, because of these retirement vehicles, market news is of nearly universal interest. Everybody who works has a chance to have his or her money grow in the stock market, tax-deferred.

Your broker is your best guide to sorting through the information you find even in reputable business publications. Again, if you see something there of interest to you about XYZ corporation, call your broker. "I just read something in the *Wall Street Journal.* What do you think?" Your broker can often evaluate the news more objectively than you can. *The Journal* may have simply reported that XYZ went up a point and a half yesterday, and that Bear Stearns thinks it's going to go even higher. But your broker can put those developments (and predictions) in perspective.

THE UNRELIABILITY FACTOR

I don't act on anything I hear on television without first analyzing it or having my firm's research department study it. That is because the media, like everybody else, can sometimes be unreliable and the stakes for you the investor are high. The network news programs, in my opinion, aren't particularly observant in their business and financial news coverage. They follow the leader, often picking up on investment stories fairly late in the game, and sometimes doing stories for the wrong reasons. For example, news directors, producers, and reporters know that a story on smoking, cigarettes, and lung cancer lends itself well to video. It's not just a talking heads piece. The cameras can show people smoking, they can show people getting x-rays, they can show some doctors conducting research. Good visuals are often what the networks look for.

The *Wall Street Journal*, and other financial periodicals, are somewhat more reliable, but, at least in my lifetime, they have rarely caused major changes in the investment world — either the market itself or particular stocks. Their stories, too, often follow the market. If a trend develops, like a surge in growth stocks similar to the one we saw in the early 1970s, the *Wall Street Journal* will usually jump on the bandwagon. If high-tech stocks are in vogue, they might run a feature, or instruct their reporters to call brokers and get comments. The story will zero in on a given trend or a given category.

However, even these reports are not truly reliable enough to act on in all cases. In a way, they offer broker-on-the-street synthesis, and Heaven knows how truly authoritative that can be. So much depends on who the reporters reach, what their experts say, and what pattern, if any, they detect in their interviews. As I can certainly attest, brokers have different opinions about everything.

THE POWERFUL HAND OF THE PRESS

Still, the media can have a strong influence on investment trends. Some of the network newscasts, like those on ABC, NBC, and CBS, now devote a fair amount of time to business-related stories, especially if they touch on consumer, health, and legal issues. In 1997, for example, long before there were negotiations about a possible settlement between state attorneys general and the tobacco industry, one network did an eight-minute segment on the industry and how that spilled over into tobacco stocks.

After such stories run, many brokers get client calls, and in a way, that's a good sign. Investors ought to pay attention to these broadcasters. It's a way of remaining mindful of their financial interests. But, if you see a network newscast allot that much air time to the relationship between smoking and lung cancer, don't sell all your tobacco stocks the next day. Instead, call your broker and tell him or her what you've seen and heard. "As you know, Mr. Broker, I own a thousand shares of Philip Morris. Do you think I ought to sell them?" Don't just take a newscast's story and act on it. Have the news evaluated by a professional who can put it in perspective.

The broker can put what the customer has seen or heard into an investment context. For example, the customer with those thousand shares of Philip Morris might have been scared by the network news story, and decided to "dump my thousand shares." But the broker can look at the whole Philip Morris picture, through a company annual report, a *Standard and Poor's* write-up, and a research department report, and calmly point out to the client that Philip Morris is no longer just a tobacco company, but the largest food company in the world. The client eventually might decide to sell all or some of the stock, but at least it will be a calm and informed decision, rather than one driven by fear and misinformation.

In that instance, the broker might also point out that, even though the network story showed a bunch of doctors talking about the direct relationship between lung cancer and smoking, cigarette sales are booming all over the world. And even though we deplore the fact that cigarettes create terrible illnesses, the fact remains that people are smoking like chimneys all over the world — Europe, Asia, Israel, Japan — and even in parts of the United States. In Altoona, Pennsylvania, the restaurants don't even have no-smoking areas. And cigars are coming back big, to the point of becoming prestige items. Some of the better brands can't be kept in stock, and consumers are paying huge amounts for them when they are available.

Unsettling financial news (and other bad news) can be used for a good purpose, though. A tobacco story on the network news may reach 15 million people, and influence one-fifth of those investing in some way. Perhaps half of *them* invest as individuals in individual stocks. If you accept my estimates, this story, however widely broadcast, has a direct impact on the investing patterns of a million people. A million people may see their own interests affected by this particular story. That becomes one of the big factors that you may want to figure into your analysis. It may even supply a reason to buy a particular stock. You might say to yourself, "I don't have this kind of stock in my portfolio. It's a trend story. I see things happening. Is there a company out there that I can jump on and whose stock I can buy?"

Thus, you have to look at the media in two ways: First, as a source of information, and second, and perhaps more important, as a catalyst for things that happen in the investment world. In fact, after a story critical of tobacco, there might be indiscriminate selling. Managers of big mutual funds and pension funds and foundations must report to boards of directors, many of whose members are environmentalists or people who, in turn, have to report to the public. Many managers might just want that "tobacco stock" out of their portfolios for public relations purposes, and their actions en masse might create a buying opportunity for you. The time to buy is when a good company is in temporary trouble. A "bad news" story might create this kind of opportunity.

COMPANY-DRIVEN PUBLICITY

As an investor, you must also bear in mind that the companies themselves go to a lot of trouble to shape financial and business news. Suppose I'm the head of a company and I'm terribly bothered by the low price of our stock. "We're a good company," I say to myself, "but a lot of people don't seem to realize it. I'll just call my friend at *Forbes* and say, 'You should do a story on us. We've been overlooked. We'd make a good, interesting story.'" He writes us up, and it's favorable. Suddenly my stock is in front of a lot more people than ever, and I start to see some stock purchases and stock price increases, all without any change in the company.

In his recent book, Al Dunlap, a well-known and effective turn-around artist, wrote about his method of turning a company's stock around. Dunlap became CEO of several major but failing corporations, fixed their problems, and brought their earnings back up to normal. Then, he went to financial analysts on Wall Street to tell them the company was back on the rise.

Dunlap admitted going to some lengths to woo financial analysts and journalists. He made a point of having direct access to the analysts, and he spent a lot of time in New York, meeting with the different analysts at the different big investment houses. Basically, he would tell them, "Here's what we're going to be doing at Scott Paper." According to Dunlap, almost immediately after these sessions, the analysts began to recommend purchase of the stock and the stock price went up.

Company executives like Dunlap can be very manipulative and mesmerizing, but good securities analysts, even when they're wined and dined on a trip to see the Puerto Rican factory, will stick to their guns and see how the numbers crunch out. In most cases, the numbers usually take priority over the spinning done by company executives.

A good article, published in a reputable publication, can definitely help publicize a company's stock. When I was a new broker, I might recommend a stock simply because I read a favorable write-up of it in *Forbes* or *Fortune*. I was hungry for ideas then, and clients could more easily relate to a stock written up in *Forbes* than an obscure high technology company in Madison, Wisconsin that nobody, including me, understood. I might say, "I just read this article about Campbell Soup. They've started a brand new division researching foods that are more nutritional and potentially more popular than what's currently on the shelves. I think the stock is about to move. How would you like to buy 500 shares?"

I don't use financial articles as often now as I did when I was a new broker. Still, those types of articles in the financial periodicals are generally reliable, and one usually can't see the hidden hand of the company trying to hype itself. The articles tend to be sophisticated and critical. If they say something positive, you can probably believe that, on balance, it's a good company being written about. But also remember: Additional (and sometimes better) sources of information may be available through your broker.

"INFO-BROKERS"

One of the biggest problems in the security industry today is the policy of letting financial people buy radio time and tout investments during their shows. These people are really not much different from advertisers. Often, they are brokers who get on the radio just for the purpose of increasing their own production. They give out information along with their telephone number, all while paying for their own airtime. Finally, regulators at the state and federal levels have begun to crack down on these infomercials, because listeners have trouble distinguishing between an advertisement and a credible journalist talking about potential investments.

If you're an investor listening to this kind of infomercial, keep in mind that the on-air person is not taking into account the fact that you might be a novice or relatively unsophisticated investor. This broker doesn't know your financial situation, either. Investments in the stock market are often fueled by greed (everybody wants to make a buck these days) and fear. When a broker gets on the radio and pitches a stock, he knows how to play on those emotions, how to hit the hot buttons. Conscientious brokers will point out that there is risk involved in a particular investment. But most people who call in or listen to such infomercials don't want to hear that. They want to make money. They hear what they want to hear.

On radio and TV and in the newspapers, I make a point never to recommend a stock. I don't want to add to the viewer's confusion. I purposely use phrases like: "Here's a stock you ought to take a look at," or: "Here's something that looks good to me, but check it out with your broker, because he or she knows your individual situation better than I do." I've never said, "You ought to buy this. You ought to sell that." I couch my responses in fairly general terms.

I go on the air to disseminate information. In my opinion, doing anything else is completely inappropriate. As a stockbroker, it's not my place to tell anyone on the radio or TV to buy something. I don't know their circumstances. They might not have any money. They might not be able to afford a risk. A lot of other folks in the media don't extend the public this courtesy. I advise my clients not to buy anything recommended to them on television, radio, or in a printed publication until I check it out.

CHAPTER SUMMARY:
TRACKING THE MARKET

1. *We are bombarded today with investment advice and information. Although it seems as if absorbing this blitz will make you a smart investor, always consult your broker before you act on what you hear, read, and see.*

2. *There are certain key media sources that I depend on for straightforward, honest information. As an investor, you should utilize these sources, but also check with your broker to make sure their advice fits your needs.*

3. *The media is not always reliable. Sometimes taking a broadcaster's advice is similar to acting on curbstone tips. And companies often try to shape the news to suit their interests.*

4. *The media can have a strong influence on you as an investor. It can also have a strong influence on other investors. This means it might affect market trends in general.*

5. *Certain brokers further complicate the situation by going on the radio and giving advice mainly to sell you particular products. They do not know you and might not have your best interests at heart.*

CHAPTER EIGHT

Mutual Funds

*I often recommend mutual funds because they provide
two things the so-called average investor is unlikely to get on his own:
diversification and professional management.*

A mutual fund is nothing more than a collection of stocks that a money manager puts together, packages, and offers for sale. If we're talking about open-ended mutual funds, which are 90 percent of all mutual funds, the package changes over time. Closed-end mutual funds have a finite or limited number of stocks in them, and they don't change.

When I started in the business 35 years ago, there were already some very well-known mutual-fund names: Massachusetts Investors Trust, Century Shares Trust, the T. Rowe Price no-load funds. Back then, I used mutual funds extensively in cases that warranted them, but they were nothing close to the important phenomenon that they are in the investing world today.

There now are about 6,000 such funds — more than there are stocks listed on the New York Stock Exchange (3,500). The real explosion in mutual funds took place during this latest long-running Wall

Street boom, when more and more money managers, seeing an ideal opportunity for profit, started more and more mutual funds. With investors over the last 15 years, these funds have been extremely popular.

In the future, we probably will see a shakeout of the mutual fund industry, and we'll probably end up with many fewer funds. Things that go around come around. The weak will be shaken. The bull market, which started in 1982, will not last forever. On Aug. 12, 1982, the Dow was at 776. Since then, an almost uninterrupted 15-year climb has taken us to where the market is as of this printing — slightly over 8,000. When the market feels the bumps in the road, so will mutual funds.

Billions upon billions of dollars — unprecedented amounts — have been going into mutual funds nearly every month. The industry keeps breaking one record after another. But, whenever there's a decline in the market over a period of two or three months, as there was in mid-July 1996, there's a net withdrawal of money in mutual funds. That means that more money is withdrawn from these funds than is deposited into them.

T. Rowe Price started out in the 1930s with half a dozen mutual funds. Now they have 50, all of them started in my hometown of Baltimore. Charlie Shaeffer started out with Mr. Price as a stockbroker with what was then John C. Legg and Company. I knew them both. Both left Legg in 1934, during the depths of the Depression, to start T. Rowe Price. Charlie Shaeffer once said to me, "We started out in an era when people not only didn't have money for professional management, which we gave them, but most of them didn't have enough money to buy 100 shares of stock." What a difference 50 years has made!

ARE MUTUAL FUNDS FOR YOU?

A lot of customers have come to me over the years with relatively small amounts of money, like $5,000. Now, $5,000 to a lot of people is a heck of a lot of money. It may be all they have in the world to invest. On the other hand, in the world today, $5,000 is a relatively small amount of money considering the fact that some people have retirement funds of $200,000 and $300,000, inheritances of more than that, and other piles of money that, in some cases, rise well into the millions.

When it comes to relatively small amounts of money, I often recommend mutual funds because they provide two things that the so-called average or small investor cannot do alone. Number one, they provide diversification, and number two, professional management.

With $5,000, you just can't go out and buy a hundred shares of this, and a hundred shares of that, and a hundred shares of something else, and get true portfolio diversification. The money will run out too quickly. It may even run out with the purchase of the first hundred shares. Let's say an average share of stock costs $40, which it does. One hundred shares at $40 each is $4,000. That's almost the end of the $5,000. But mutual funds provide diversification to investors without a lot of money.

Plus, the mutual fund gives professional management to the relatively small individual investor. You as a "small investor" (how I hate that term) can't hire a professional money manager with a $5,000 investment. But in a mutual fund, you receive professional management because the manager is managing your money for you along with thousands of other people's money.

Mutual funds today are also terribly important as a way to do international investing. If you're going to invest in the Czech Republic or Thailand or Hong Kong, you're better off buying an international mutual fund than hand-picking Hitachi and Toyota and other individual stocks from the stock exchanges of these foreign countries. In the first place, an analyst can't visit the head of Hitachi as easily as he can visit the head of The Rouse Company. He'd have to go halfway around the world to do it. Plus, he would encounter both a language barrier and a currency barrier.

When you do your foreign investing via mutual funds, you get the diversification you need. You can invest in an American-based international mutual fund, or you can look for funds and managers based elsewhere. What you're really doing is hiring companies with the staffs to follow foreign stocks. Not that either decision is foolproof. I personally invested in a Japanese fund that's been a semi-dog. I bought it at the wrong time, when the Japanese economy was about to conk out.

Some people perceive mutual funds as a savings device. Mutual funds have greatly encouraged this perception by encouraging automatic monthly deposits. They set things up so that on the same day every month, $100 or $200 or $300 can be debited from your checking account and transferred automatically into *their* mutual fund. Not only is such forced investing a clever and marvelous sales pitch, but it works out well for the investor. If it is up to John and Jane Doe to send their mutual fund $100 every month, on their own, they probably won't do it because they'll see an automobile tire they need or a trip to Washington they want to take with the kids. The mutual fund investment will come last because it offers no tangible and immediate result.

When the money is automatically deducted from their checking account, however, it's forced saving. And it is possible to survive on the money that's left in the account. As I have said before, "If you can live on 100 percent of your salary, you probably can live on 90 percent of it." (Mutual funds, incidentally, are not the only way you can invest automatically. You can also invest in individual stocks by having the monthly amount automatically removed from your checking account. Certain firms, like Westinghouse or Procter & Gamble, have automatic stock purchase plans for their employees. They're good to take advantage of, because eventually that money will grow, or at least it has in the past.)

If you have more than $5,000 to invest, you don't want to stick all your money in mutual funds, no matter how well they're doing. I believe that owners of a $300,000 stock portfolio ought to have 20 percent of their money in mutual funds — split up between an international fund and a growth fund. With $300,000, people can do a great deal of individual stock picking as well, and I think that is for the best. That's a pretty good size account, and you can often make more money (if you have enough to start with) by investing in individual stocks.

Mutual funds may be stellar investing devices, but so far, the average investor I see with a $300,000 portfolio isn't saying, "Look, I don't want to go through the aggravation of picking individual stocks. I'm just going to put all my money into a couple of mutual funds." These investors like to buy individual stocks so they can follow them in the papers.

About 20 percent of the investors I know are invested solely in mutual funds and don't bother selecting individual stocks. They'll do as well as the market does, but no better. When people buy individual stocks, they are purchasing a part of companies that usually raise their dividends every year. If they go to the right brokers to help them pick their stocks, it is not hard to find the good ones. Mutual funds really don't do that. They don't raise their dividends periodically or annually like individual stocks and pass them along to the shareholders. They aren't oriented to dividend increases.

If you come to me with $5,000, and we put it in the Franklin Templeton Foreign Fund, that fund issues new shares to accommodate your purchase. With such an investment, you do pay an annual fee for the management of the fund. This fee, usually a small percentage of your earnings, comes out of your dividends. Even the funds that say they're no-load are the first to admit — and it's stated right there in their prospectuses — that some management fees are charged. That word "load" simply means commission. Management fees are something else, and they apply to just about whatever mutual fund you buy. Remember: The no-load fund managers aren't driving Mercedes convertibles because they sell their professional services for nothing.

MUTUAL FUNDS IN YOUR 401(K)

Mutual funds have become more important than ever because of the growth in 401(k) plans and other retirement programs offered by companies. With 401(k) plans, employers supply the worker with a choice of mutual funds — money market funds; growth funds; income funds; and bond funds — to invest in. These plans, and especially 401(k) plans, are becoming, in effect, the private pension funds of this country. They're a huge force in the investing world. Frequent issues of *Money*

Magazine and *Kiplinger's* are devoted entirely to them.

A woman wrote me recently. She said she worked for the DuPont Company, had $8,000 of her 401(k) retirement fund in a Wells Fargo fixed income fund, which is a bond mutual fund, $15,000 in a Merrill Lynch capital fund, and $13,000 in Fidelity Magellan growth fund. DuPont, she told me, gave her other choices. Already in her 401(k) fund, she said, was $36,000, and she was adding at the rate of $5,000 a year, or a good 14-15 percent of her income. What, she asked, would I recommend she do with her 401(k)?

My response was: First, get out of Fidelity Magellan. I also recommended that she move her money out of her Wells Fargo fixed income fund. At 36, she's much too young to be investing so heavily in fixed income investments.

She said she had five other funds that she could put her 401(k) money into, one of which was an international fund. I recommended that she take advantage of that opportunity.

This woman also had the option of putting her 401(k) money into the purchase of her own company's stock. I did not suggest exercising that option. I said, "You have your whole working life ahead of you. Why put more money into company stock? Something could go wrong with the company and it's not as if DuPont is doing anything special to entice you to buy more company stock, like matching your contributions with its money or selling you shares at a discounted rate."

If she follows my advice, and decides to take the money out of Magellan Fund and put it into Franklin-Templeton Foreign Fund, or maybe one of the other growth funds, I think she will do much better. To make the necessary changes, she merely tells her benefits department. She may or may not have to do it in writing, though I recommend she give and get some sort of documentation of the change.

As a 401(k) participant, she is allowed to make changes four times a year in her selections, but you should not be making a lot of such changes, and certainly not four times a year. Instead, take extra time in the beginning to make the right allocation. Go to people who know what they're talking about. Someone in the benefits department might be able to help, though most employees of such departments know nothing about picking investments. They administer benefits, and are not investment professionals themselves. Some bring in an expert to talk to employees, to guide them in their allocation. Mark and Morry and I are occasionally asked to do that, and I know it's helpful to plan participants.

Without proper advice and understanding, many plan participants simply select some appetizing "income funds" that look to them as if they'll generate more income that way. But those funds can easily turn into dogs. You can lose money in an income fund, even though you might not think so.

This is an instance where, if you were making decisions on your own, you should pull out *Morningstar*, and see how it analyzes and rates the funds in question. Someone recently called me on TV and asked me about a mutual fund I'd never heard of. I said, "Check *Morningstar*," I said, "and see for yourself. If it's rated four or five stars, it's good." There's just one caution about that: To repeat the same good results reported by *Morningstar*, make sure the same management is still in place.

CHOOSING A MUTUAL FUND

When choosing a mutual fund, don't buy one that's "fully invested." The fund you want has some cash reserves to take care of a decline, like a hundred-point drop because an Alan Greenspan comment rattled the market the night before — he said there was too much euphoria on Wall Street, that making money had become too easy. Markets here and everywhere took a terrible tumble.

We're in a strange era when many of the mutual fund managers are so young that they have not lived through down cycles in the market, as I have. They've been doing their thing only while the market's been going up. In my opinion, this is a hazard for mutual fund investors. If I were an investor, I would rather go with a fund manager who is experienced enough to have lived through ups and downs. Younger managers won't know what "downs" feel like until they've been through one, and much higher returns than the Dow Jones Average. The ad may be truthful. But at the same time that the Bull and Bear Fund was up 42 percent, many of the same company's funds, which they don't advertise, might have been dogs. Obviously, the mutual fund and its advertising people pick *the* fund that has done the best. Their other funds could have been major failures. The Bull and Bear Fund could even be a major failure this coming year. The problem with the advertising is that people don't differentiate between funds within a family. They think, "My God, up 42 percent last year. Dow Jones up only 16. Let's go ahead and buy something from XYZ." Then this year, that particular fund could be a clunker.

But if you look at a five or ten year performance record, you'll have a much better idea about the history of a fund. You don't want to invest short-term in a mutual fund anyway; that's not what they're for. So you have to do some homework when you pick a mutual fund, and you have to look into its past. There are reference books that supply these performance records. As I've suggested, *Morningstar* publishes the best and most useful, but there are other worthwhile ones.

A lot of people talk and worry about the fact that there's no insurance on money invested in a mutual fund. Mutual funds are not like bonds. They are usually a collection of stocks. People put their money into them, and, theoretically, at least, can get nothing in return. However, bear two things in mind here. First, no mutual funds have, in effect, depreciated to nothing. And second, there's no insurance on individual stock investments either. Stocks can and sometimes do go to zero. For example, Merry-Go-Round stock was up to $15 or $20 a share at one point a few years ago. It's not worth 10 cents now. The same thing can theoretically happen in a poorly crafted mutual fund, but it's not very likely. Mutual funds are a little bit safer than stocks, but not as safe as bonds.

One of the bigger problems with mutual funds is that there are so many of them, and they all compete against one another. There is, as a result, intense mutual fund competition for higher returns. They even compete against funds within their own family. When there's that much competition, mutual funds can end up spending a huge amount of they're no fun. In 1973-74, the Dow dropped from 1,100 to 577. It was an absolute nightmare.

Experienced fund managers manage their funds quite differently from many who have not lived through these down markets. For one thing, they don't put all their eggs in one basket. They keep some cash reserves on the side. First, they won't get killed if their stocks drop, and second, they have buying power in case something they want hits an attractive level. They don't have to sell something (possibly in a lousy market) to buy it. With cash reserves, they can program their computers to tell them when Merck, which is selling at 90, drops down to 85, at which point they'll buy 50,000 shares.

The market recently declined because inexperienced people (especially inexperienced brokers) failed to build portfolios that news bulletins wouldn't affect. When some financial stories break, like the one where Greenspan accused the market of being overly exuberant, I told clients, "Stay the course. Hang in there. The good corporations are going to be around a long time. Don't let Alan Greenspan run your investment portfolio. Don't look in tomorrow's paper to see which holdings weren't affected by his statement and conclude, 'They're good stocks.' Most likely, all stocks got hit and hurt. It would be the rarity for a stock not to be affected by that sort of statement." When people get scared, the market falls. But you the investor don't have to be hurt long-term by that tumble.

I also have told investors, "Never buy mutual funds on the basis of one or two year results. And don't change your mutual funds too often, whether they are doing really well and are 'too high' or 'not doing well enough.'" This is important, because it's very hard to well-time your ins and outs of a mutual fund. Also, mutual fund advertisers muddle our decisions by making it seem like buying their fund guarantees immediate profit.

Let's say one of the giant mutual fund organizations, in January of a given year, publishes a full-page ad in Barron's or the Wall Street Journal that says, "XYZ's Bull and Bear Fund Up 42 Percent Last Year Versus Dow Jones Average Up Only 16 Percent." This ad wants you to choose that fund or any fund that XYZ runs, and it practically promises money to get the investor's attention. The more funds that keep spinning off, the more people say, "The average investor doesn't know about my fund. I have to go on television to tell them." So these days, mutual funds are running expensive television ads with some frequency. And there are tons of print ads, each one bigger than the last. No longer unusual are full-page ads in *Forbes, Money, Barron's,* and *Kiplinger's.*

When the marketing of mutual funds is very expensive, and funds are relatively new and small, the ratio of marketing costs versus money actually invested can keep increasing. It is ironic that, in many instances, the cost of advertising actually makes such funds financially undesirable to you, the investor. Who wants to spend money on a fund that will use a great deal of your money to get more customers? Still, it's important to realize that high expense ratios get hidden, in effect, when the funds grow. If a fund is managing $75 billion, $2 million spent on advertising isn't a large part. It's like anything else. The more the sales volume increases, the lower the expenses are, as a percentage, compared to revenues.

As a result, you should be wary of selecting start-up funds. To get noticed in the beginning, new funds must spend quite a lot on advertising. And, since they have few investors and little money in the beginning, their expense ratios are logically going to be higher than an older fund. Start-up funds might also take extraordinary risks to show high early results, and such risks can backfire in the second and third year of operation.

One type of mutual fund that has done well recently are index funds. An index fund has many different stocks and attempts to mirror or closely track their relative index. One index fund, and probably the most known, is the S&P 500 index fund. Because of the number of the stocks invested in, an index mutual fund relieves you the investor of the responsibility of picking individual stocks and allows you to do as well as the market. If all you want to do is duplicate what the market's doing, buy an index fund.

But if you want to do better than the market average, and you should, do your homework. You should work hard to find mutual funds that outperform the market on a consistent basis, rather than simply buying a mutual fund that mirrors the market. Go to people who know what they're talking about, who use the tools available, like *Morningstar* and the *Lipper's* rating services, and try to find funds which have outperformed the market over the years. There are a lot of them. In their glory years, Fidelity Magellan outperformed the stock market by a lot — enough to make an investment well worth your while. It was run by a guy who really knew what he was doing, Peter Lynch, and he described in detail what he was doing in those two great books of his.

Some mutual funds are sector funds. They invest in a certain sector of the economy that looks strong, like the high-technology sector. Sectors go in and out of style. A sector can have a very good year this year, and be a dog the next. Again, the one trap that people don't want to fall into is buying mutual funds with merely a good one-year record. Any fund can look good for one year. All the manager has to do is hit a hot sector like high-tech in 1996.

Just as it's very easy to have one really good year, it's fairly easy and fairly normal for a mutual fund to have one isolated very bad year. It's a special hazard if the sector it specializes in is having a bad time of it. Fifteen years ago, when interest rates shot up sharply, utility stocks got killed and utility mutual funds got killed along with them. In general, sector funds alone are not a safe long-term investment for your money.

When choosing a mutual fund, don't get too attached to no-load funds, especially if you are not using a broker or investment manager to manage your portfolio. A no-load mutual fund may not charge a commission, but, as my partner Morry Zolet often points out, "No load means no help." You don't get any assistance.

Perhaps even more important, the fact that you don't pay a commission when buying and selling shares in a no-load fund encourages you the investor to move too frequently in and out of funds. On the whole, no-load funds may perform as well as load funds, but not for investors who get in and out of the funds every 14 months (the average for no-loads) versus every 34 months (the average for load funds). Many no-load investors get in and out at the wrong time, rather than investing for the longer-term.

If you buy a load mutual fund from a stockbroker, however, the broker should and will keep an eye on it. If the fund is under-performing because of bad management, he will get rid of it, or if it's under-performing for seemingly temporary reasons, he might buy more. When a customer says to Morry, "I think I'll invest in a load fund, but I'll buy it from a discount brokerage," Morry always responds, "Would you go to a discount brain surgeon?"

He obviously believes that professional advice is important even in selecting and shaping your portfolio of load mutual funds, because (again, still, and always) each individual investor's situation is different. Therefore, putting certain mutual funds in a client's account takes a little more doing and a little more thought than just going to a no-load mutual fund and saying, "I want to buy this and I want to buy that." It still requires professional guidance.

Also, as basic as it sounds, it's important to emphasize: Don't compare dissimilar funds with one another. Better put, compare one international fund to another international fund, or one growth fund to another. Don't sell your international fund because its 12 percent return is considerably less than the 30 percent appreciation of your growth fund. When you do that, you're forgetting why you bought the fund in the first place, and you're simply not comparing apples to apples. Alas, this is something I see many mutual fund investors do.

Lastly, don't be over-influenced by the generic and sometimes suggestive names of the mutual funds you investigate, like Basic Value Class A, Global Holdings Class A, Blue Chip, Value, or Aggressive Growth and all that stuff. Like a baby's name, a mutual fund's name means nothing. As an investor, you should not make decisions on the basis of a fund's name.

BOND MUTUAL FUNDS

If you come to me and say, "Westy, I have $10,000 sitting in the savings bank earning 2 percent interest. Can you do better?" I'll say, "Sure. Let's buy a U.S. government bond. We'll get you 5 or 6 or 7 percent." Yet, it does not follow that I'll also recommend a mutual fund that invests only in government bonds.

None of the bond mutual funds are as yet insured. I tell everyone to read the bond fund's prospectus carefully. If they did, they would see that they can lose money in that investment, that it's not a risk-free investment. When people buy a government bond, they lend money to Uncle Sam. They know when they will get their money back, how much money they will get back, and the rate of return that the government will pay them. When they buy a bond fund, however, they aren't buying a bond. They are buying a basket of bonds that somebody has put together, with no obligation to pay investors back.

Government bonds themselves are risk free. If people go out and buy a $10,000 bond at the bank, or a savings bond for their children, they are guaranteed to get their money back when the bond matures. A bond *fund* invested in government bonds sounds gilt-edged, and its leaflets show beautifully printed government bonds. But people can lose money on these funds — not because of management costs, which are hardly excessive. To make them attractive with high rates of return, bond managers load these bond funds up with long-term and often low-quality bonds. When interest rates go up, long-term bonds come down sharply in price.

Here's an example. Let's say that you give me $10,000 today. I buy you a long-term government bond fund yielding 6 percent. To take a wild example, let's suppose that in the next few months, the Federal Reserve raises interest rates. The bond rates go up to 9 percent. It's obvious that no one has to pay you $10,000 any more for your 6 percent bond fund, which brings you $600 a year in interest, when new people coming into the market can get $900 a year for bonds paying 9 percent. The value of your fund has dropped sharply in price. Now, had you put that $10,000 in an individual government bond, the bond would also have declined in price in the period before it came due. But when it comes due, you are guaranteed to get $10,000 back. In a bond fund, there's no such guarantee.

CHAPTER SUMMARY: MUTUAL FUNDS

1. *Mutual funds are an important addition to your portfolio. Especially if you don't have that much money to invest, they will help you diversify. They often have plans which take money straight from your checking account, and this is a good way to force yourself to save and invest.*

2. *Mutual funds also help you get international stocks into your portfolio. This is a necessary part of diversification.*

3. *The rise of 401(k) plans has added a lot of importance to mutual funds. There currently are a lot more mutual funds than there are stocks listed on the New York Stock Exchange. Making the right selection is not easy.*

4. *There is rampant competition today between the various mutual funds. Stick to the five- to ten-year history of a mutual fund when deciding what to buy.*

5. *Index funds, like the S&P 500, will generally do exactly what the market does. If you're relatively risk-averse, they might be a good thing, but you can do better than that if you do your homework.*

6. *Start-up funds are not usually the safest investment. Sector funds are not reliable long-term investments. Both can fizzle after a year or two.*

7. *With no-load funds, you don't pay a commission to buy or sell. But you're on your own. And you tend, therefore, not to be a patient, long-term investor. You're more inclined to move swiftly in and out of no-load funds, and therefore fall prey to the difficulties of timing your investments.*

8. *Mutual fund names don't mean anything.*

9. *Mutual bond funds are not insured the way bonds are and may be a bit risky as an investment. I don't particularly like them, at least compared to bonds themselves.*

10. *Be fair to yourself. Compare one kind of mutual fund to a similar one (like international to international; growth to growth, etc.).*

CHAPTER NINE

Bonds and
Fixed Income Investments

"Bonds are the house we live in." — *Milton Westheimer (my late father)*

My father used to say that bonds are the house we live in. He meant that bonds, and other fixed-income investments, are safe. They are like the roofs over our heads — a protected place in which we dwell. "Out there," he would say, we can get hit by a car or lose all our money. But in here, in our homes, we are secure. We're not going to accidentally get rich on our house, but we know we won't lose anything on it, either.

No wonder, then, that in any discussion about investing, fixed income investments often take a back seat to stocks, which are much more glamorous. People buy stocks with the goal of making money, and people who have bought stocks and stock mutual funds over the years generally have accomplished that goal. Meanwhile, bonds have remained boring and dull. They provide slight protection from inflation (in other words, they exceed inflation only by a little). And they're generally considered an "old person's" investment.

Bonds also have a reputation (undeserved) for being cumbersome. They used to be thought of as something of a nuisance for individuals to handle, at least compared to stocks. That's not true any more. Bonds no longer come with coupons. No longer do you have to snip the coupons and send them in to the company in order to receive your interest payment. Now, you simply sit there and as a matter of course receive your money on a regular basis.

As for government bonds, the process has also been much simplified, but in a different way. If you buy your government bonds from the Federal Reserve, they don't send you a check for your interest payments. It's easier for them to pay you electronically, and it's much better for you. You don't have to worry if your interest check is sitting in your mailbox while you're away. You don't have to be concerned if you didn't get the check. And you never have to fear receiving a check mutilated in transit. Now the interest payments go right into your bank account, via computer, just like a monthly social security payment. Once the transfer is consummated, it shows up on your bank statement. Because of the ease of the process, the Federal Reserve doesn't just offer direct deposit of interest payments. It insists on it.

As my father suggested, bonds and fixed income investments are a safe, necessary part of every investor's portfolio. We all need a roof over our heads. Bonds ensure your protection in the case of a big stock market crash, or a huge economic devastation. They are not the exciting part of investing; they are the pragmatic side. As such, a limited amount of your portfolio should be invested in fixed income investments. I'll explain in detail later, but take the number 120 and subtract your age. Whatever the resulting number is (let's say 75 if you're 45), subtract it from the number 90 to get the percentage of your portfolio that ought to be in fixed income investments (15 percent if you're 45 years old).

BONDS ARE SECURE

When you buy a bond, you are lending your money to an organization, government, or corporation. When you buy a U.S. treasury bond, also known as a U.S. government bond, you are lending money to the U.S. government. The government promises to pay you back the amount you have invested, plus a specific rate of interest that never changes during the life of the bond. You can buy a ten thousand dollar, ten-year government bond from either the Federal Reserve branch in the city where you live or from a stock broker. As I write this in July 1997, you can get one that pays about 6 percent interest. You will thus earn a total of $600 per year on your ten thousand dollar loan to the government. Over the span of 10 years, you'll earn a profit of $6,000 in interest. That interest is free of state and local income taxes, but is still taxed by the federal government. At the end of the ten years, you get your $10,000 back plus interest, guaranteed. There has never been a default of a U.S. government bond. Of course, this is in part because the government has the printing press. The government can always print enough money to pay off its bonds.

As strange as it may seem, some investors don't like the secure aspects of bonds. They put all their money into stocks because, to them, bonds are unexciting. Others think they are too young for bonds, and want to make big hits. If these investors know the risks, that's fine. I often say, "Some people would rather eat well than sleep well." You may well do a lot better financially than those who keep some of their money in fixed income investment devices. Ten thousand dollars invested in stocks some time ago is now worth $6 million. That same ten thousand dollars invested in bonds would be worth far, far less. (*See Appendix for charts on bonds and stocks.*)

On the other hand, there are some people who put almost all their money in bonds. Many of these investors suffered through the Depression, or lost everything in the stock market crash. I advise those people that being a bonds-only investor is not the most prudent course. And yet, investing solely in bonds is not the worst thing you can do, either. When you get old, your money doesn't have to grow all that fast anymore. You have a limited number of years to spend your money, and you may only want to avoid losing it. Government bonds are a ticket to safety because you never lose your money in a bond. Its value may decrease if inflation shoots up, but the principal is always there. If you hold it to the end, you'll get your money back.

BEFORE YOU INVEST WITH BONDS

As I've stressed several times, when we begin working with clients, we require them to fill out a comprehensive questionnaire. On it, we ask, "Do you have a mortgage, and, if so, how much do you owe on it and at what rate?" If someone comes in with $300,000 to invest, and they have a mortgage rate of 8.5 percent, we usually say, "Naturally we would like to have your money to invest. That's how we make a living. But from our point of view, the better course is to start chipping away at your mortgage, because if you're paying 8.5 percent on your mortgage, paying it off at that rate is the same as investing it at that rate with no risk."

Furthermore, as you grow older and approach retirement, you should reduce your debts so you have fewer obligations to worry about. When you pay down or pay off your mortgage, your cash flow increases at a time when the tax deduction from mortgage interest payments may be less important to you.

Many investors don't see the big benefits from taking this approach. We try everything to get it across, including this example, which I like: If you walked into a bank and borrowed money at eight and a half percent from one window, would you then take that money to another bank window and deposit it into a savings account paying three percent annual interest? Most people wouldn't. Yet, some people keep lots of money in savings accounts getting three percent interest, while paying out eight and a half percent interest on their mortgage. So we urge people to use money from savings, if they have enough of it, or from recent inflows of money, to chip away at their mortgage principal, before they even delve into bonds or stocks.

CHOOSING BOND INVESTMENTS

Individuals don't invest much in bonds partly because they don't really understand them, and partly because there are so many variables. Who guarantees them, what's their rating, what kind should they buy? It can be confusing. For the sake of simplicity and safety, I generally recommend purchasing Treasury bonds or tax-free bonds.

The older you get, the more bonds you want. The simple formula for determining how many stocks you want in a portfolio, which is the reciprocal of how many bonds you want, is to take the number 120 and subtract your age from it. It's not carved in stone, but the resulting number roughly represents the percent of stocks you want. (Of course, you also probably want about 10 percent of your money to be in cash.)

So if you're 45, you want 75 percent of your portfolio to be stocks, approximately 15 percent to be bonds. For years, I started the calculation with the number 100, but I've recently changed my mind because people are living longer. One hundred is thus too conservative as a starting number. It doesn't give you enough stocks. I use 120 now because, over the years, stocks have given the investor ten and a half percent return a year, which is double what bonds have supplied.

To decide which bonds to invest in, we have to bring in the economic concept of inflation, because that's obviously one of the key determinants. During a long stretch in the late 1970s, inflation raged, but within the last seven or eight years, inflation has been very much under control — rising at anywhere from two to three percent a year. Have we licked inflation? If so, is there now a greater incentive to go with bonds? The answer, in my view, is either "no" or "we don't know." If we thought inflation were dead, we'd buy more bonds. They reward us at a certain interest rate agreed upon well in advance, but they are a poor hedge against inflation.

U.S. government obligations come in various maturities: short, medium and long. Short government obligations are known as Treasury bills. They come in three and six month maturities, although occasionally a one-year bill will be issued. The chief differences between a

Treasury bill and a Treasury bond are the length of maturity and method of payment. Treasury bills are sold at a discount of their eventual value at maturity. This discount is how you get paid your return. Most other bonds pay interest every six months, but you invest the face value of the bond.

In between bills and bonds are something called Treasury notes. Generally, these are two, three, five, seven, or ten-year notes. (Bonds are generally of 20- or 30-year maturities.)

The federal government also issues savings bonds in various face amounts. With one exception, savings bonds don't pay income that you can spend. After buying a regular ten thousand-dollar government bond, you get an interest check from the government twice a year. When buying a savings bond, you merely sit there for 10 or 12 years and watch the bond grow into its face amount (like $50 or $100). There are no coupons to clip and no interest payments sent or received. (The one exception: if you convert your EE bonds to H bonds, you will receive regular interest payments by check.)

In any event, we are well past the point where anyone should buy U.S. savings bonds, other federal government bonds, or bonds of their particular state out of some sense of civic responsibility. As I've often said, you can show your patriotism in other ways. Earn more money and pay more taxes. Wave a flag on the Fourth of July. Go to a parade. Visit Fort McHenry. And remember: Government bonds are generally *not* for young people.

WHICH WAY INTEREST RATES?

If you think interest rates will come down for the next several decades, buy the "longest bond" you can, because that's where you'll find the highest interest rates. Interest rates may decline during the life of your bond, but your rate of interest will remain the same.

If you bought a 30-year treasury bond in July 1997, you'd earn 6.6 percent interest. And the same tax implications would apply for it as for a shorter bond. Nothing changes except the maturity dates. A bond is what it says — it's a bond. Lender and borrower are bonded with and to each other, and the rates never change throughout the life of the bond.

Several professional companies rate bonds, like *Moody's* and *Standard and Poor's*, but they don't rate government bonds. Government bonds don't have to be rated because they carry the full faith and credit of the United States government, and as long as the world is still spinning on its axis, government bonds carry no risk — none. As a last resort, the U.S. government can always print enough money to pay off its bonds. That's something U.S. Steel can't do.

If you're going to do bond investing right, the concept of staggered maturities is a very important one to understand and use. You should buy some short-term bonds, some mediums, and some longs. This works a little bit like diversification in your stock portfolio: It protects you from the unexpected. If you buy all short bonds and interest rates come down, you're going to get hurt, because every time your six-month bond or your one-year bond comes due, you are going to roll it over into lower and lower and lower interest rates. On the other hand, if you buy all long bonds and interest rates go up, you're going to get hurt because immediately after new bonds come out at higher rates, your long bonds are worth comparatively less.

My best advice is, don't get caught in these traps. Don't try to guess which way interest rates will go, because nobody really knows. By buying some short, some medium, and some long, you're guaranteed to avoid this pitfall. By buying a staggered series of maturities, you limit your losses and allow yourself an important luxury: You can invest in common stocks, which carry a degree of risk, but which also carry the potential for high reward.

Suppose, again, that you're 45, and, according to my formula, you should have about 15 percent of your portfolio in bonds. You should diversify that 15 percent in terms of the bonds' maturity. Don't put all 15 percent of your bond money, let's say a total of $100,000, into 30-year government notes paying 6 percent. All of a sudden, if inflation takes off, interest rates go up, and new bonds start to pay 9 percent, you're

MY FAMILY HISTORY

My father (top row, far left) and his seven brothers (pictured alongside and below) were born and raised in St. Joseph, Missouri. My grandfather, Ferdinand Westheimer, came from Germany to this country at the age of 19. After being an itinerant peddler around the New York area for a number of years, he chose St. Joe, on the banks of the Missouri River, as the site for his dry goods store. Gold had been discovered in the west and, at mid-century and beyond, prospectors were outfitting their caravans and setting sail from St. Joe in quest of the valuable nuggets.

After getting his business established, my grandfather was asked to join the executive board of a bank in St. Joe. One Saturday he called all of his sons together and said, "Sons, I'm on the executive board of such and such a bank, and the bank is going to fail and shut down next week. I'm calling you together because I want to be sure all of your family and business deposits go into the bank over the next few days. I never want it to be thought or said that any Westheimers didn't make their regular deposits in a bank about to close its doors because they benefited from my position in it." The deposits went in, as usual, and the Westheimer family probably lost money. The sons followed instructions out of respect for their father, and for the good of the family name. It is a kind of respect that doesn't really exist anymore.

When I think about my father, Milton Westheimer, I try to keep that kind of respect in mind. Dad died in 1956, but he has had a profound influence on my life, as well as on my conservative investing style. I think of myself as living in the shadow of his presence — or better, on the shoulders of his life and his father's. ♣

going to lose your shirt.

You can sell these bonds through a broker, but you'll take a beating on what you get for them. In this scenario, where interest rates go up and new bonds come out tomorrow paying nine percent, your $100,000 investment is immediately worth quite a bit less to others, though it's still worth $100,000 plus $180,000 in interest income to you over the next 30 years. When they can get bonds yielding nine percent at the same $100,000 price, no one's going to pay you $100,000 anymore for your investment. Over the space of 30 years, they'll make $90,000 more than your bond; $270,000 including interest.

That's why you want to buy some short, some medium, some long. If you want to take a risk, and you should, take it in the stock market where there's usually a greater hope of reward. When investing in very long-term bonds, you take some risk without any hope of great reward.

In the bond diversification program I advocate, there can be so much difference in what the bonds pay that it really makes sense to do this staggering or laddering. The example I used is a wild one: six percent rates on long bonds will tomorrow become nine percent. But odd things can happen. The U.S. can get into a war in the Mideast, and the government would have tremendous demands for ammunition, planes, boats, missiles. Because of the resulting boom in the American economy, corporations could be borrowing money like crazy. Interest rates could go to eight or nine percent fairly quickly. (At various points within the last 15 years, the government has paid 13 percent on bonds.) In my earlier example, you gained or lost $90,000 on your $100,000 investment depending on which day you purchased your bond.

Because you can encounter a large gap between bonds issued not very far apart in time, you should stagger or ladder your bond maturities. That way you don't have to worry about the direction of interest rates. Believe me, as I say over and over again, nobody can ever truly know which way interest rates are headed. Not long ago, the chairman of the Senate Banking Committee looked down at the Federal Reserve chief, Alan Greenspan, and said, "Mr. Greenspan, we've heard your testimony this morning. Very interesting, very illuminating. Tell us, which way are interest rates going to go?" Greenspan said, "I don't know." And that was short-term! So I contend that if Alan Greenspan doesn't know, and the Federal Reserve doesn't know, and the Senate Banking Committee chairman doesn't, nobody does.

It's not for lack of data or study. The Federal Reserve carefully monitors the economy. The Fed's huge staff of economists, 250 in all, regularly presents the chairman and the Board of Governors with economic forecasts. These can change markedly from one month to the next. And different chairmen have different goals. Greenspan happens to be more worried about inflation than a strong economy and tries to use interest rates as a way to either cool inflation or to speed up the economy. The Greenspan board has been a reactive body, fundamentally, but it's been remarkably successful.

In addition, nobody really knows very far ahead of time whether we're going to have a strong economy or a weak one. If the economy booms, interest rates will increase, because businesses, now more profitable, will want to expand. When businesses want to expand, they need to borrow money. The more demand there is for borrowed money, the higher goes the price of money, and another word for "the price of money" is interest rates.

In that framework, businesses are in effect competing against one another for a limited supply of money. And they're competing against the government, too. If it sees itself in budgetary trouble — that is, it expects a big deficit — the government, which has to borrow money to pay off its bonds, will pay any rate it has to. And that raises rates for all the rest of us. If its budget is balanced or nearly so, interest rates should stay down. Because we don't often know which budget scenarios will play out, it is best to stagger your bonds.

CORPORATE BONDS

Corporate bonds offer a higher rate of return than the government's, but the income you get from them can be completely taxable. On the other hand, we use corporate bonds in a lot of individual retirement accounts, pensions, and profit-sharing accounts. (Because the bond income won't be realized until later in life, taxes are of less consequence with such accounts.) Generally speaking, corporate bonds tend to be especially appealing to charities, foundations, and other non-profit institutions which are tax-free already and don't have to shelter any of the interest income from taxation.

The government generally pays you less in interest than corporations because part of your interest payments are sheltered from state taxes, and because payback is guaranteed by the United States government, which makes the risk to you the lender minimal. The amount of interest you pay, whether you're an individual, or a corporation, or a government depends on your credit rating. The lower it is, the higher interest rate you must pay. People who pay 18-20 percent on credit card balances don't have anything close to the same financial stability as the government does. It's the same way with corporate bonds. A very high interest rate might mean that the payback of the bond is in jeopardy.

In the 1980s, for example, a lot of so-called junk bonds were bought and sold. Many of them were issued to capitalize leveraged buyouts and mergers and acquisitions. People and organizations, using computers and staffs quite sophisticated at researching such offerings, did their homework, evaluating the corporations, getting all the documents necessary, reviewing the prospectuses, and analyzing the financial statements. Back then, you could make a lot of money in junk bonds if you found companies sound enough financially to pay off the bonds' high interest rates at maturity. But whenever someone suggested or showed me a junk bond, my eyes quickly glazed over. It was an area where I was neither interested nor especially adept. And that is still the case today. Junk bond investments can be highly profitable, although I tend to be extra cautious about them when the economy is lousy.

There's nothing inherently inadvisable about investing in junk bonds. Just as with stocks, your investment turns on the company financials. Will it survive long enough and perform well enough to pay off its debtors? If you're going to buy junk bonds to get additional yield on your investments, I suggest junk bond mutual funds because they give you additional diversification and professional management.

During the 1980s surge in junk bonds, I was telling my clients to stay completely away. Most junk bonds don't default now, nor did they then, but I didn't deal in them because I just didn't want to leave myself or my clients open to that possibility. I didn't want my name tied in any way to a defaulted bond. I had a reputation then for dealing in high-quality securities. I didn't want to get the last nickel out of an investment, as a junk bond buyer might, and I still don't.

Moody's and *Standard and Poor's* evaluate corporate bonds, before and after issue, with ratings that go all the way from Triple A down to Double A, Single A, A minus, B, and even Triple B. Junk bonds are anything below Double B. So, for example, if a PepsiCo bond were now paying roughly 8 percent, a junk bond would be paying 10 or 11 percent. The big difference is explained this way. With the junk bond, you might not get your money back, because it's guaranteed by Bill Whoever. That's not true of the Pepsico company, which is prospering all over the world these days.

The 1980s surge in corporate junk bond issues was cyclical and thus likely to be repeated — when the generation that lost a ton of money on junk bonds is long gone and the lessons of the era are forgotten. As I said, I don't deal with junk bonds, so I don't know them too well. But if suddenly your broker calls you up and says, "Hey, how about investing in this bond? It's going to pay 11 percent," you ought to at least know that he's trying to sell you a junk bond that carries a certain level of risk.

When corporations want to borrow large amounts of money, they hire an investment brokerage firm to form what's called a syndicate. Corporations will entice bond purchasers by upping the rate of a bond's return to well over what government bonds pay. Hundreds of brokers, all working for syndicate brokerage houses, will be enlisted in various meetings to market the corporate bonds. Brokers, like those at Ferris Baker Watts, will call various customers at foundations, charities and pension plans, which are also tax free, to buy the bonds. Corporations, in effect, farm out the security-selling job to us, much as they would for stocks.

Say my brokerage is allocated a certain percentage of a bond issue. If Company X is looking to raise a 100 million dollars, my firm might be allocated a half a million dollars' worth of Company X's bonds. We, of course, are more likely to sell them to organizations than individuals, though some individuals in lower tax brackets may want them. Even so, it's more in our interest to sell big blocks of bonds to institutions than to sell much smaller blocks to Mrs. Widow Brown.

Suppose you read in the *New York Times* about an established company that's developing a new piece of equipment that will diagnose a major health problem and thereby help sick people get better. You the investor check it out and conclude, "This is a strong new product that has a monopoly in its field." You can buy that company's bonds or its stock, but you can't decide which.

Be aware of the difference between stocks and bonds. When you buy a company's bond, you don't get anything directly out of the company's new piece of equipment. Even though the company itself may be very profitable because of it, you are merely a creditor of the company. All you've done is lend your money to it. You can't get one more nickel out of the bond you invest in than the amount you put in. When you buy a stock, however, you are a part owner of the company. When the company profits, you eventually will also.

My advice, again, is to go to a professional who has done some work on this problem and who can advise you. If I were meeting with you, the client, and said to you, "I'm really high on this company and we have checked it out," your decision on whether to buy the corporate bond or the company stock would primarily depend on your age, your own particular investment needs, and your portfolio. Chances are, though, that if you're an individual, you're not going to want to buy a corporate bond, unless it's in a retirement account and avoids immediate taxation. Otherwise, there's no tax break in it for you at all.

In some senses, there's little point devoting a great deal of attention to corporate bonds because it's a very small segment of the overall bond market. Most people buy either U.S. treasury bonds or tax-free government bonds. Companies don't rely very much on individuals for loans, either. Generally, the biggest buyers of corporate bonds are "institutional" — like foundations, pension funds, and mutual funds.

TAX-FREE MUNICIPAL BONDS

The U.S. is not the only government entity that issues bonds. States, counties, municipalities, and agencies of these different governments do, too. In fact, state governments are some of the bigger money-raisers in the bond market. They know that they must keep outside funds coming in to supplement their tax and other revenues. The State of Maryland, for example, has what's called a Triple A bond rating by *Moody's*, which is the highest rating a state can get. Maryland has always enjoyed a very high credit rating, which tells you, the would-be investor, about the safety of your bond.

The higher a state's credit rating, the lower interest you the lender are going to get. It's a simple matter of supply and demand. When the state has a high credit rating and its bonds carry virtually no risk, it doesn't have to pay you the lender an above-average or extraordinarily high rate of return to get your money. No Maryland bond has ever defaulted in the history of the state. Nor has there been a default by any county or subdivision in the State of Maryland.

There have been defaults in other states on bonds, but it's been a very rare occurrence. An agency of the state of Washington, for example, issued some water power bonds (known familiarly as WOOPS), which defaulted. Some counties in a few states have defaulted. Though they did not default, the bonds of Orange County, California dropped in price when the administration there unwisely invested in some derivatives.

States need bond money almost all the time, and in large amounts, to finance their capital projects, like highways and bridges. And the states know the consequences of default. But unlike the federal government, they can't print the money to repay their bondholders. They do offer one big tax advantage the federal government doesn't extend. State bonds are triple tax free: no federal government taxes, no state taxes, *and* no local taxes are paid on the interest payment the investor receives from them. That's one of the incentives for you to buy them, and one of the reasons they don't pay as much as many federal government bonds. Federal government bonds today (July 1997) are paying about 6 percent interest, while state bonds are in the four-and-one-half to five percent area.

As long as we're talking about government bonds on the one hand and state bonds on the other, let me offer this piece of advice: If you're in a relatively high tax bracket, you want tax-free bonds — bonds of states or cities or counties — in your portfolio. If you're in a relatively low tax bracket, you want government or corporate bonds. The break point today, the place where the lines begin to cross, is roughly the 28 percent tax bracket. Anything above that, you'll want to go with the tax-frees. Below that, you should be going with U.S. government or corporate bonds.

ZERO COUPON BONDS

The zero coupon bond is worth discussing, in part because a lot of people use it to finance their kids' college education. With a zero coupon bond, money is not paid back to you during the life of the loan, but you know you're going to get the face value of the bond back. If you don't need the income, a zero coupon bond is a perfectly fine way to put money away for a child's college years. If you want $10,000 in three years through a zero coupon bond, you put down $9,100 now. But I advise doing at least one thing before saying yes: Ask the bond issuer what the interest rate is so you know pretty much what you're being paid.

For example, when a friend's children were born, the grandparents bought zero coupon bonds for both of the grandchildren with the idea that by the time they were 18, they would each have $10,000 to put towards their college education. That's a pretty secure way to accomplish what they wanted with their gift. They could not lose money on the zero coupon bonds, unless they had to sell them in the interim, at which point they might have lost money because interest rates were quite high at the time they bought them. But if they hold the bonds until maturity, they'll not lose money, and, in fact, they'll do quite nicely.

Take the zero coupon bond bought for a client's grandson born in 1983. Interest rates for those bonds were very high, something like 13 percent, because those were the early inflationary years of the Reagan Administration. By the time the grandson goes to college in the year 2001 and redeems the zero coupon bond, he will have gotten a very good return on the grandparents' comparatively small but timely purchase. On the original $2,000 investment, he'll get $10,000. The bond issuer made the commitment to pay that high rate of interest all the way until the bond's end, having factored in all the calculations, including the possibility that interest rates could drop. The grandparents made a wonderfully good buy. They or their grandson would have to be idiots to sell the bond before it reaches maturity, because they'll never get zero coupon bonds with interest rates that come close to that today.

Interestingly, there were some government bonds issued around that time that yielded 15 percent. Nobody bought them because rates were supposedly going up yet higher and people were saying, "Oh, I'll wait till they go to 19." That's another instance of market timing gone awry. Now those same people look back and say they were foolish for not purchasing the government bonds at 15 percent. All of us have 20/20 hindsight, but it should have been clear, even then, that those folks were trying to get the last nickel out of the deal. Their strategy backfired.

CASH RESERVES AND
MONEY MARKET ACCOUNTS

As I said earlier, you always want to have 10 or 15 percent of your investment portfolio set aside in cash reserve. We not only advise clients to put that amount into a money market fund, but we urge them to, because it's good for the client and it's good for the broker. The client knows that the money is always available on demand, dollar for dollar. The broker likes it because it's a pool of money that he can use to invest. As brokers, we can say to a client, perfectly honestly, "Mrs. Gotrocks, this is a very painless transaction. You don't have to send us a check. We don't have to send you a bill. The money is right there in your account. We'll just move it from the money market account into these General Electric 7.5 percent corporate bonds," or some other investment that we think is suitable.

In fact, in my view, it's better to have a bit too much money sitting in cash, in a money market account, than to put too much money into bonds. The money sitting in the money market account not only functions as a sleeping pill. It's there to take advantage of a buying opportunity in case stocks get dramatically cheaper and you want to make a purchase. Believe me, the broker's financial interest does not control this bit of advice. The brokerage firm makes nickels, dimes, and pennies from having a client's reserves reside in its money market account.

Some say that when you put investment dollars in a money market reserve fund, you are merely "parking your money." And in some ways they are right. The fund *is* basically a parking lot for money — a place where you put your money at a fairly low rate of interest. But the money market fund is a place where you're assured of getting your money back dollar for dollar, and with some small amount of interest.

And it is not necessarily foolish to leave a lot of money in a money market account for a long period of time. Here's an analogy to explain: When you park your car, it's usually just for a few hours. If you go to Europe for two months, you may want to park your car in the long-term parking area at the airport. The bill may be astronomical, but you know your car will be there the minute you get back.

Some people leave money in money market funds for an especially long period of time. I called a man recently who had just inherited $300,000 from his mother, and he was so busy at his own craft, and working against such tight deadlines, that he really wasn't ready to talk to me about investing the money. I had some immediate suggestions for him, and tried to make an appointment with him to come in to talk about the deployment of his new money. He said, "I certainly want to do that. But I want to wait until later in the year, after I've gotten past my deadlines."

This particular client realizes that he's only getting a nominal return on his money — maybe four percent — in a money-market account, and that he could be getting twice as much in a corporate bond, and maybe two or three times as much in a stock that behaves well. But he's so preoccupied with his work responsiblities that he's willing to let the inheritance quietly sit there. He knows the money will always be there, and he sees the stock market, long-term, as a good place for him to invest.

Money market funds, then, are a pool of safe money that doesn't yield very much income but carries little or no risk. As far as I know, there has never been a default of a money market fund in this country. It's all invested in government securities, and usually very short-term, high-quality ones, like three or six-month government bonds.

Some brokerage firms operate their own money market funds. Some banks do, too. Brokerage firms like to build up these accounts so they're available to salesmen and registered representatives, in case a good investment idea comes along and they can call a client and say, "Mrs. Gotrocks, you have $50,000 in your money market fund here and it's only yielding 3.9 percent. I have something available this morning, a corporate bond, AAA, guaranteed by the GE company at 7.5 percent. Now it's true that in a money market fund, Mrs. Gotrocks, you can get your money out any time you want, and that particular GE bond runs a ten-year period. Nevertheless, getting 7.5 percent is a risk worth taking for a ten-year period when you can virtually double the amount you're getting in the money market fund. As long as you have $50,000 sitting right here, why don't we take $20,000 of that and move it over into the GE bond? That will still leave you $30,000 for any reason you might have, like taking a trip or buying a car, or taking advantage of some other good investment opportunity that comes along."

Most brokerage firms use money market funds that operate out of New York. The brokerage firm I am affiliated with uses one called the Reserve Fund, which is the oldest money market fund in the country.

I do want to make it clear that contrary to public opinion, money market funds are not insured, nor are their deposits guaranteed by anybody. They are not the same as a checking account at a bank, which is insured up to $100,000 per account.

Before investing, you the investor should probably investigate what a money market fund does with its money. Few investors do this. At the very least, put your money with a reputable outfit that you've heard of. Get a prospectus. Every firm that uses a money market fund has a prospectus that spells out the fund's objectives, investments, and managers, but I don't think anyone's ever asked me for one.

The fact is, I see very little advertising for money market funds. Such funds can't make much money because their spreads are so narrow. When the lender is getting a four percent return, there's very little left on the table for the fund managers to make, no matter how much money they're managing. Just by way of comparison, there's more of a profit potential with the sale of long-term bonds because there's a much more substantial markup on them. The spread for the seller is much greater.

CERTIFICATES OF DEPOSIT

If someone comes to me with a definite foreseeable need — college, a house, a trip — I say, "Stay out of the stock market because the market could be 20 percent lower by the time those bills are due." I may put that client's money in a five-year certificate of deposit (CD), or a five-year government bond, to be sure that the money will be there when the client needs it.

(To figure out how much a college bill will cost in another five or ten years, take the current price and add inflation. That way, you know that if the present rate of inflation continues, the college bill, instead of being X, will be X plus some-percent. Anybody can do the calculations from there.)

CDs, then, can make sense for this purpose. As opposed to money market funds, a CD offered by a bank or S&L is insured up to $100,000 per account by the FDIC. Of course, not all bank CDs are equal. And, fortunately, there is a way to compare CDs. Every month *Kiplinger's* and *Money Magazine*, and every week *Barron's*, publishes a list of the highest CD rates. It all comes from a company in North Palm Beach, Florida that compiles the "Bank Rate Monitor," as well as something called "100 Highest Yields."

If you're shopping for a CD, be somewhat careful when dealing with out-of-state institutions you've never heard of. I personally prefer not to get the last nickel. As my dad used to say, "Son, let the other guy have the last ten percent." I'd rather deal with a bank that I know and whose people know me.

With CDs, you can buy short term, medium term, and long term. You'll need some time and patience to compare all the ads and offers. Suppose you have $10,000 and will need the money in three years. You don't want to hear anything about effective yields, percents, or yields on maturity. Ask only one question: "How many dollars will I get back in three years?" Then compare the numbers and take the top one. You can do that in an hour on the phone from home.

It is easy, though, to get confused by all the different measures of yields on a CD. Games are often being played. "Effective yield to maturity," "percentage yield," "daily interest," "monthly interest." The effect, if not the purpose, of using the different terms in the ads is to prevent you from being able to do comparison shopping. So bank A says, "Our effective yield is this," Bank B says, "Our daily interest rate is this." Both banks are counting on your inability to compare apples and oranges.

Some banks will say: "Our introductory rate is 9 percent." You need to know: How long will that last — three months? And will the rate drop to six percent after that? Ask for the number of dollars you'll get after three years, compare three or four CDs available, and take the best one. It is my experience that when you call up a bank or Savings and Loan and say, "Just tell me how many dollars I'll get from your CD at the end of three years," they will give you straight answers. These financial institutions want your business. They make money on you. They'll tell you.

If you decide to buy a CD, be sure to get what they tell you in writing: "The Bank of X guarantees to give to Mrs. Gotrocks $11,134 on September X, 199X." Be sure your CD is insured, too. Get a little leaflet that says, "Insured by the FDIC," then lend them the money and put the CD documents in your safe deposit box.

But — and this is a big "but" — it's my experience and my clients' experience that you must specifically ask for that written commitment, otherwise you might not get it.

And if you haven't gotten that statement and they've only told you, "Mrs. Gotrocks, you own a $10,000 CD with an effective yield of 6.83 percent," you may have problems. You've given them your money, but they haven't said how many dollars you'll get in three years.

At that point, it's hard to go back to them and say, "No, I want something specific, in writing, that will say exactly how many dollars I will get on maturity or I will take the money out." It might be too late by then. Measure twice, cut once. It's an old slogan in carpentry and textiles. It makes a lot of sense in investing. Be more careful at the beginning.

REAL ESTATE INVESTMENTS

If you're looking at alternative ways to invest your money, definitely take real estate and REITs (Real Estate Investment Trusts) into consideration. A real estate investment trust, in regular language, is a package of real estate holdings that you and others invest in. You're actually buying into an organization of real estate professionals who assemble and manage real estate properties, shopping centers, office buildings, nursing homes, hotels.

Growing up, I remember hearing the phrase over and over again, from friends and relatives alike: "He lost everything in real estate," or "They changed their standard of living after losing everything in the Florida real estate bust of the 1920s and 1930s." I imagine there were booms and busts in lots of other places, too. But the one I (and others) heard the most about was Florida's. People were chasing real estate down there like it was the gold rush. All of a sudden, two things happened — an oversupply of real estate, caused by a corresponding lack of demand. No one wanted to buy the raw pieces of raw land being sold. Demand was killed off by the stock market crash of '29, which set off the depression of the '30s. It was a progression of horrors.

Interestingly, the people investing in Florida real estate did not think they were involved in a super high-risk, even speculative, investment. People originally invested in Florida because the Sunshine State was going to be the resort haven of the east, a place where people would go on vacation to get warm. They did not foresee a new housing boom — people back then weren't talking about living out their retirements in

Florida. If you retired then, during what was a period of relative austerity, you continued to live where you had worked. It was quite unlike today, when so many people come in and say to me, "I'll work three more years and then I'm going to kick back and go to Florida, or Arizona, or California, to stay warm for the rest of my life."

People like REITs because they pay extraordinarily high income. In order to escape or avoid taxes at the corporate level, REITs must pay out 95 percent of their income as dividends to stockholders. In practice, that forces them to supply income at a rate of eight to 10 percent a year. By comparison, the dividend on the average stock today is a hair's breath under two percent.

Investing in the right REIT is a good way to assure yourself high dividends, and many investors are so inclined. Most didn't live through the Florida land boom and bust. Because they're in their 40s or 50s, these investors don't immediately throw up their hands and say, "I don't want any part of real estate." And they've been rewarded for their openmindedness. Commercial real estate has performed fairly well except during the late 1980s and early 1990s, when it became overextended and fell on hard times.

My only personal adventure in the field was with a very wellthought-of real estate professional. A good buddy of mine, with whom I worked about four or five years ago, told me that three local guys were making a huge amount of money purchasing hundred-thousand-dollar units of real estate from this real estate pro. They were investing in limited partnerships, and not REITs (there thus was no organized market where you could resell your investment later).

Without anybody's prodding or pushing, I asked my friend if he would split a unit for me, so I could get in on this seemingly great opportunity for $50,000. He said yes, and my limited partnership bought me half a unit in a warehouse in New Jersey. It was never rented and I lost every nickel, though I got a few tax write-offs on it. It's the only time I ventured into something I didn't know anything about. It was a good lesson.

If a salesman approaches you about a new REIT involving Mexican hotels and resorts, here's how to assess it as an investment. First, you must have faith in the broker who's selling it to you. Unfortunately, many brokers don't know much about REITs. When the product is there to be pitched, the brokers will say to you, "This REIT is appealing today because there isn't much else out there. Stocks are terribly overpriced, selling at the highest P/Es in X number of years, and providing the lowest dividend yields in market history." REITs are in fact attractive today because, by their very nature, they must pay out most of their income. They are bought and sold like stock.

REITs do have to pass certain criteria in order to be sold, but there is no regulatory assurance that the shopping center a REIT invests in will succeed. Other criteria, like market capitalization and debt ratio, are used. If they make money, REITs must pay out 95 percent of their profit. But it could be 95 percent of zero profit. In the Mexican example, the REIT might buy all the wrong hotels.

Don't buy REITs because you're looking for a tax shelter. A limited partnership has some tax write-off potential, which I realized as an investor. But a REIT is a tax shelter only for the owners and operators of the property through depreciation.

So if I were investigating a REIT myself, I would think mostly of the quality of the properties involved. The problem is, I don't know how to assess real estate. I, like my clients, would have to rely on someone knowledgeable suggesting that I buy a particular REIT. My partners, who know a lot more about REITs than I do, might say to me, "Westy, Mid-Atlantic Realty has some great properties, as does First Washington Real Estate, which owns the Festival at Woodholme (in suburban Baltimore). That property has turned into an amazingly profitable enterprise. Now it's got the Mercantile Bank, Bibelot Book Stores, Sinai Hospital, one medical building, and another under construction. It's a real bell-ringer. They found the right site at the right price. They know what they're doing." So it's back to the same Rule Number One. Apply it as you would in selecting stocks: Is management any good?

For our clients, we see REITs as a good way to diversify and get income. When people throw up their hands and say, "Oh, real estate is terrible, real estate is in the doghouse," we point out that it has a positive side too: "All of the cash flow comes through to you the investor, and that may be better than having all of your income-producing investments in utilities. "

In my experience, First Washington Realty as a stock has been quite successful. I only started to follow REITs recently. Their stock prices have been fairly flat for the last couple of years because everything else has been booming. REITs continue to pay high income, and as long as they do, people don't care whether the stock prices go up or down. The stock's failure to rise is simply explained by supply and demand. Not many investors have been chasing REITs lately. They're just not as popular as some of the other sectors of the market, like high-tech.

Some investors might decide to buy a REIT rather than stock in a real estate company per se. One thing you often get in the REIT is diversification, whereas you might not get that with an individual real estate company. From all the materials I've studied, my conclusion is that you the investor shouldn't overlook REITs. Have them in your portfolio, but not too much of them — at most, 10 percent of your total portfolio.

ARE ANNUITIES FOR YOU?

Annuities are fantastic ways to invest money and enjoy tax-deferred compounding. I suggest annuities for my clients seeking a shelter from taxes and as a supplemental retirement plan. Once investors have taken advantage of retirement plans at their place of employment, whether it be their 401(k), profit-sharing, or IRA, I suggest using an annuity to further build the asset base for retirement.

Both the fixed and variable annuity are retirement accounts — investors cannot gain access to their money until age 59 1/2. If they do, they are subject to a 10 percent penalty.

Fixed and variable annuities differ because of their rate of return. With a fixed annuity, the insurance company that issues it gives you a fixed rate of interest for a set period of time (usually between 1 and 10 years). Secured is both your interest rate and principal. It's the kind of annuity that's best suited for the CD type of investor. Not surprisingly, fixed annuities tend to be most popular when interest rates are high. Investors like to lock up that rate for a long period of time.

If you buy a fixed annuity, make sure that it's for a period longer than one year, and that you are guaranteed a set rate of interest for the entire period of the annuity. A five-year annuity should give you the same rate for five years, and not just the first year.

If you have a longer time horizon in mind and can handle the ups and downs of Wall Street, I prefer the variable annuity. With a variable annuity, you select your investment choices (and rate of return) from a menu of options offered by the insurance company. You can allocate your investments through options called subaccounts, which allow you to be as conservative or aggressive as you wish. You are free to move your money from one subaccount to another without paying any taxes on the gains achieved along the way.

Variable annuities offer you a much greater chance to out-perform inflation, provided you have your money in growth funds or international investments. Investors who grow nervous can move to a fixed income option or money market option, and their switch does not trigger any tax consequences. Most insurance companies reserve the right to require you to start taking money out of the annuity at age 85. A lot depends on the company issuing the annuity, and you may not get this call until you're 90 or 95, but, for many companies, it is standard practice to enforce this rule when you hit age 85.

Insurance annuities are an especially useful investment device for those who want to build up their nest eggs, tax-deferred, for their later years. I do a lot of annuities for clients, but I never structure them alone because they're complicated. But if you don't need the current income, an annuity allows your money to compound tax-deferred until you have to take it out, and it can thus grow like topsy. At nine percent, your money will double in eight years, and at eight percent, it will double in nine years. That's the rule of 72.

In some ways, the annuity is a competitor of the mutual fund. But, like the mutual fund, variable annuities offer professional money management through mutual fund type programs that allow your money to compound tax deferred.

Many annuities have another very valuable aspect called a death benefit. If a husband over time puts $30,000 into an annuity, his surviving beneficiary, his wife, gets all of the money that's been invested, regardless of whether it's accumulated some return. So it's a hybrid kind of product — a guaranteed death benefit and a chance for appreciation.

Until the account holder dies, the money in an annuity keeps building up tax-free at a very fast rate, because neither the state nor the federal government takes anything out for taxes. It's like an IRA, but it has one feature that's better. In an IRA or a 401(k), at age 70 and a half, you have to start taking out roughly 1/20th of what's in there. In an annuity, you don't. You can let it continue to compound tax-free until much later.

And the annuity is insured, usually by an insurance company. So it's generally a safe investment with some special benefits that work well for you, in life and in death. With an annuity, you take advantage of a loophole in the tax structure, an entirely legitimate one, that authorizes you to build up money for your "Golden Years." (Whoever named them that ought to be tarred and feathered in the village square. Your teeth fall out, your eyes get blurred, your feet develop corns, your hair falls out if it hasn't already, and your digestive system becomes very tenuous.)

I can recall some examples of where I have advised clients to go into an annuity. A widow got some insurance money from her recently deceased husband and she was at the age where annuities were appropriate. I wouldn't sell an annuity to anyone under age 40 or over 80. If a widow of 55 or 60 gets her hands on $100,000 and doesn't need the income, I may persuade her to buy a tax-deferred annuity.

I also recommend annuities as part of a more diversified package of investments.

After you stop working, annuities can pay you income for life.

ARE METALS PRECIOUS?

As for precious metals, I made one investment in gold, and it nearly turned into a horror story, though it's not over yet. When gold got up to around $500 an ounce, a friend and I bought lots of one-ounce gold Krugerrands. Our thinking at that time was that gold was going to hit 600, 700, 800 dollars an ounce. We were sorely tempted not just by a rising market, but one where the sky seemed to be the limit. As of July 1997, gold was worth $350 an ounce. I gave some of the coins to my daughters. When I went to my safe deposit box the other day, I gave one to my secretary.

Many so-called experts recommend that you put money into gold. To most investors, it seems pretty unwise to plunk down so much money for so little. The rationale for investing is that if we ever have a financial catastrophe, gold, gold jewelry, and precious metals will be the only things of value. Neither paper money nor stock will be worth anything, but jewelry, because it's always liquid, will always command a price. In case the financial world collapses, and you need to buy gasoline or food, gold coins and other precious metals may be considered the only acceptable currency.

On radio and TV, I used to advise putting five percent of your net worth into gold coins, then burying them in a secret part of your backyard. "Don't put them in a safe deposit box," I'd say, "because if there's a catastrophe, the banks will be closed." In response, a lot of people have teased me, "Can we come over to your house and dig up your backyard?" The fact is, though, that my wife's family, and so many other families, got out of oppressed lands in the 1930s and '40s only because they had valuable jewelry to sell.

If you decide to buy precious metals, such as gold, go to a licensed coin dealer. The Yellow Pages are full of them. By shopping around, you can have some idea whether you're paying the right amount.

Very few of my clients have invested in precious metals. It assumes an absolute worst-case scenario. Another problem with gold is that it doesn't pay any income. It has what we call negative income: it actually costs money to store it in a safe deposit box.

A real sharp guy around my age, a genius when it comes to knowing what to do with money, bought U.S. quarters when nobody else was because they were made out of real silver. Now they're not, but he made a lot of money. But, as he would probably tell you, trading in precious metals requires some special know-how. This is not the stuff for most investors. In the end, I say, "Stick to what you know."

CHAPTER SUMMARY:
BONDS AND FIXED INCOME INVESTMENTS

1. Bonds and fixed income investments are the protected shelter in which your money dwells. They may not be the most glamorous investment opportunity. But, unlike stocks, when you invest your money in fixed income, you always know it will be there at the end.

2. Before you invest in bonds, pay off all your debts, especially the ones on which you're paying high interest rates over a long time period. You will probably not get as good a guaranteed return from any other investment.

3. Don't buy U.S. government bonds out of a patriotic duty.

4. Invest in bonds with staggered maturities. Buy some short-term bonds, some mediums, and some longs. This protects you from interest rate fluctuations.

5. Corporate bonds usually offer a higher rate of return than government bonds, but, unlike government bonds, they are fully taxable (unless they're part of a retirement account).

6. Corporate bonds are different from stocks. When you buy a company's bond, you don't get any benefit from the company's gains or losses. You are simply a creditor who will be repaid when the bond comes due.

7. Individual states also sell bonds. It is rare but possible for them to default on payment. The really good thing about state bonds is that they are triple tax free: no federal government taxes, no state taxes, and no local taxes are paid on the interest payments the investor receives from them.

8. You always want 10 to 15 percent of your portfolio in cash reserves. We advise our clients to put their cash in money market accounts. But don't use money market accounts as a "parking lot" for all your cash and forever defer investing most of your money. ➡

9. *Certificates of deposit (CDs) are good investments when you have a date you want to get your money back for a specific use. They are rated in Barron's, Kiplinger's, and Money Magazine. Ask the bank or S&L what you will receive at the end of the time period you are considering, and make them put it in writing before you buy the CD.*

10. *REITs and other real estate investments can nicely round out your diversified portfolio. They are also a good way to assure yourself high dividends. When considering REITs, look at the quality of the properties involved. You probably need to find someone you can trust who knows something about them.*

11. *An annuity is a tax-deferred investment that the government has authorized so people can build up a nest egg for their later years. The annuity invests your money in mutual-fund type accounts, long-term. I wouldn't sell an annuity to anyone under age 40 or over age 80.*

12. *Investing in precious metals can be very profitable, but is also quite unpredictable. When trading in precious metals, know what you're doing. They are not right for most investors.*

CHAPTER Ten

Stock-Picking

On an iffy double play in baseball,
it's best not to try for too much. You can end up allowing both batter
and runner to reach base and eventually score.

It's the same with the stock market. Be sure to get one out.

A sensible investor has a lot of alternative strategies when it comes to picking stocks. I will list a few good methods, some great stocks, and a few bad ideas, so that you can recognize and understand them.

Coca-Cola, Merck, and American Home Products, three of my favorite stocks, first came to my attention through research professionals. The one thing that has attracted me to the entire pharmaceutical industry, like Merck, American Home Products, Bristol-Myers Squibb and Schering Plough, has been that these companies, rather than paying out large dividends to stockholders, plow back a large portion of their earnings, sometimes up to eight or 10 percent a year, into research. This has enabled them to develop new products, where substantial profit margins are achieved before competition sets in. For example, Merck has been able to come out every four or five years with a blockbuster product because of the money it allocates to its huge research laborato-

THE RAG BUSINESS

After college, I worked at Julius Gutman's, a family-owned department store in downtown Baltimore opened in 1877 by Julius Gutman, my mother's father (I was named after him). By the 1950s, it was an institution. I worked in all areas of the store. I was a buyer, a merchandise manager, and much more. I worked there because my parents urged me to go into the family business (from left to right in photo above, that's me, my first wife, my father, and my mother). In those days, people did what their parents told them to do. Besides, the store was a booming business in the Depression because we undersold the big stores. What other stores sold for a dollar we sold for 94 cents. What other stores sold

for $2 we sold for $1.77. During the Depression, when people saved nickels and dimes, those differences were huge. When I first joined Gutman's, my mother's brothers ran the store. Later, I was slated to go higher than the other employees because of my blood relationship with the family. I was being groomed for a top position.

When I was in my middle 30s, I was named president of the store. It was prestigious for me to run a highly respected Baltimore store, but, unfortunately, it went downhill during my presidency because of several factors. I wasn't cut out to be an executive, leader, or merchant. I soon discovered that. When I took over, our department store was known as the lowest priced one in the city, and yet it had a good reputation. We weren't Hochschild's, Hutzler's, or Stewart's, but we dominated the corner of Park and Lexington. But soon, Baltimoreans began to desert downtown in droves and moved to the suburbs. Their shopping habits moved with them. Under my leadership, we neither had the courage nor the money to expand materially to where the shoppers ➤

ries. You follow these companies long enough, and you almost expect those breakthrough discoveries and products to happen rather regularly.

Peter Lynch's system of finding stocks is seeing which products he and his family members like in everyday life and examining them on a financial basis. As head of all Fidelity mutual funds, and particularly its giant, Fidelity Magellan, he made a fortune on Johnson & Johnson (Mylanta, Band-Aids, etc.). He sensed a trend and said to himself, "I'm going to put my chips on my intuition." Then, his research verified that

J&J was a good company. The stock went absolutely through the roof. He did the same with other companies.

He wouldn't buy Dunkin Donuts stock just because the coffee tasted especially good on an initial visit, or even when he went back several times, checking on himself and finding that the coffee was indeed superior. He had to do the arithmetic first: What are the balance sheets like, what is the history of earnings, what is the history of dividends? When he found answers to his liking, he went heavily with his initial instincts and scored big with Dunkin Donuts, among others.

Lynch says, "Keep your eyes and ears open to what people are buying." In one of his books, he gives this example: His wife went to the supermarket, and, on arriving home, reported that women were grabbing L'eggs pantyhose off the counter by the dozens. L'eggs were made by Hanes, so he did his research, bought Hanes, and earned handsome rewards. I have to say, I think that Lynch's method is slightly oversimplified for the average investor. Just because people are buying a lot of a company's product doesn't mean that its stock will quadruple. Even if you go to a supermarket a week later and find out that the same product is being purchased in record numbers, you're merely gathering informa-

are now — the suburbs. Meantime, the little stores on Lexington Street closed one by one. Our business started to go downhill in the middle 1950s. It was a terribly rough time in my life.

I'm a good communicator and, I think, an articulate public speaker, but neither of these attributes worked for me in the "rag business," which is what we called the bargain department store business. I couldn't use any of my real talents. And I didn't have those I really needed. I still don't. I'm a poor negotiator. When I buy a car, I usually pay close to the list price or whatever they quote me.

When we merged with Brager's, our new "partner" won controlling interest of what used to be our store, and it put in its own president, Paul Sowell. A lot of people told me that there wouldn't be any more room for me, so I decided to look elsewhere. In 1960, during a lunch in the Southern Hotel with two or three people I respected — one was John Motz, who was president of the Mercantile Safe Deposit & Trust Co.; another was Harry Green, a lawyer — I sought advice on where to look. John Motz said, "Westy, Baker Watts is looking for a good Jewish broker." I was immediately interested. ❧

tion anecdotally. You have to analyze the company figures. If you can't do it yourself — and the average person can't — have a broker help you.

But the average person can keep his or her eyes open and then say to the broker, "Send me a report on this company (Johnson & Johnson or Wrigley's Gum or Philip Morris), will you? I'm thinking of making a big commitment. I want to know what your research department thinks."

I occasionally find a product that I personally use and like, and follow the Peter Lynch advice to find out about the manufacturer. For example, there's been a huge amount of comparative advertising lately for all of these antacid products. "This one is stronger." "This one will act faster." "This one came onto the over-the-counter market more recently." "This one's recommended by more doctors." It's pretty impossible to sort out all the sales angles. The antacid my doctor likes and recommends is Pepcid AC. As it turns out, Johnson & Johnson makes it, and jointly distributes it with Merck, another of my favorite companies. J&J is more of a marketing organization of pharmaceuticals, but one of the product's ingredients was apparently discovered by Merck.

Merck is big in ethical drugs, or drugs that have been approved by the FDA. Among other things, it makes and sells Proscar, Diuril, and this new drug I take to lower my cholesterol, Zocor. In the case of Pepcid AC, Merck realized that it made sense to enter into a joint venture with Johnson & Johnson. By choosing not to go the prescription drug route, it could get the product to the public more quickly, and thus bring about more widespread consumption more rapidly.

Another good company might put a lot of emphasis on research and product development. And, instead of sending you a large dividend check, which is taxable (so you only keep two-thirds of the gains), it might invest that money in research, which works out better for you in the long run than if you got a large short-term dividend. The reinvestments often produce new profits and higher profit margins, and enable the stock to go absolutely straight up.

I've had practically a lifetime love affair with American Home Products, which is a widely diversified company with several divisions. One of them, an ethical drug division, frequently brings new drugs onto the market. The company as a whole has built up a huge multi-level marketing organization to distribute and sell its over-the-counter products. I'll bet you have at least 10 American Home Products in your home — such household products as Anacin, Dristan, Easy-Off Oven Cleaner, and Preparation H. (I probably have most of these in my own home, except for Preparation H.)

You don't hear very much about American Home Products. Its corporate name is not very well known. At one point, its general phone number wasn't answered "American Home Products." AHP takes a very low profile. Because it's widely diversified and raises its dividend every year, though, I've not only stayed with the company ever since I first bought its stock in the 1950's, but I can honestly say I have never lost my affection for the company. Only on research, development, and advertising does it spend liberally. But, for them, that has proved a remarkably simple and successful strategy for profit.

TAKE ANECDOTAL EVIDENCE WITH A GRAIN OF SALT

Over the years, many of my clients have passed along to me personal anecdotes that support their ideas about buying or selling a particular stock. They have not always been on cue. When making decisions based on these personal experiences, they often need a broker to evaluate their personal judgments. Sometimes they won't let me change their minds, but they often are better off if they give in to my instincts and experience.

A woman once came to me and said, "Westy, buy me some Holiday Inn. We just came back from vacation and stayed at a Holiday Inn. We loved the place. They were so nice at the desk." I bought it for her and her husband. If people want something badly enough, I buy it for them. If I don't and the stock quadruples, they'll remember, and Heaven help me. Sometimes, though, there's a middle ground, where I can say, "Holiday Inn sounds great. Let me have a look at the fundamentals just to be sure you're not going to buy a dog." That is the best course to take, in my opinion. Let your broker have a look.

Sometimes with anecdotal evidence, the best thing to do is the opposite of what you first think of doing. For example, Texaco's stock got into immense trouble as a result of very adverse national publicity in 1997. If you owned stock in Texaco, and saw a huge scandal about to unfold, your initial instincts told you to bail out, for either pragmatic or moral reasons (racism at the company's higher management levels was alleged). If you're a woman or an African-American who might otherwise make or retain an investment in Texaco, your first reflex action may have been to say to yourself: "The heck with Texaco. There are plenty of other places where I can put my money." And there are. But the stock will probably come back, just as Exxon's did after the Valdez oil spill and just as Johnson & Johnson's did after the Tylenol scares.

But here's the other part of the equation. When there is a big sell-off of a company's stock, especially of individually owned blocks, the company is sent a very clear message. In addition, it hears, directly or indirectly, from large foundations, large pension funds, and large insurance companies managing giant portfolios. Many become reluctant to buy or hold Texaco stock because of the difficult public relations position they're thrust into because of the allegations. When individual and institutional investors appear to be bolting in huge numbers, a company under siege has no choice but to respond immediately.

I advise an investor under such circumstances to realize that he's going to see some massive sell-offs at the beginning of the crisis, but to stick with the stock because the company will probably take steps to contain the damage. The first day after the 1997 Texaco/racial discrimination story broke, the stock lost $800 million in value. The second day, it lost $500 million. The third day, as the company president sought to resolve the situation, the stock came back and recovered $400 million. But its stock lost nearly a billion total dollars in value in three days.

No wonder. Many institutional investors decided to dump Texaco. African-Americans on the boards of directors of many institutions did not like the suggestion that Texaco was anti-black. They reasoned, "Look, we don't want to be holders of this stock. Besides, if we are, our own institutions are going to take their own very bad public relations hits."

Yet, the Texaco stock will not stay down forever. Ten years ago, Union Carbide went through something similar with the Bhopal disaster, when a battery manufacturing facility in India blew up, causing huge and devastatingly large casualties. Many big lawsuits were threatened, filed, and eventually resolved. In time, the company stock recovered and moved much higher. So did Johnson & Johnson.

Texaco, which is a Dow Jones stock, came way back after its early sinking spell in 1997. The workers' threatened class action suit triggered the inevitable costly settlement, but a product boycott by consumers, also threatened initially, never materialized. Texaco products are advertised and sold directly to consumers. Wisely, the company resolved the matter quickly to keep African-Americans from boycotting their stations in droves. And, in the end, the company itself was so big that even the huge settlement agreed to proved pretty much a drop in the bottom-line bucket. If Texaco continues to have good and rising earnings over the next few years, the bad smell from this episode will go away.

Particularly in times of company scandal, the mature investor says again to himself, "Build a portfolio and don't let every headline buffet it or kick it around." If you're a mature investor, you may take some bumps along the way, especially when controversy strikes, but you will commit more errors by following the headlines than not. In Texaco's case, the smart investor reasons, "Look, I like Texaco. It's been around for a million years. Like other good companies, it has a good distribution system, a good franchise system, and good name recognition in the marketplace. In addition, the price of oil and gasoline is pretty stable, so the company is probably making a healthy enough profit. Not only will I hold what I have in a fundamentally sound company, but I might think about buying some more shares."

By thinking through the situation this way, some sophisticated investors bought Texaco when it was on the bargain counter. They didn't care so much about race relations as about making money. They knew they would make a bigger and more major mistake by dumping the stock in panic than by staying the course. They could foresee some temporary heartache, and even some temporary financial loss. But they, like

I, probably realized that more investing mistakes are made by letting every headline influence your decision than not.

Are there special cases that justify the rapid-fire, wholesale dumping of stocks you own? Suppose that you're an 80-year-old retiree who's got 40 percent of your portfolio in stock, with 10 percent of your holdings in Texaco. You know you're not going to live forever. You realize that the Texaco stock will eventually come back up in price, but it's probably going to go down or stay down first, because the lawsuit, for a while at least, is going to keep generating more bad publicity. At that realization, you might say to yourself, "I can't wait five years for this stock to come back. Let me sell it now; I'll lose a few dollars and buy something that maybe won't be quite so buffeted by this kind of a thing." Your assumption — that the problem will persist for five years — leads you to dump the stock. That assumption is probably wrong, and your decision to jump out of Texaco might be wrong as well. In a situation like this, usually the best thing you can do is hold through the rough spots. Eventually (and probably sooner than later), the stock will recover if it is a fundamentally good company. But when all is said and done, you have to be comfortable with your investments. It is, after all, your money.

There are times when I wish older investors would make greater use of personal experience in their investment decision-making. Because they come into daily contact with them, older investors could have a special affinity for companies that manufacture and sell products that respond to the medical and health conditions of the aging. Unfortunately, as investors, older people hold themselves back from investing in these companies. Without a steady income from their former occupations and their previous businesses, older retirees must supplant that money with income from other sources. So they're leery of growth company stocks that make the products with which they come into contact every day. They prefer companies that do not plow their profits back into research, but distribute it to them as dividend income.

They shouldn't necessarily strike growth stocks from their list of investments. Instead of buying utilities that yield six percent dividends and whose stock prices rarely fluctuate, older people should think about buying companies like Pfizer, Inc., whose stock has been upwardly mobile for a long time. Instead of expecting a large dividend, which they're not going to get from Pfizer, they can, as the Pfizer stock price increases, sell off a few shares to live on. Unfortunately, the members of my older generation were taught very young never to touch principal. Because they had no money then (few people did), they were never to touch a nest egg of capital. It was practically sinful to spend or tap into it.

This, it turns out, is bad advice today as well as mathematically flawed. As I say again, income and principal are two pockets of the same suit. I'd prefer to have a growth stock appreciate, sell off a few of its shares to live on, and just watch the rest grow. That is far more profitable than buying utilities with dividends, taxable at ordinary income rates. Besides, utility stocks can decline, too.

Negative personal experiences often unduly influence investors. On the one hand, no investor has ever said to me, "I just bought this great car. Buy me five hundred shares of the car company." It's usually the reverse. A very affluent woman from New Jersey once gave us discretion to handle her portfolio as we saw fit, with one exception, "Don't ever buy any Ford Motor stock." She had had a bad personal experience with a Ford — a lemon she bought and couldn't get rid of. My partners and I decided we were not going to fight her. It didn't matter to her that Ford was expanding and taking off. "I don't give a damn if it does," she'd say. "I don't want it on my list." We allowed her to have her way. Her instruction to us became her method of retaliation and revenge. Of course, the fact that she was not going to buy 200 shares of Ford didn't hurt the company any.

This kind of thinking is much more rampant with tobacco stocks. "I don't care if Philip Morris is in the Dow Five," clients will tell me. "I don't want it." So we pick a sixth stock and put it in there instead of Philip Morris. The people who haven't bought Philip Morris have suffered because they didn't buy it. The stock has been a real bell-ringer.

A broker can never make you do anything you don't want to do. If you insist, your broker will not force you to buy or sell anything. But you will probably make more money if you take advantage of your broker's analytical skill, while realizing that it's sometimes silly to let your hates keep you from making money.

THE "HOLD-EVERYTHING" PHILOSOPHY

At one of my numerous talks on investing, a man with millions of dollars in his portfolio asked me this unusual — but thought-provoking — question: "Westy, what do you think of my investment philosophy? I never sell anything." It caught me a bit by surprise, but it shouldn't have. My response was, "I'm sure that your portfolio contains some dogs that have gone down to nothing or next to nothing (he agreed). But, in my opinion, your philosophy is basically a good one. I can assure you that, over the years, more mistakes are made by selling what turned into home runs, or great investments, than by buying promising stocks that turn out to be dogs."

And the arithmetic to prove it is fairly simple. Let's say you buy a thousand shares of a stock at ten. That's a $10,000 investment, and the stock drops to zero and you lose it all. The most you can possibly lose is what you put in, or $10,000. You'll have a few of those kinds of stocks along the way. If you buy a stock at 10 that goes to 20, where you sell it, you take your $10,000 profit and pay taxes on the capital gain, leaving you with roughly $6,000 in profits.

However, if the company you sold turns out to be Schering Plough or Intel, and the stock goes past 20 to 30, 40, 50, then splits two-for-one and goes back up to its previous high price, you say to yourself, "If I had only held on, my $10,000 investment would now be worth $100,000." That realization can make you quite sick, both financially and emotionally. You sold the stock completely, but you're still following it. You can't help but look at it, especially if it becomes a very big deal and a household name, like Microsoft or another of those high-tech companies. You would have been much better off just holding on, or selling just part. In that way, the never-sell policy can pay off big.

The "buy-and-never-sell" approach, while more right than wrong, does depend on who you are and what your resources are. My first wife's mother was an intrepid, unquestioning follower with the resources to sustain her. Widowed in 1934, during the Great Depression, she inherited from her husband what was then a medium-sized portfolio. For 50 years, until the day she died, she made not a single investment change, and managed to live well on the growing dividends that her list, dominated as it was by the bluest of blue chip stocks (GE, GM, Caterpillar, etc.), provided her. I knew her for at least 40 of those 50 years, and I was a broker for at least 25 of them. I tugged and I slugged to get her to make at least one change, but she wore me down. "Julius," she would say, "if these stocks were good enough for us in the good old days, they're plenty good enough now."

If you're going to follow this "hold-everything" system, there is one pre-requisite: you must have enough money to cover the losses incurred by your losers, while still finding the money to buy more stocks and bonds if you want them. Not that many companies drop to pennies or to nothing, but some stocks can go down precipitously and turn into dogs. Over the long pull, particularly in the bull market we've gladly ridden for 15 years, the right thing to do has been to hold everything. When Clinton was elected in 1992, the Dow was roughly 3,100. By 1997, it had more than doubled and was headed toward tripling! Without even getting out of bed, many investors doubled their money, which is absolutely unheard of. In a bull market, "sell-nothing" investors are going to do extremely well. In a bad (or bear) market, those investors will probably still do well, assuming they are smart enough to buy good companies, which usually don't get killed in a declining market.

If you are using the "hold-everything" philosophy, stick to it. To see why, follow along on this real-life situation. Your computer guy comes over to your office and says, "You won't believe what's happened to the price of memory. It has completely collapsed. It's gone from $45 a megabyte, where it's been for years, down to $5 a meg almost overnight." "What caused the huge and rapid drop?" you ask. He says, "Two other companies came into the marketplace manufacturing and selling memory. To gain a part of the market, they drastically lowered the price on a computer commodity that was not inherently expensive to make. The $45 was clearly a price held very artificially high because of the absence of competition. All three companies are battling it out now and dropping their prices like crazy."

If you invested in the original, dominant memory company, track it, hold its stock, and do not despair. First, the tide of fortunes could turn, as it often does. The two new competitors might fail to gain a big chunk of the market. The chief engineer, the genius driving one of the competitors, might die in an automobile crash. Your company might decide to buy out one or both of its competitors (assuming the government approves).

My family trust manager in New York bought me Intel at $13 a share, adjusted for splits, but came within a fraction of an inch of selling it when some bad news came out — it was the big controversy about a minor fallibility with one of the Pentium computer chips it manufactures. His intuition said not to sell. Intel easily managed to overcome that flap. Today, it remains the dominant chip provider. As of July 1997, the stock was worth $95 per share.

Selling Intel under those circumstances would have violated your total stock philosophy, if you believed in "holding everything." By selling, you would have lost the integrity of your investing system, and you would have become victim to the everyday wonderment of, "Is this stock going down? Or is it going up? Should I sell it? Should I hold it?" If you have carved in stone, "I rarely sell anything," you don't have to worry. You lead the simple life of a systematized investor, one whose philosophy is fundamentally that of the eternal optimist. You believe that if you wait long enough, most everything will go up.

Sam Hopkins, a retired partner of Alex. Brown, told me that he followed one piece of advice all his life, and had been successful: "Ninety percent of the time," he said, "it pays to be an optimist." I guess he's right. I was brought up in a household that stressed exactly the opposite.

"Things are going to crack. Be careful. Don't do this. Never take a chance. Stay on the safe side." I can still hear these admonitions ringing in my ears, mostly from my mother.

If you're like me, better to remember the saying: A rising tide lifts all boats — new boats, old boats, leaky boats, lousy boats, big boats, little boats. There have been some amazing success stories in this market. If the tide is rising, for Heaven's sakes, ride it.

DIVERSIFYING BY SECTOR

A recent CNN report suggested that, for one of the first times in history, focusing your investing on a particular sector is proving not very effective. In the old days, companies in the same sector were buffeted by the same economic conditions, so, in effect, they moved up, down, or sideways pretty much at the same rate. Now, some companies in specific sectors do exceedingly well, while others in the same sector do quite poorly. Performance is all over the map. If that is true, and I believe it is, the need becomes all the greater to focus intensely on a company's fundamentals, perhaps concluding, "Well, I think this is going to be a good next year for technology companies that are making modems and I'll invest in 3-Com because they bought U.S. Robotics, which makes a great, speedy modem."

The 20-25 main sectors of the economy appear in the "Value Line Composite Index." The one that immediately comes to my mind is health, which includes HMOs and hospitals. In that sector, there seems to be a lot of consolidation going on, with companies merging, or buying up a great many hospitals and becoming conglomerates like Helix and United HealthCare. Airlines are another main sector, as is automotive, which is more industrial (General Motors is not in the transportation index, but the Dow Jones Industrials). The transportation sector, which is a big one, includes airlines, railroads, trucking companies. There's also telecommunications.

In my opinion, you're better off to diversify *by sector* than to concentrate your holdings *within* a sector. A woman called me on TV to say that some of her mail indicated that the high technology sector looked good to her now. "Why did it?" she asked me. "For the simple reason," I said, "that the high technology sector has been a very good performer and people have a tendency to buy what's doing well, which is often a mistake, and to turn their backs on a sector that's doing badly, which is another mistake."

If I call Mrs. Gotrocks — I picture her as living on the top of a hill with a garden — I'll get an order quickly by saying "Intel, which manufactures more computer chips than anybody else, is up from 35 to 50 in the last three weeks. That's after a two-for-one split, and the split came after the company survived a brief but major flap about an alleged fallibility in one of its newest chips. I think you ought to get in on that." I like placing that kind of call a whole lot more than one where I say, "Bethlehem Steel stock is down from 15 to eight. I think you ought to have some of it." Most people would rather buy a high flyer than a low flyer.

It's not surprising. As a broker, almost automatically, I can have greater enthusiasm for what's succeeding than what's apparently poised to turn around. Not that I can't be cheery enough about that scenario. If I believe Mrs. Gotrocks ought to buy Bethlehem Steel, I would tell her, "The stock is fairly depressed, the company's fortunes are turning around, and I've read some very optimistic reports recently on the company." I might add, "They've developed a new technique in their mill for grinding out steel at a much cheaper price than U.S. Steel, and that should help earnings for the quarter." It's easier for brokers like me to sell something by focusing on the positive than by dressing up the negative with a positive spin.

INITIAL PUBLIC OFFERINGS (IPOS)

IPOs are another kind of investment that can be part of your portfolio. IPOs are shares of a corporation just going public for the first time. The corporation offers its stock for sale in order to raise the capital necessary to begin a new company or to further capitalize an older one. Brokers are the ones who sell IPOs. (There are also secondary stock offerings, and so on.)

I myself haven't done much selling of IPOs recently. When I was younger and more aggressive in the business, I peddled a lot of IPOs. Some did very well, and there was a good profit in them for me as the broker. Brokers are not paid a commission as such when they sell an IPO. An IPO's profit is built into its selling price. On an IPO that sells originally for ten dollars a share, for example, the broker might make 30 cents a share, which is three percent.

Some brokerage firms get a lot of IPO shares to sell to their clients. So, if I thought it was a good stock with honest management and a nice presentation of its product or service, I would add it to a client's portfolio. Brokers save IPOs for their best clients, commonly telling them that they only have a limited number of IPO shares to spread around. That makes the clients feel special, and it is, on the whole true. The fact is that many IPOs are good both for the broker and the investor, and their sale in this fashion is quite proper.

The more I read about IPOs, the more I feel you should resist the temptation to buy them at their initial offering price, and instead wait a few months until their price settles. Often, if an IPO begins at $10 per share, it will settle down to $8.50 when the bloom's off the rose. When the IPO is first offered, demand usually outstrips supply, especially in a strong market, because of the hype brokerage houses and financial periodicals generate for it. That almost always guarantees an immediate gain for the stock. However, this gain can be unnatural and unwarranted and the stock price usually levels off after a little while. Some IPOs may go straight from $10 to $20, and stay there or go higher, but many drop down in price later and settle in at that lower level for a while.

IPOs are always brought out in a strong market. That in and of itself means that many IPOs are overpriced or overvalued. If the market dives before an IPO is scheduled to be brought out, the offering could be canceled "due to market conditions." When the market is low and buyers discouraged, the company can't get its asking price because everyone is feeling suspicious and gloomy. If the market dips after an IPO is brought out, the IPO will often drop in price before it begins to rise, and sometimes it can drop sharply.

DON'T GET INFATUATED

One big thing to avoid as an investor is becoming infatuated with a certain stock. We know about infatuation in the sense of man/woman relationships, where you get blinded and just don't see the rest of the world. In investing, one of the harder things to know is whether you've gone into an unnatural swoon over a particular stock. Suppose someone comes to me and says, "Look I've been using computers and software for a long time so I know something about them. I read all the computer magazines. I know it's a risk, but I want 50 percent of my holdings to be in Microsoft. I think it's destined to be the absolute Godzilla of all stocks. It's going to take over the world. I can see where its technology is headed. I've read Bill Gates' book. Microsoft hasn't fully tapped into the domestic market yet, let alone the international. I want this stock big-time."

If we were having an honest, client-to-broker discussion, I'd say, "Those are all good reasons, but they're not good enough to be so heavily invested in a single stock. If you want to go ahead with this, that's your decision. But I'd rather you reassess. When you get infatuated with a woman, you see only her gorgeous features and none of her flaws. It's only after you divorce your wife and marry this other woman that you begin to see her flaws emerge: Your sentiments had clearly blinded you, and kept you from having a more level-headed, balanced picture of your new friend.

If the client badly enough wants 50 percent of his holdings to be in Microsoft, and is sophisticated enough to appreciate the risk he's running, sure, I'll let him do it. Microsoft might be the new big thing. Its stock might quintuple. But, savvy investor or not, I would point out to the client that prudent investing involves not letting any one stock dominate your portfolio — because unexpected things can happen even with the best of companies. Six or seven years ago, the insurance giant USF&G tumbled from 38 to 5. Maryland National Bank dropped from 40 to 2. In the case of Microsoft, Bill Gates might decide to quit, and the company, without him, could lose its way. There's no way to anticipate any of that.

There *are* ways you can anticipate developments within the competitive marketplace, though. For example, you might see the Borland Company suddenly coming along, dominating a couple of particular software areas where Microsoft had been a leader, and you might conclude, "All right, my love affair with Microsoft has ended. I'll take it down from 50 percent to 10 percent of my holdings. I now realize things are not quite a good as expected."

In addition, it's not totally unreasonable to expect Bill Gates to announce that, in four years, he's leaving the company he founded. "At the age of 45, I'm going to devote my life to philanthropy." When Peter Lynch announced he was leaving, Fidelity Magellan ran into hard times. When you are infatuated with a stock, you are unable to believe that its stock could ever fall. But if it does, and you have 50 percent of your holdings in it, you could be destroyed.

When I think back to my Xerox, Texas Instruments and Polaroid days, I remember feeling euphoric when making the purchases of these industry leaders. I had become infatuated with the one-decision, growth-stock theory of investing. I thought I would remain in those stocks for the long haul. I turned out to be wrong. Some of them dove so sharply that they've never come back. Polaroid, for example, was going great guns. Nobody had any technology to compete with it.

One of the lessons I learned then, and relearn every day, is that there's no such thing as a perfect stock. It might be good today, but you never know who's coming out tomorrow with the new software blockbuster and will leapfrog your investment. Everything is ephemeral. You can hope that your companies are going to remain good for a very long time, but none of them can be so good for so long that it pays to be so heavily invested in them and them alone.

DON'T OVERLOOK DOW FIVE AND TEN THEORIES

In spite of all these cautions, there are a few theories based on the Dow Jones Industrial Average that I am actually beginning to think are almost foolproof. The theories are based on mathematical formulas and have been extremely profitable because of absolute adherence to their rules.

The Dow Jones Industrial Average, about which we hear daily, is made up of thirty stocks picked by a blue-ribbon committee. The *Wall Street Journal* prints the 30 stocks that produce the much-mentioned Dow Jones Average every day on page C3. The list of stocks generally stays pretty constant, although it has changed from time to time, including recently. In the old days, the 30 Dow Jones stocks were what we called "smokestacks." They were the industrial stocks — mostly companies like U.S. Steel (which is still included), American Smelting, Texas Gulf Sulphur, and General Railway Signal.

More recently, the Dow Jones 30 has been modernized. Today's Dow Jones Average is composed of a new breed of stock, like American Express, Coca-Cola, Disney, and McDonald's. The Dow Jones doesn't have any "high technology" stocks as such, but it does include companies like General Electric, AT&T and IBM, which are up to their ears in technology. A few "smokestack stocks" remain, like Caterpillar. I consider each of these 30 listed companies to be "blue chip" stocks. They meet certain profit qualifications just to be listed.

The best "system" of investing that I have heard about and used so far is the Dow Five, which uses the Dow Jones Average to achieve truly remarkable earnings. My partner, Mark Dyer, discovered the Dow Five several years ago in a book called *Beating the Dow* by Michael O'Higgins. Mark told me that we ought to do something with the idea. We've done a lot with it, and now that we have, other firms are doing so as well. I don't blame them. It's a great plan.

The Dow Five is not the philosophy I have consistently subscribed to in my 35 years as a broker, but it has added a lot to my present strategies. For two main reasons, the Dow Five strategy really appeals to me as a broker and should to you as an investor: the quality of the companies in which you invest, and the spectacular monetary results you can achieve. Because the companies are so strong, it's an investing style that carries reduced risk.

Dow Five stocks are all of very high quality. They should be. They are plucked from the 30 Dow stocks that are among the finest companies in the country. They are as far away as you can get from the unheard of, untested company you decide to invest in because of some tip picked up at a backyard barbecue. Over the last 24 years, a $10,000 investment in the Dow Five strategy has grown to over $1 million. That is a 20.9 percent annual rate of return, including both growth and dividend income. Because of the stocks' high quality and especially the incredible results achieved, I must confess: Even the first time I heard about the Dow Five, I wasn't the least bit skeptical. This I must add: If the results have been this good for 24 years, you have to think about trying it. If the results for the next 24 years are as good as the last 24, or even half as good, you have to think about using the theory for a goodly portion of your stock portfolio.

To get the Dow Five, take the ten highest yielding stocks on the Dow Jones Industrial Average; this is the Dow Ten. Anyone can find them in half an hour by reading the *Wall Street Journal*. Look for the ten Dow stocks with the highest dividend yield. The Dow Ten stocks are not usually listed in a group. You must find them yourself or ask a broker to find them for you.

From the ten highest yielding stocks, extract the five lowest priced ones, on the valid assumption that the lowest priced stocks have a tendency to recover quickly and thus rise more percentage-wise than higher priced but lower quality stocks. (The Dow Five list can change every day, but it usually doesn't.) Then, in equal dollar amounts, buy the five stocks that have the lowest prices and the highest yields.

Don't do anything for a whole year. Then, at the end of the year, if nothing has changed, and these five Dow stocks are still the lowest priced and highest yielding of the ten highest yielding stocks, stand completely pat. If, on the other hand, some of these stocks have moved up in price and out of the Dow Five, as they most likely have, kick them out, no matter how much you love them. Sell them and put in the new arrivals.

You probably won't want to add these new arrivals. They are unfamiliar to you, and haven't been as good to you as the stocks you are kicking out. Some of the stocks that have been in the Dow Five over the last three or four years and then moved up and out are Philip Morris, Merck, and Union Carbide. The beauty of the theory, which is stated right there in O'Higgins' book, is that the customer doesn't have to pick the five stocks for himself. It's an automatic system, an automatic plan. Emotions don't get in the way.

As I've said, the results of this system have been spectacular. From 1973 to 1995, a $10,000 investment in the Dow Five would have appreciated to beyond $1 million. If that same $10,000 had gone into the 30 Dow Jones Industrials, it would have grown to just $208,000. So you are doing five times as well with the Dow Five. Now, I can't guarantee that the increase has been or will be the same each year. We check every three or four years, and the results have been very strong, more than 20.9 percent per year on average.

Dow Five and Ten strategies are especially suitable for retirement accounts because the investments produce large capital gains that go untaxed in 401(k)s and 403(b)s.

To get the sought-after results of the Dow Five theory, you cannot tinker with the system. You have to follow it to the letter. One client called me recently. She had invested in the Dow Five, asking me to call her to let her know of the yearly changes I would make before I made them. On television that morning, she had heard that one of the new Dow Five stocks, General Motors, was having some sort of a problem (a prospective strike, I recall). I told her that, with the Dow Five, we typically don't call our clients to inform them of changes we make to a portfolio; we do whatever the Dow tells us to do. The Dow Five is carved in stone. We bought her General Motors and she just had to deal with it.

The only problem with the Dow Five is that you need a certain minimal amount of money to invest to make the strategy financially worthwhile. We suggest that you don't buy the Dow Five with anything less than $20,000 (total) because the commissions otherwise may be too high. On the other hand, if you don't mind paying high commissions, you can plug in to the theory with any amount of money. Certainly commissions are peanuts compared to the gains produced by this system. There is also a cheaper and potentially easier way of acquiring the Dow Five. You can buy shares in the Target Five Equity Trust with as little as a few thousand dollars. This trust duplicates the Dow Five, and the commission paid on buying in is 2.9 percent.

If you do have the suggested minimum of $20,000, you can invest directly in the Dow Five theory by buying the five individual stocks at the outset. You would pay the average New York Stock Exchange commission of 2.5 percent. That means that $500 of your initial $20,000 would go to the broker. At the end of the year, when you readjust your portfolio, you will again pay the broker a commission for selling and buying the appropriate stocks.

If this system works so well, you might wonder why the whole world has not bought into it. The reason is simple: Most professional money managers have their own individualized systems. Some can get you returns that are just as high as, or higher than, the Dow Five. Especially in the last few years, that has been relatively easy to do. Besides, if a money manager started using the Dow Five system, he wouldn't have much left to do!

Recently, there has also been some concern that the Dow Five might no longer work if it became too popular and too widely followed. I disagree. This is a bit different than a stock becoming "overdone" by bidding its price above earnings. The Dow Five theory requires you to discipline yourself to buy stocks that are currently less popular than their peers. And without doubt, that is the best time to buy stocks, even though (and mostly because) everyone else has stopped buying. When stocks are out of style is the right time to buy them.

To some people, an approach like the Dow Five is both boring and predictable. To me, it is both conservative and lucrative. The Dow Five system gives you a sense of assurance that enables you to buy high quality companies you might never buy on your own. You need only look at the companies' high dividends to know they are of high quality. Companies don't issue dividends if they aren't making money. The Dow Five companies are successful; their stock prices just happen to be deflated for one reason or another compared to their 25 colleagues on the DJIA.

By deciding to subscribe to the Dow Five theory, you will have to let go of a few of the pieces of advice I have been dispensing throughout this book, especially the idea that you fully understand a company before investing in it. The Dow Five may cause you to put 25 percent of your investment dollars into companies you don't necessarily know, and to make several leaps of faith. You won't know the committee members who chose the Dow Jones 30. You may not know why a company's stock price has declined. You don't know for sure that it will come back. F.W. Woolworth, which was a Dow Five stock a year or so ago, has now stopped paying all dividends, and no longer is included in the Dow Jones 30. It was a real dog and may not survive. But at one time, it was part of the Dow Five. That said, the Dow Five is a well-grounded, reasonable mathematical theory that works.

Another theory that also gives you extraordinarily good results in the stock market is the Dow Ten. This means you invest in the *ten* highest yielding, lowest priced stocks of the Dow Jones Industrial Average. If you had followed the Dow Ten strategy over the past ten years, you would have beaten the performance of 99 percent of all actively managed mutual funds. In at least one respect, the Dow Ten is better than the Dow Five — you spread your money out twice as far and get double the diversification. But in other ways, the Dow Ten is less promising than the Dow Five, where you get an extra boost from buying stocks with especially low prices.

One problem with both the Dow Five and the Dow Ten theories is that they don't provide you very much income. Usually the amount of annual income from the Dow Five or the Dow Ten lists is rather negligible, so if someone has to live on income, I don't recommend either of the theories, unless you take a slightly unpopular approach. Because the value of the Dow stocks multiplies so quickly, you can take some money out of the principal every year to live on. (Many people remain reluctant to do that.)

Investing in the Dow Jones 30 and the related Dow Five and Dow Ten theories is a good way to go. The stocks are safe but sound, and the system is easy to keep track of. Plus, by sticking to a system, you keep yourself from panicking when little thing goes wrong: You simply force yourself to wait and see what happens. All in all, it's a great way to invest that I enthusiastically recommend. I daresay that, if my father were around today, he'd do the same.

PROS AND CONS OF INVESTING LOCALLY

I've written and talked a good deal about the advantages of investing in local companies. You can know something more about them, you can visit them easily, and you can even talk to the management personally. Local company investing has worked out well for me and my clients. Whether a company is local certainly has been a factor in our decisions to invest or not to invest.

There've been some very good success stories among local companies here in Baltimore. For example, people made fortunes on Noxell, which was bought out by Procter & Gamble. Local investors have done well, too, with McCormick, the Rouse Company, the local bank stocks — First National, Mercantile, Union Trust, which is now Signet (and soon to be bought by First Union, an even larger bank), Equitable Trust (which was acquired by Maryland National, was in turn bought out by NationsBank) — Black & Decker, Fair Lanes, and Maryland Cup, just to name a few.

I don't often visit these companies myself, but our research people (Ferris Baker Watts) do. These researchers concentrate on local stocks because the companies are convenient and easy to visit. They can do it in a day without staying overnight. And local companies are very happy to entertain researchers and analysts, to wine and dine them. As I said earlier, putting out a favorable report on a stock has a tendency to push the price of that stock up, which enriches the top company people, who, because of inexpensive stock options, often own a large number of shares.

Because companies are local, local investors very much want them to do well. They may know members of management. They may know company employees. Make sure that the local stock you are being asked to buy, or are interested in buying, measures up. Request your broker's research reports. Ask yourself and your broker: "If this weren't a local company, would we be so interested?"

One reason brokerage firms like to sell local stocks is that they have the shares in their own inventory. Some local stocks are not traded on the recognized exchanges, but are sold directly by the brokerage firms. They're called over-the-counter stocks. And there's a somewhat bigger profit in stocks that the brokers have in their inventory than there is in AT&T, which trades on a major market.

That information — that we brokers make a market in a particular local stock — must, under new regulations, be disclosed on the person's buy ticket, with something like, "We make a market on this issue."

In the end, knowing that the brokerage firm will make a few extra bucks on local companies should not dissuade you from buying their stock — not if you and your broker think you can make money on the purchase.

CHAPTER SUMMARY:
STOCK-PICKING

1. Use the "anecdotal evidence" philosophy sparingly. It can help turn you on to good products, but sometimes it can make you put far too much into one stock or avoid a stock that is a big money-maker. Let your broker evaluate your intuition with solid information.

2. If you have the resources and the temperament for the "hold-every-thing" philosophy, it can help you avoid a lot of heartache.

3. You're better off diversifying across various sectors than concentrating in one.

4. Beware of Initial Public Offerings. It is usually good to wait a few months to see where the prices are going before buying.

5. Utilize the Dow Five and Ten theories if you are looking for a simple, lucrative investing system.

6. Use care when you invest locally. Make sure to get all the needed information on a company, and maybe even visit it yourself. Make sure you're not "going local" simply because the company is local.

CHAPTER ELEVEN

To Be A Savvy Investor

When shopping for investments,
pay more for something that fits.

There are a number of techniques and strategies that can help you become a more educated, comfortable investor. Let's run through these concepts, some of them confusing to the novice, so you can understand them, discuss them with your broker, and possibly use them.

To be a good investor, you have to know and follow the basics. A good company will grow and should make money for you. If you know what makes a good company, you can make solid judgments about which stock to buy.

SPREAD YOUR RISK

Recently, I was visited by a middle-aged man whose father had recently died. The client never made much money, but the father had left him quite a nest egg — almost half a million dollars worth of stock in Baltimore Gas and Electric (BG&E) and $15,000 worth of a few other stocks. A badly misshapen nest egg. My partners and I hauled out all the traditional arguments about why he should sell half his BG&E. We said the utility's nuclear plant could blow up (it probably won't). We said over-regulation could become a problem. We said the stock could drop substantially. It wouldn't be the first time a stock had lost 40 percent of its value. The son was very reasonable, but he had such loyalty to his father that he couldn't let the stock go. His father had put almost all his money into BG&E, made a tidy profit, and lived off the dividends. And because the son had grown up hearing all about BG&E's fine qualities at the dinner table, he was not ready to trim down his company holdings.

But having that much money in one stock is excessive and dangerous. First, by so concentrating his holdings, the father had essentially ruled out investing in other stocks that might have done even better during the same period, including utility stocks which paid better dividends, like Potomac Electric Power, or the Duff Phelps utility fund. If this man's father had put his original investment money into 19 stocks other than BG&E, the son might have $5 million now, rather than $500,000. Second, by continuing to hold onto so much of one stock, and not diversifying, the son makes himself financially vulnerable. We never know what will happen, but if, in the unlikely event, BG&E's Calvert Cliffs nuclear power plant experiences a Three Mile Island-like disaster, the stock value could plunge, and much of the father's money, which is now the son's, could be lost.

To see such gross under-diversification is not unusual for me. Lots of people put all or most of their money into just one stock. Assuming a portfolio of $200,000-$300,000, my rule of thumb is to have no more than five to ten percent in any single stock, while owning approximately 20 different stocks altogether. Some people just choose five stocks and stick to them exclusively. I think that's way too small a number of companies to invest all your money in. It can vary a little bit, but not significantly. At the very least, you never want to have more than 25 or 30 percent of your investment nest egg in any one stock. Lots of people do and it's very risky.

There are a few reasons why people put all their money in two or three or five different stocks. Most are based on emotion. Look at the stocks taking up the most room in your portfolio. The fact is, you are emotionally wedded to stocks that have appreciated in value over the years. That's why you have so much money invested in them. We all have a natural tendency to fall in love with stocks that have done well for us, and we hate to sell them. However, our emotions often lead us astray. The fact that the stock has become a very large percent of the portfolio probably means it's gotten too large. And if something bad happens to it, you will lose both financially and emotionally.

That's another reason I recommend diversification. You never want all your money in one place. In baseball, if you are in the field, you go with what you know will help you win. You'd rather take your time and be sure to get one out on a ground ball than mess up at both ends of an attempted double play, allowing all men to reach safely. That's the way it often is with the stock market. If you try for too much, you can often lose money. By contrast, if you have only five to ten percent of your holdings in a company, and it drops, you won't feel overjoyed, but at least you won't be devastated. And if the stock completely fails, you can be a little more objective about it, rather than becoming emotionally glued to it.

USF&G, a major insurance company headquartered in Baltimore, saw its stock crash quite a few years ago. Because USF&G employs so many people in Baltimore, the city in which I work, many Baltimore-area investors had very large holdings of this stock. Hundreds of people had built up their positions by working for the company, and others had huge blocks of the stock passed down the generations of their families through inheritance. Some new clients came to me with over 50 or 60 percent of their holdings in this one stock. When USF&G slipped, probably the result of factors both external and organizational, it lost about 80 percent of its value. If that happens to five percent of your portfolio, you aren't going to blow your brains out. But if it happens to 60 percent of what you're worth, you lose your appetite and a ton of money. As a result of USF&G's crash, some families in Baltimore had to change their standards of living and really downsize. We had warned our clients to lower their holdings in that stock, not because we knew what was going to happen, but because "Murphy's Law" operates in the market, and unexpected things can knock your socks off. But these clients held on because of emotional attachment, they lost quite a lot of money and are still feeling the effects.

When some people lose money this way in the market, they often want to sell the stock that did so poorly for them. Others want to keep the stock, hoping it will come back in value. When people ask for my advice, I stick to the 5 to 10 percent rule — generally no more than 5 to 10 percent of the portfolio in any one stock. If the stock has sunk to 5 to 10 percent of the portfolio, where it belongs, keep it if you want to. If it is still greater than 5 to 10 percent, level it off so that it represents only that percentage of the portfolio, because the stock price could go even lower. If you want to get rid of it entirely, do that too, so long as you keep only 5 to 10 percent of the portfolio in each stock that you own.

There's one big reason people often give me for not wanting to sell the big blocks of stock needed to adhere to my 5-10 percent rule. They say they "don't want to pay capital gains taxes," which, until recently, were roughly 28 percent of their gains. I think that's a bit silly, and usually respond with one of my favorite Wall Street sayings, "Don't worry about gains and taxes. Worry about losses. What's wrong with paying a capital gains tax?" And I'll add, "I'd rather do that than lose all my money." My clients told me for years that Washington would reduce the capital gains tax. Finally, in the summer of 1997, Congress and the President pulled off the feat.

I would rather worry about what I might lose by holding onto a stock than worry about the little I must lose by letting go. Besides, capital gains payments are not what's really keeping these clients from selling the big block of stock. It's emotional attachment. If the capital gains tax were lowered, as they were in 1997, they would come up with some other excuse for not cutting back.

Interestingly, the tax excuse may have made sense to the father who had all the BG&E stock, but not so to his son. It was for the best that his father, while alive, did not liquidate all his BG&E holdings because first, he would have paid a huge capital gains tax on his increase in wealth. But when you die, your tax cost gets updated to what's called the "date of death" evaluation. If the man had died in 1995, when BG&E was at 25, and at time of estate taxation was 27, his only tax would have been on the two dollar a share gain. If selling a large part of his BG&E stock was necessary so that his portfolio was more balanced, paying the tax on that $2 gain would have been a small price to pay for this man's financial security and peace of mind. His tax payment of about $8000, which is 28 percent of 14,000 shares times a $2 increase in stock, is peanuts compared to what his $350,000 investment could make elsewhere.

DON'T OVER-DIVERSIFY

Although you don't want most of your money in any one place, you also don't want to have your money divided up among too many stocks. Again, my rule of thumb is, "Don't have more than 20 or 30 stocks at a time." If you do, housekeeping becomes really complicated, both for you and the broker. Unless you have a multi-million dollar account, most brokers will be unhappy handling a portfolio of 50 or 60 stocks. Even if one out of your 50 stocks goes sky-high, your gain in dollars will often be meaningless

For example, I recently advised a couple with an account of $250,000 and 35-40 individual stocks. The shame of it was they had hardly any money invested in some of the stocks; they had 25 shares here, 50 shares there. The market value of many of their investments was around $3,000. Even if one of those stocks had tripled, it would have made no big difference in their portfolio. So I had to trim down their number of stocks. I wanted them to establish meaningful positions with their money. With a total of $250,000 and a portfolio of 20 stocks, they should have invested about $12,500 in each stock. Then, if the stock tripled, they would make a meaningful gain.

Some people, especially inexperienced investors, get pleasure out of owning lots of companies. For them, it's a bit of a hobby, like collecting stamps or coins. And it's not that they have bad judgment. They will choose stocks for good reasons, especially if they like a new product. There's nothing terribly wrong with it, but it doesn't allow them to make meaningful profits on any of their holdings. One wise investor once said, "Have a set number of stocks like 20, and if you see something else out there that you must have, don't buy it unless you're prepared to sell something to make room for it." I agree with that advice.

As to what's actually in your portfolio, I recommend a mix of stocks. To use Peter Lynch's terms, singles and doubles are stocks that go up between 8-10 percent per year. If you can get a portfolio that goes up 10 percent steadily, you are tripling the inflation rate, which is enough for me. But since you never know exactly what the market is going to do, you want to have a few home run stocks in your portfolio just to be safe — stocks like Microsoft or Bristol-Myers Squibb, which have tripled or quadrupled over a three to four year period. Generally speaking, though, I am not too aggressive when I invest in the stock market. I don't try to put more than a few potential home-runs into the portfolio. I've already moved aggressively by going into stocks in the first place. I prefer and recommend diversification, and sticking to high quality stocks.

As I suggested earlier, I think that about 10-20 percent of your portfolio should be made up of mutual funds. I also recommend that between 5-10 percent of your portfolio be in the international field. Even if you are a broker, it is quite difficult to choose individual stocks of companies in Germany or Japan. It is harder still to talk to the management of a foreign company to find out what it is up to, or to do much independent research on these foreign companies. International mutual funds help you diversify without forcing you to choose specific stocks about which you know little. You the investor should always know something about what you're investing in.

STICK TO FUNDAMENTALS

The investment world has gone through some explosive changes during the 35 years I've been in the business. The rapid rise and huge growth of mutual funds and tax-deferred retirement programs like 401(k)s, 403(b)s, and IRAs have made a huge difference. However, during all this time, I've dropped very few of my "most important" approaches, theories, and philosophies of investing. I've never stopped focusing on company fundamentals. The fundamentals of investing haven't changed that much in 35 years, nor should they in the next 35.

The fundamentals come from focusing on the answers to such questions as: Is this a consistently growing industry? Does this company have a good record on dividends? Has the management been aggressive? Has the company been gaining or losing its share of the market? If you've ever been in business, those are fundamental criteria you can appreciate.

As an investor focusing on the fundamentals, there are ways to distinguish between a company that is poised to turn around and increase in value and a down-and-out, not-going-to-turn-around company. Research professionals can often do this "spade work" for you, answering a number of key questions. For example:

- What are the barriers that keep other competitors from entering the industry?

- Is management the same or are they bringing in new people with new ideas?

- How much does the company spend on research?

(The more a company spends on research, the more new products it will bring out, and the more quickly it can bring those new products onto the market. If a new product is marketed in a field where there's not much competition, the company can charge pretty much what it wants. It therefore can rack up higher profit margins. Over the long haul, a company's stock price will relate fairly closely to the company's profit margins.)

If you're focusing on the fundamentals, you also want to know if the company's new products have the same high profit margins as the earlier ones. Take, for example, a drug or pharmaceutical company like Pfizer, which spends between eight and 10 percent a year, year in and year out, on research. Or take Bethlehem Steel. It survives and prospers because, through its investment in research, it comes up with new processes to produce steel in a less expensive way.

In that instance, the savvy investor wants to know: How major a breakthrough is this new technology? Who are the company's competitors? How long will it take them to catch up? How confidential can Beth Steel keep the process? Do foreign competitors have something comparable? Those are all the things that you look to research to answer, and those are some of the questions a fundamentalist like me typically asks.

Some people are real technicians when it comes to stock — and there are a bunch of them on Wall Street. They use complicated "point and figure" charts and graphs to indicate good times to buy and sell. They watch the market action of the stock, track the volume, both on the "outside" (the public) and volume on the "inside" (company officials). As an investor and an advisor, I've never been much of a technician. I'm a fundamentalist. I believe in earnings, growth, etc. I'm more bottom-line oriented.

Using statistics so extensively in decision-making isn't confined to the stock market. In a playoff game between the Baltimore Orioles and the New York Yankees in 1996, everything centered on Orioles ace pitcher Mike Mussina. I later read in the paper a fascinating statistic about Mussina, which highlights the newly technical side of baseball. They figured out that from pitch zero to 80, the opposing teams over the year were batting .214 against Mussina. When he went from 80 pitches to 100, the opposite teams hit a much higher .250 against him, and when he labored on from 100 to 120 pitches, the other teams were smacking him around at a very healthy .350 clip.

Some managers may keep track of Mussina's pitch count and remove him when he hits 100 pitches in a day. Other managers may take numerous other factors into account before making a call to the bullpen — like how Mussina says he feels, his overall physical condition, the day's weather conditions, the state of the bullpen as a whole. I don't know which kind of baseball manager I'd be (more likely the latter than the former), but I do know that, when it comes to stocks, I'm not really interested in their highly technical statistical side. I'm much more interested in company fundamentals.

LET DIVIDEND INCREASES BE ONE GUIDE

Over the years, I've tried to educate investors on what they should incorporate into their knowledge base and how to apply it. One important way to determine a company's quality is by looking at its dividends. We have no control over whether a stock goes up or down. Standing here today, we can't know what's going to happen to the stock price over the next ten years. And even if a stock doubles or triples during that period, it really doesn't do you the investor much good because, until you sell the stock, it's just a gratifying paper gain. And we rarely recommend selling stocks of good companies.

But we can find stocks that raise their dividends every year. A company's growth in income — its growth of dividends — is fairly predictable. Let's take the case of an individual who buys the stock of Procter & Gamble. P&G's 1987 dividend was $.68 a share; 1989 — $.75; 1991 — $.98; 1993 — $1.10;1995 — $1.40; and 1997 — $1.80. Those steady increases represent nearly a 164 percent increase in dividends over a ten-year period starting in 1987.

We have no way of knowing whether our favorite stocks are going to rise within the next five or ten years because a great deal of the movement of stocks is affected by human emotion, which is unpredictable. What we do know is that if we select stocks of companies with steady or huge profit increases, those companies will usually be able to pay their shareholders an increasing share of their profits, year in and year out. They do so despite the prevailing psychology of the stock market — the forces which push stocks up and down. Generally speaking, about half the movement of stocks is emotionally affected. The other half is affected by company earnings.

In other words, the price of a stock is governed by so many different factors that it is almost completely unpredictable. The earnings of the company, the general level of interest rates, the psychology of the stock market in general, and world events — all of those are completely unpredictable and uncontrollable. And all of them can send stock prices headed in either direction. Yet, such companies as BG&E, Bell Atlantic, Exxon, and Procter & Gamble have been extremely profitable companies.

The growth of your income, the checks that these companies send you in the form of dividends, are fairly predictable. That's because they are based not on psychology, not on outside events, and not on the level of interest rates, but on the profitability of the company and its ability to pay you the stockholder an increased share of profits every year. Companies like to raise their dividends partly because doing so means more profit for company officials who own, or have options to buy, a great many company shares. They also do it to entice more investors to buy their shares. However, the important thing is that you the investor profit from these dividends.

Some of these companies paid very low dividends to start with, but when you can see an increase of 215 percent in your income, you're getting something substantial. In Bristol-Myers Squibb's case, the 1985 dividend was 47 cents per share. Ten years later, adjusted for splits, it was up to $1.52 a share, which is a healthy increase and a decent amount of money. The stock price has also tripled and quadrupled over that period. Bristol-Myers Squibb is currently not a big income payer because they plow a lot of their earnings back into research. (In addition to being a big over-the-counter drug company, it produces and sells such consumer products as Clairol and Excedrin.)

In 1997, Bristol-Myers Squibb was paying a very, very small rate of return — about two percent. The stock was selling for roughly $80 a share, which means it was paying $1.52 a share as a dividend. Customers who want immediate income may say, "I'm not taking any three percent deals. I see ads in the paper for CDs at six percent."

But those folks are only looking at today's stock-generated income — and their own personal living expenses. Like many people, they live from paycheck to paycheck. When they come to us with a block of money and we show them a two percent stock, they don't see the full picture. They tend to think of the dividend as the *only* valuable aspect of the stock and, when they compare two percent to all those other potential investments, Bristol-Myers Squibb, in their minds, is a loser that doesn't make any sense to invest in. But the fact that its dividends keep going up indicates that the company is increasingly profitable, which means that one component of this price/earnings ratio puzzle, the price, will go up as the other component — the earnings — goes up. That usually means that the stock value down the road will also increase.

Bristol-Myers Squibb is only paying two percent dividends today. Investors don't really care what it will be paying in ten years — that's too far away to bother with or to foresee. They prefer to hear their brokers say, supported by several reasons, that "Bristol-Myers Squibb is good because we think the stock will double." The prediction that the stock will double is something they immediately relate to. I don't use that chatter very much, nor do my partners. I think dividends are still a great way to judge a stock.

Some brokers may say of a certain stock, "It's selling at $50 a share now, but it looks to me like a $75 stock within a year. That's a 33 percent increase in a year." There's actually nothing wrong with saying, "In my opinion, because of certain factors that I know about Bristol-Myers Squibb — that they're quadrupling their television advertising, that the FDA has just given its approval to one of their anti-headache drugs — I think the stock is going to go from a hundred to $200." If I were writing orders, I could write ten times as many with that sales pitch than the one about the company's growing dividends. The average guy wants to hear how he can make big bucks quickly on the stock market

But dividend increases are a definite assurance that the company is doing well and that the stock should eventually follow, no matter what

MAKING IT CLEAR

I grew up on Slade Avenue and I've lived in Baltimore all my life. I had a fairly cloistered background. Despite that, I've been told that I explain certain difficult financial concepts in a way that breaks through to people of various economic backgrounds who never understood them before.

I do have a sense of compassion for the down-trodden. Every year I spend some time and money at Our Daily Bread soup kitchen, which is run by Catholic Charities. Once or twice a year I will spend two hours there between eleven and one, on a Saturday or Sunday, giving investment advice to people who either bring in a check for $25 or a bag of food. I publicize this on radio or TV and we usually have a mob scene — more people than my partners and I can handle. And I have always had a semi-soft spot in my heart for people without any money. I'm not a big giver to charity, but I rarely turn down a solicitation. If I get something in the mail for Action for the Homeless, and it's bitter cold out, I send them a hundred bucks.

Sometimes someone will call me on TV and say, "I just inherited $100,000. What should I do with it?" First, I say, if they have a mortgage or any other debts, pay them off, because by doing so they don't have to pay interest. The second thing I say is, share some of that money with charity. Now, I know nobody wants to hear that, but it's what I believe. I don't say that to prospective clients when they come to see me. They don't need me to be their rabbi or advocate for the homeless. But that is what I believe, and it's a belief I hope I have acted on in my own life. ♣

your broker mentions or downplays. Let's say, for the sake of discussion, that you the client don't think the stock price of Bristol-Myers Squibb will necessarily appreciate by 33 percent in the next year, but you still think it's a good investment. In that case, your judgment would be validated by its dividend history. Any stock whose payout is up 22 percent in ten years is an appetizing company to own.

WHAT IS THE PRICE/EARNINGS RATIO?

Let's take Bristol-Myers Squibb as an example to get a handle on the elusive concept of the price/earnings ratio. It's one of the concepts investors have the most trouble comprehending. The financial pages in a lot of newspapers and publications now print a company's P/E ratio, but you have to know what it means to be able to use it.

A ratio is a relationship. And the price/earnings ratio is nothing more than the relationship between a company's earnings per share and the price of its stock. So, for example, when the price of the stock continues to move up (let's say from $20 to $40 a share) and company earnings stay flat (at, say, $1 in earnings per share), the price/earnings ratio increases (from 20 times earnings to 40 times earnings) — and therefore becomes a potential danger signal indicating that the stock may be overpriced.

Always compare a company's P/E ratio to industry P/Es and to its own historical P/E, not to the market's P/E ratio. A company's historical P/E can be obtained from *Value Line* or your broker.

Bristol-Myers Squibb stock, as of August 1997, was selling at 27 times earnings, which is somewhat high compared to the average P/E ratio (in July 1997) of roughly 22 times earnings. However, sophisticated investors are willing to pay a premium for Bristol-Myers Squibb stock because of its rapidly accelerating growth rate. When earnings are moving up sharply, investors are more willing to accept a higher P/E ratio. A faster grower is worth it.

For another example, let's suppose a little book publishing company were a publicly traded firm. It's putting books out that are selling extremely well. Its earnings are increasing, as are its gross proceeds. By all measures, it's doing well, but nobody's buying its stock. For whatever reason, investors don't think much of it, and the stock price has stayed pretty much still (and low). For sake of discussion, let's say its stock price is $10 a share, but its earnings per share has risen to $2. Its P/E ratio is thus five-to-one. Its stock is selling at five times earnings.

I as the broker would be saying to my clients, "This publishing company is making profits and they're sending a good share of those profits back to you, the shareholder, every year in the form of the dividend." One of these years, somebody or a whole bunch of somebodies will wake up and say, "You know, that publishing outfit has been making money every year. They keep putting out best sellers." When that happens, early investors can realize quite a windfall. They've made what they consider to be a good investment, and eventually more people will agree.

And they will, because, increasingly, investors all over the country are asking their computers to supply them the names of companies whose earnings are increasing rapidly and whose stock prices are not. In those instances, they suppose that the stock will eventually sell at a higher price — say seven to ten times earnings — and someone will grab it. If the stock price is very low compared to what it ought to be, and eventually the crowds realize this, they'll start buying the stock, and that will move the stock price up.

If you bought a young stock at 10 and it catches on with the investing public, going to 50, you will have made a lot of money on paper — a windfall really. I personally don't use a computer to scour for companies whose earnings are increasing rapidly and whose stock has been overlooked, but some investors do bottom-fish in this fashion (with or without the computer). People will buy a huge block of stock because eventually its worth will be recognized by the investment community, and they are willing to wait until then. The price of the stock is stagnant, while the company's earnings are moving up, so, in their minds, eventually the P/E ratio will grow and their early investments will pay off.

A stock like this hypothetical book publisher could be overlooked for a lot of reasons, one of which is that the company has not been very good at marketing its stock. Maybe there was an initial public offering (IPO), but the company's executives didn't visit very many of the right analysts, to do the usual "road show" touting their stock. Years later, they might get savvy, calling on the publishing analysts at 25 brokerage firms on the East Coast and saying, "We'll be in Philadelphia next week. We'd like to take you and your group to lunch, and tell you why you shouldn't overlook us any more." Follow-up road shows like that help to increase the price of the stock. It's a sales tool that eventually helps the stock and its investors.

WHAT DOES "EARNINGS PER SHARE" MEAN?

The concept of earnings per share is a little different from the P/E ratio, but it's yet another useful way to compare one stock with another. To get earnings per share, you take the total earnings of the company, the profit, and you divide that by the number of shares outstanding. Suppose a company had made $100 million in profit, and has ten million shares of stock. You divide 10 million shares into $100 million. That then becomes $10 per share. Bristol-Myers Squibb's earnings-per-share went up every year starting in 1985 — from $1.40 that year to $2.00 in 1989, to $2.40 in 1991, to $2.88 in 1993, to $2.96 in 1995, and then to $3.04 in 1997.

Someone can pick apart that bit of information by saying, "Gee, the earnings per share were 47 cents back in 1985 and it's increased 220 percent since then. It was pitifully low in 1985. Of course, it's going to go up. What does that increase show?" Stated another way, "You gave me two peanuts ten years ago, and now you're giving me ten peanuts. They're still peanuts." In a sense, that's true. But if I can build a portfolio of stocks whose income goes up 10 or 12 percent a year, that triples the inflation rate, I've done well for my client. Of course, I try to pick stocks that I think will go up in price, but you never know. The whole market might go down in the next ten years.

A lot of people mentally turn off at this point because they think this is too complicated and cumbersome. After they obtain the required data about stocks, which itself isn't all that readily available, they think they need to employ fairly decent math skills. And even if they come up with this number representing earnings per share, many still don't know what to do with the information obtained. That's the problem. You've gone through this whole exercise, now what? That's what a broker is for.

ONE SIZE DOESN'T FIT ALL

Another much-misunderstood concept revolves around the price of a stock. Sometimes I'll suggest a stock to people, like Avon. "How much is it?" they'll ask. "Seventy dollars a share." "Oh, that's much too expensive," they'll say. Most investors, I'm convinced, would rather have 100 shares of a twenty dollar stock — an investment of $ 2,000 — than 20 shares of a hundred dollar stock, which is $2,000, too. Most people think that a stock at a hundred dollars a share is "more expensive" than a stock at $20 a share, whereas in reality it might be cheaper. A stock selling at $20 might have poor earnings; it might be earning only 20 cents a share, so it's selling for 100 times earnings, which is frightfully expensive. Avon, at $70 a share, might be earning roughly $2.60 a share — thus selling at only 27 times earnings. That is not nearly as expensive.

The number of shares you have doesn't matter in many cases. Berkshire Hathaway, as an extreme example, sells for nearly $50,000 per share. And it's been one of the great success stories of the 20th century under the guidance of the gifted investor Warren Buffett. All you needed was 10 or 20 shares of his stock and you became a millionaire. But most people would rather tell others, "I've got a hundred shares of this or I've got a thousand shares of that."

The thinking of the unsophisticated or novice investor would seem to be: "Well, if I have a hundred shares and it goes up ten points, or ten dollars, then I've made a thousand dollars." But an inexpensive stock rarely goes up ten points. If it does, it's risen a full 100 percent. A higher priced stock is actually more likely to go up that dollar amount. For it, a ten dollar increase is far smaller a percentage increase. You don't find $10 jumps happening often with cheap stocks, but you see it all the time with more expensive stocks.

Here's another reason to shy away from the low-priced stocks. An investor says to me, "I just bought a thousand shares of Rocky Mountain Gold at a dollar a share." He thinks that's cheap, but gold's expensive to produce, and the company might not have any earnings. As it happens, the lower the stock price, the greater the likelihood that the company isn't going to have any earnings. Many people don't understand that fundamental fact.

Many investors continue to think that, if they own one thousand shares in a cheaper company, they're richer and more important investors. These are the folks who say, "If I only have 20 shares of Avon, I don't exactly feel like a big player." In fact, in that instance, they're much bigger players because they have the same number of dollars invested in a very high quality stock which has demonstrated its success, whereas their thousand shares of a much less expensive stock may have nothing behind it except its cheapness.

Somebody might say to me, "Gee, this stock is selling at only ten dollars a share. Isn't that cheap?" To make my response clearer, I often use this real-life analogy: "If you went to a store and saw a men's sport jacket selling for half price, which was real cheap, but it was not your size and not your color and didn't fit you, it wouldn't be cheap. In fact, you wouldn't think of buying it. It wouldn't be worth anything to you. You're better off paying a little more and buying something that fits. If it doesn't fit your requirements, it's not cheap."

Part of the challenge of being investors is to be able to relate financial matters to things that we routinely do and understand in everyday life. This price/earnings ratio business doesn't correspond to anything we do in regular life. Fortunately, you can be a good investor without understanding the P/E ratio because the people you go to for professional advice understand it and use it as one of their guidelines in investing. Even if you do understand and use the price/earnings ratio, you shouldn't look at it in isolation. But when you're comparing one possible investment to another, it's a way for you to determine which one to prefer.

DON'T BELIEVE EVERYTHING YOU READ

Various newsletters that aim their message at savvy and sophisticated investors regularly suggest that the market looks like "it's going to take a tumble." They'll say, "Get out of your equities, put your money into cash (meaning money markets), and wait for us to tell you when it's safe to go back into the equities market again." That's nonsense. I read up to 40 newsletters and magazines a month. That piece of advice is offered by people who badly want to get customers. They preach market timing, which has never worked out consistently. The problem is, if I predict Armageddon on the stock market, once in a while I'll be right. As the old saying goes, "Even a blind hog finds an acorn once in a while."

There's nothing unethical about what they're doing, but in my opinion they're riding the wrong horse. I don't know of anyone who has successfully timed the market consistently. But the ads, especially from newsletter gurus, are appealing. "Big crash coming. Put your money in a money market." These ads generally run during a period when the market is declining and investors are already frightened. The gurus think that, by urging people to get out of the stock market, they can get their money now and invest it properly some other time.

In fact, as I sum it up, an "expert prediction" about the market is something of an oxymoron. Every month, the *Wall Street Journal* runs a feature called the "Dart Board Theory." Regular people throw darts at the stock pages. Then, the results of their predictions are compared with those of a certain group of stock experts. Half the time the random throwers are more accurate, half the time the experts.

Some brokerage companies put out their own reports to draw the investor's attention. "One-decision stocks" were popular at one point. "One decision" meant that you concentrated all of your effort on finding the best growth companies possible. After buying these stocks, you in effect held them forever. You made only the one decision to buy. You never had a reason to sell or make another decision. It turned out to be hogwash. The 1973-74 crash destroyed the validity of that one-decision concept.

When you the investor look at expert predictions, particularly about specific companies, the first thing you must realize is there's something in the brokerage business called the "bullish bias." I have rarely seen a brokerage firm put out a bearish or unfavorable report on a company. There are a couple of reasons for that. Number one, it doesn't generate any business for them. If they put out a bullish report on McCormick, the whole world is their oyster. Everyone can buy the stock. There's huge potential. But if they put out a bad report on McCormick, they're only talking to a tiny percentage of people who own it.

Furthermore, McCormick will hesitate to see them again. They won't even host their brokerage's analysts for awhile, because their negative report has hurt their company's stock.

I've now given you two big reasons to be skeptical about research reports. I'm not saying to pay no attention to them. But I have rarely seen a brokerage firm put out an unfavorable report on a company. As a broker who knows this, I'm comfortable saying, "Yes, our research department did strongly recommend the purchase of this stock. But if it were up to me, I wouldn't buy it." Still, it's far from easy to fight your own company's recommendation.

The research people work hard at my company, just as they do at other brokerage houses. You *can* trust them. Just take them, like every-one else, with a grain of salt. In the old days, generalists would cover var-ious industries for the brokerage houses. You could trust the research departments then a lot less because their analysts could not necessarily assess a company accurately in an industry they didn't know well. Today, the research departments in the brokerage firms, and in the investment advisory firms, are highly specialized. They all have analysts, for exam-ple, who specialize in the drug industry and who read every publication that each pharmaceutical company puts out: press releases, house organs, quarterly reports, medical literature about the new drugs.

Mutual funds today will hire a pharmaceutical expert to follow the drug industry, or an engineer to cover the construction industry. They may get a former Pepsico product manager to cover the soft drink industry because they know the lingo, they know the people to contact, they've been there. That means they're more skeptical of company claims, and so they can be more realistic, less accepting of everything at face value. In a Pfizer annual report, the chairman of the board may say, in glowing terms, that the future looks bright. The new pharmaceutical specialist in the brokerage's research department might say, "Oh, yeah. How about this?"

Once, on radio, someone called in and either asked directly about Giant Food, or wanted to know which companies I liked in the super-market industry as a whole. I generally don't recommend stocks on the air, but if someone asks about a specific company, I might say nice things about it, which I apparently did that day about Giant Food. My boss called me afterward to say, "Hey, we put out a bearish report on Giant Food, and here you are plugging it on radio. What goes?"

The firm's report on Giant Food was not entirely negative. It was a report on the supermarket industry and Giant was in a column that was labeled semi-favorable, which could be translated to, "You can live without this stock."

I said nice things about Giant because I had followed it over the years and considered it a good company. I saw Giant concentrating on private brands, which is where much of the supermarket profit is made. It earns far more profit by selling Giant brand corn flakes than Kellogg's Corn Flakes. When a Giant supermarket sells Kellogg's brand products, it can earn only a tiny profit margin because Kellogg's does all the advertising and adds that cost to the price of the product. Giant doesn't advertise its private brands as much as Kellogg's advertises its, but, as a grocery chain, it has customers in its stores, and can sell its own corn flakes product a half a buck cheaper. In many ways, Giant is piggybacking on Kellogg's advertising. It takes advantage of the demand thus created for corn flakes, and then, when Giant puts its own version next to Kellogg's, some Giant customers say, "If it's basically the same product and much less expensive, why not buy it and save some money?" For a family that doesn't have the money, the store-brand offers nutritious, stomach-filling food. When I spoke favorably of Giant, the stock might have been going through a not terribly favorable period, but, in the long run, I thought of it as a good investment.

My main point is this: With their reports, brokerage firm researchers may not always be offering you long-term analyses and investment advice. In fact, in the long term, Giant Food as a company and stock has done well. My boss and I weren't that far apart in our view of Giant Food but, on the day in question, we, in effect, had a slightly different timetable in mind. So if you get a research report, analyze it yourself, with the appropriate timetable in mind, or have a broker analyze it for you doing the same.

CHAPTER SUMMARY:
TO BE A SAVVY INVESTOR

1. Don't have too many stocks and don't have too few. Each stock you own should be no more than 5-10 percent of your stock portfolio. For appropriate diversification, you should hold approximately 20 stocks.

2. Stick to fundamentals. Human emotions make the stock market unpredictable, but a solid company will generally prevail.

3. Use the company's dividends to figure out whether it is worth buying its stock. A company's regular and rising dividends can reassure you that, even if the stock is down, the company is still doing well.

4. Pay attention to the Price/Earnings Ratio. Use this concept to figure out the comparative cost and value of a stock. A high P/E ratio makes the stock more expensive, but sometimes it is worth paying for high growth.
   A too-high P/E ratio might mean that the stock is overvalued (and therefore not a good buy).

5. Research departments can be useful, but their recommendations should be viewed cautiously. You should evaluate all information you read with a broker you trust.

CHAPTER *TWELVE*

Savings and Earnings
for Your Future

You should be in the stock market
at every point in your life.

First, a bit of a refresher when deciding what percent of your total assets should be in the stock market. Follow my formula based on the number 120. Take the number 120, and subtract your age from it. The resulting figure is roughly the percent of your investments that you want to have in common stocks. If you are 40 years old, therefore, approximately 80 percent of your money should be in stocks and stock mutual funds. And, according to my formula, which is more a guideline than something carved in stone, you would have to reach the age of 120 before you stop investing in the stock market. (Because these are just guidelines, you don't have to make your stocks/bonds/cash reserves in perfect or exact ratio.)

Originally, I was more conservative about my formula: I used 100 as my base number, and so my clients had 20 percent less in stocks than they do now. I have adjusted this because I want to protect my clients from inflation and because the stock market continues to perform extraordinarily well. My recommended course has become more aggressive because, over the span of years, stocks clearly have appreciated in value far faster than the inflation rate. Inflation has been running lately at about three percent a year, while stocks have yielded an average of 10 percent per year total return (gain plus income). Bonds, meanwhile, have yielded roughly five and a quarter percent — slightly better than inflation.

According to my 120 formula, you should be in the stock market at every point in your life. Each person has differing needs, and the different times in your life lead to different kinds of investing. Most investing is not about greed or need: It is about saving and earning money for the future.

FOR YOUR RETIREMENT

I'll be the first to admit it: It's hard to make plans for the future when so much is unsure. For starters, few of us know how long we will live.

I recommend planning for the best case scenario — for a long, healthy life. Don't underestimate your own life span, as many people do. Don't decide to worry about your later years *later*. Perhaps your parents did die young. But we live in an advanced and sophisticated era for health and medicine. People frequently outlive their forebears because they don't smoke, or because they watch their diet more carefully, or because the U.S. is no longer a true manufacturing society any longer, and we suffer much less factory pollution and ill effects.

Above all else, medical technology makes it possible for us as human beings to overcome far more than we could even ten years ago. (My publisher refers to me as a "human Volvo: I'll roll on for 200,000 miles, but before the odometer stops, practically every part of the car will be replaced or repaired at least once.")

For all these reasons, I tell everyone to plan for as long a life as possible. The worst thing that can happen to you is to be older than you expected, and not have any money left. Stated another way, the financial risk of life is not that you will have a short life, but that you'll live a long one. If you're only going to live a few years, you probably have enough money to do whatever you wish. The financial risk is that, with better medicine and better nutrition, you will live a long life, but your money will run out before you do. The way to protect against that possibility is to have high quality stocks that raise their dividends every year to protect you against inflation.

Therefore, put as much money as you can into any retirement program offered you. Because these investment programs are tax-sheltered, their value compounds when you leave them alone. In some 401(k) plans, employers even match or supplement your contributions as an employee. Unfortunately, too many workers do not understand the benefits of such retirement programs, or such generous company contributions, and don't get or earn the money they deserve.

Right now, the biggest money we brokers see comes from retirement accounts. After a lifetime of saving, these accounts are often worth $300,000, $400,000, and more. When you put money into these programs week after week, paycheck after paycheck, the money builds up quickly. When they are a deferred part of your pay, your investment dollars are freer to grow than inheritance money. Because these retirement dollars escape income tax, I like to think of them as my windfall from Uncle Sam.

There is just one exception: Individual Retirement Account (IRA) money is generally *not* tax deductible if you are covered by another retirement plan. If you're not covered by another plan, you may deduct up to a certain level of income. In either case, when you retire, you can roll your retirement money into a self-directed IRA without paying the tax. Then, you are taxed only when you turn 70 1/2 (or if you took the money out earlier). At that age — 70 1/2 — you have to starting taking approximately 5 percent out of your IRA each year.

With the growth of small businesses in the United States, a growing number of employees do not have specific retirement plans at their place of work. If you are in such a situation, fight to get one. Eventually, all employers will need to have them in order to remain competitive in

LOUIS RUKEYSER AND ME ON MY 80TH

I have to admit it: I love TV. Every day I look forward to going on the WBAL-TV set. Every day I get a tremendous adrenaline rush when those two red lights go on and I'm on the air. On "Wall $treet Week With Louis Rukeyser," I always feel a tremendous rush. Except for the question from the viewer, which we get as panelists on Wednesday morning, everything is spontaneous and unrehearsed. I get so eager for the show that my boss has told me to come in completely unprepared, so that I have to listen to questions before I answer them. Sometimes, I get so excited that I launch into a whole speech without ever answering what Louis has asked.

Another confession: I also love seeing my name in print. In February of 1977, I launched my current print journalism career by suggesting a regular column, called "The Ticker," to the late Phil Heisler, then the managing editor at the Evening Sun. Over lunch, I pitched him the idea and gave him a few samples of what I wanted to do every Monday on financial news and the stock market. He agreed to it right away. Soon, the column became popular with readers, and I started writing it for publication two times a week, on Monday and Thursday (now Wednesday and Friday).

The column and I have survived five financial editors, four managing editors, and five publishers. In 20 years of writing "The Ticker," I missed only one deadline, despite trips, blizzards, illnesses, and detours — for open heart surgery. If I've learned anything, it's that you hold territory by occupying it.

Today, I have four careers: a column at the Baltimore Sun, my on-air work at WBAL radio and WBAL-TV (they're separate activities, though I do both in the same building), and my brokering job at Ferris Baker Watts. I wrote this book to preserve my memories, my father's teachings, and my collected knowledge. Perhaps, through this brief foray into the book-writing world, I can make a positive difference in people's lives now and long after I'm gone. ❧

the job market. If you can't make your employer set up a retirement program, invest as much money as you can in your IRA. The money is taxed when it comes from your paycheck and not invested, but it grows in the IRA tax-free.

Even if you don't have a lot of money to save, plan for your retirement. Social Security is not intended to fully finance your post-working years. If you need to pay your bills or take care of your family's basic needs, do so first. I believe that once services are rendered, you must and should pay for them immediately. But any money you can have deducted from your paycheck and put into a retirement program is a very worthy investment. In fact, you have an obligation to your family and yourself to look out for your future. In order to do this, I recommend giving up some "discretionary" spending, like an extra dinner out or an extra trip to the beach, and putting that money into a retirement account.

And, although planning early is the best system, it is never too late to begin planning for your retirement. The rule of 72 says you can divide the number 72 by the interest percentage rate on your money to get the number of years required for your money to double. For example, if you are getting 10 percent on your retirement money, it will double in 7.2 years. If you are getting 8 percent on your money, your money will double in 9 years. So you can calculate how many times your money will double depending on the rate at which your investment dollars are earning interest during the years before your planned retirement. If you start early, it could double or triple while sitting in your retirement account.

One way mutual funds help you plan for the future is by taking money regularly from your bank account — with your authorization. This type of direct deposit makes sure that some of your money gets put away into investment-related savings every month. Of course, direct deposit isn't for everyone. But it is a good way to force yourself to save and invest.

The mere existence of IRAs and 401(k) plans has had some interesting results in our society. More and more people want to retire when they are young — often younger than they can afford to. When your money is invested in a balanced portfolio, very conservatively count on netting a yearly spendable income of five percent. Thus, to generate a yearly income of $50,000, you must invest $1 million. Of course, it is possible to do better, if your stocks grow. Over the long pull, the "total return" on investments in the market (gain plus income) has been approximately 10 percent, so, in this way of thinking, you can figure on needing $500,000 to produce an income of $50,000 per year.

The problem is, you can't count on that sort of return every year in perpetuity; it is not a guarantee, and trends have a habit of turning around. Stocks do grow, but we have no way for sure of knowing when or how much. You could wait a long time to see growth in your stocks, and all that time you will not be making $50,000 per year.

Something else retirees frequently don't realize is that they will need an increasing income over the years to protect them against inflation. Bonds are useful, but, with them, no growth in income is possible, because bonds pay the same interest throughout their lives. A bond means that you lend your money to somebody; the income flow to you is fixed. That is why, for most retirement investment portfolios, you need a liberal helping of stocks and stock mutual funds, as well as a much smaller portion of fixed income generators. It's true that you get a high initial income from what we call fixed-income investments, which are CDs, bonds, corporate bonds, treasury bonds, etc. But what you don't get are two things that you really need in order to be well-off in retirement: you don't get any growth of principal and you don't get any growth of income.

You may not realize it, but we are in the middle of an investment frenzy fueled by baby-boomers. They, like everybody else, are investing in the market not because of greed. They are doing it for their own protection. They are afraid that, when it is time to retire, inflation will have destroyed their accumulated wealth. This new consciousness is causing big changes. Most people begin thinking seriously about retirement around age 49. As of 1992, there were 2.8 million 49 year-olds in this country. In 1997, there are 3.1 million. By the year 2010, there will be 4.1 million. And many of those turning 49 will be investing in earnest in the stock market a full 15-20 years before they retire. That points to a major increase in investments, which may well indicate that the market will continue to go up (hence, a DJA of 8,000 in 1997 could become about 20,000 in 2010). For this reason alone, now seems like a very good time

— perhaps one of the best ever — for investing in stocks. There is no way to tell if people will continue to invest in the market in such numbers with so many dollars. But if this trend continues, the stock market, by 2010, could double or triple from where it is now.

Another good thing about investing in stocks for retirement is that some of them pay increasing dividends over the years, no matter what happens to the stock market overall. Retirees' quality of life won't turn on whether the stock goes up or down. If their stock goes up, retirees won't eat an extra meal — until they sell the stock. But, if they have enough money invested in the right mix of stocks, they may be able to live on the dividends.

On average, stock dividends are now very low — much lower than they were back in the 1950s and 1960s. But that is not necessarily a bad thing. Dividends are now around 1.9 percent of the selling price of the average stock. But this is only because stock prices are so high. Low dividends often send a danger signal about the stock market, suggesting that stock prices are too high compared to earnings, and some people won't want to invest if they are not getting regular income from a stock dividend. Instead, they put their money into bonds and CDs. It is true that the stock market continues to go strong, despite the fact that many high technology stocks don't pay dividends at all. Still, I encourage buying stocks that raise their dividends every year, and there are a lot of them that still do.

Generally speaking, you should have about 10 percent of your money in cash. Fixed income investments, such as CDs, treasury bills, notes, and bonds, can make up the rest of your income portfolio. There is no possibility of losing when you invest this way, but you can also never gain more than the investment said you would earn in the beginning. The money that you make in a fixed income investment seems like a lot when you buy it far in advance. But often by the time you cash in that particular investment, it is not worth as much as it was before, and you haven't gained much. Still, there is virtually nowhere to put your money so it will be unaffected by inflation.

If inflation is rampant, there is no worse situation than to have your money worth its original value ten years later. That is the drawback of fixed income investments.

For fixed income investments, I recommend government bonds with a laddered maturity pattern. I would put the rest of your non-retirement fixed income savings into tax-free bonds so that your money can grow without being hindered by taxes.

FOR YOUR CHILD'S FUTURE

If you have enough money, I'm all in favor of being as financially generous to your children as you can. But, for the sake of family harmony, I also recommend making approximately the same sized gifts to every child. If you put your gifts in the form of stock, I even recommend putting all the money in the same stocks, so there is no resentment if one child's stock rises and the other's crashes. My friend's children chose their own stocks when they were young, and one stock far outdistanced the other in earnings. Because they chose them themselves, there was not a lot of resentment. But if you choose the stocks, put each child's money in the same one. You don't want one child coming to you in ten or twenty years to ask why he's the poor one in the family.

It's no big surprise that many parents see college education as one of the scarier goals of investment planning. When they think of saving enough to cover tuition costs, they probably sense that the sky is the limit — as if prices will never stabilize. If you have a child late in life, it is especially important to plan your retirement early, because you may end up paying for a college education *after* you retire. If you can afford it, start by giving the child some money every year, even when the child is very young. The more money you invest and the earlier you invest it, the easier the cost of college can be offset. Doing this also lowers your estate tax. However, I would not recommend giving away more money than you can afford to. My partners, Mark Dyer and Morry Zolet, often tell clients, "The best gift you can give your children is your own financial security so they never have to worry about you." I think they are right about that. You don't want to impoverish yourself, even for the highly worthy goal of paying for your child's college education.

If you do have more money than you think you will need to live on, give it to your children as you grow old. You are allowed to give $10,000 to as many people as you wish without filing a gift tax return. If you are married, you can give $20,000 to as many people as you like. That gift money is completely tax-free to the recipient because it is a gift. This lowers your estate tax and also allows you to watch your children enjoy your money.

If you are going to give these kinds of gifts, though, make sure to keep enough money in your own account to satisfy your own comfort level. Don't forget that you need to sleep nights, and, in a long life, there may be many more nights than you originally thought. If there is any risk that by giving away money to your children you will suffer later, do not do it. Your children will be okay and would rather see you self-supported than have extra dollars show up in their bank account. Only after you've done that old-fashioned but necessary thing of taking care of yourself should you be generous to the people you love.

When you are putting money away for the future, one thing I definitely do not recommend is putting your child's name on your stocks in a joint account. Some people do that so their child won't be taxed on inheritance. But that can really complicate things because your child will not always be young or a dependent. For example, you could put your daughter's name on your investments when she is young. Later on, if she gets married, her husband can say he wants half that money, and because they are now married, he can claim that he deserves it. Let your money be yours and your daughter's money be hers. Tying your money to a parent or a child is not a good idea, and it doesn't even save taxes, because estates under $600,000 were, until 1997, exempt from federal taxes. Under a 1997 Congressional enactment, estates under $1,000,000 will now be exempt. Most people don't have that kind of money.

And, of course, be sure you have an updated will. Let *it* govern where your money goes after you're gone.

OTHER PEOPLE'S MONEY

Non-profit entities like charities often need to invest, just as individuals do, but they are very different from individuals. If you are on the board of a non-profit organization, as I was for many years, you have to be a little more careful than if you are managing your own investments. You might miss some big investing opportunities because they are too risky, but the most important thing is to cautiously make sure you protect the organization's assets. A non-profit often has to live off its investments, while a working person can go out and earn money if too much money is risked and lost by investing.

One other thing: When forming an investment committee for a non-profit group, pick people who are sophisticated in the investment world: bankers, brokers, and investment managers. Inexperienced investors can be too cautious or too ruthless to handle the necessary risks of non-profit investing.

FOR RICHER, FOR POORER

Women are something of a new element in the stock market. Currently, sixty percent of all women in the United States work outside of the home. Many of them now have the challenge of investing their own 401(k)s, doing their own pension plans, figuring out their own investments for the future. In the past, men were the dominant players when it came to stocks. But today, women are more influential in the stock market than ever.

I have always felt that women make good stock pickers, partly because they are often the main consumers in the home. In many cases, they do the shopping, they choose the products, they clip the coupons and watch the advertisements, and they talk to other women about the products they use. In a simpler, less technical way, they analyze product competitors. I consider women a very welcome addition to the stock market. When they use their intuition, like stock brokers did in the old days, they are often quite successful. When they learn the basics of investing, they perform as well as men, if not better. In investment clubs, many of them organized by women, they are going great guns. In the next 20 years, women will be just as big a force in the investment world as men.

Some married couples set up joint stock accounts, and for people just beginning in the stock market, I recommend that. But, I wouldn't want a joint account set up where only one member of the couple takes an interest in and control of the investments.

Some spouses, and mostly men, don't share their financial information with their wives. They seem to think they have the divine right to take care of the family finances alone. But sharing this information with your spouse is important for so many reasons. First of all, history has shown that men are more likely to die first in a marriage. When a wife is left with the financial portfolio after the husband dies, she can be easy prey in a financial jungle. Many a widow has come to me in tears and said, "My husband never told me about the family finances." All too often, they're right. My own mother never knew much about the family stocks and bonds. My father always told me I would have to take care of my mother if he died first. Not involving your spouse in investment and financial decisions is a mistake — not only because she is left out, but also because men and women sometimes see things differently, and this can help diversify and solidify a portfolio. I have not seen enough teams where husband and wife work together to invest.

If your spouse does not seem inclined to share this financial information with you, it is time that you ask some very spirited questions. Doing so can help save you much heartache in a very difficult time. For example:

- Do you owe any money?

- Where are the stocks and bonds physically located?

- When can you and I look at our list of stocks and bonds together?

- When can I provide some valuable input?

- Where is the family safe deposit box and where are the keys kept?

- When did you most recently update your will?

- Who is your broker, and when can I meet him or her with you?

- Who is the trust officer at the bank to whom I will be going if something happens to you, to find out how your estate is to be settled?

- Exactly what does your will say about me? How will I be provided for?

- If your earnings stop, how much money will I receive to keep the wheels turning for the first six months? And then for the next five years? (Ask for specific numbers.)

I strongly believe that this information should be out in the open so everyone is taken care of and the right things are provided for in the event of someone's untimely demise. It is your right and your obligation to know how you will be provided for.

Every December, I make out a list called "Where Things Are." On it is such information as: Where my bank accounts are, what stocks and bonds I own and where they are located, who my lawyer is and what his telephone number is, the name of the person who manages my family trust investments, what insurance policies I hold, and where my safe deposit box is and who has the keys. I don't include the number or any really personal information. I give this list to my wife, my lawyer, my accountant, and my secretary. I also put a copy in my safe deposit box. I feel good after I complete this list. It gives me the feeling that whoever I leave behind won't be puzzled as to where my stuff is and what it means.

If you survive your spouse, definitely go to a broker to discuss your investments and find out how, if necessary, to reorganize your spouse's portfolio. Even a very successful portfolio for a married couple is probably not appropriate for a widow or widower. When such widows or widowers come to me, we reconstruct the original portfolio, which is now usually a package of stock certificates at a brokerage firm or in a safe-deposit box. I usually have three meetings with those who have lost their spouse. The first visit is to find out the financial situation of the surviving spouse, and his or her needs or wants. The second is for more fact-finding: putting together the existing portfolio and also learning about insurance, social security, and other benefits. Then I usually sit down with a committee in my firm and together we redesign the portfolio. I usually schedule another appointment within 10 or 14 days. At this third appointment, I make my recommendations.

The death of a spouse is often a serious financial change in the survivor's life. If the deceased member of the family was working, and was the family's sole source of income, the portfolio may need to be reorganized so it brings in income on which the surviving spouse can live. One widow came to me after the death of her husband, whose job brought in $70,000 a year. She had no earnings at all, and I had to explain that she needed a lot of different stocks to produce an income she could live on. I also told her that her lifestyle was going to be changed by a significant drop in income, because, with the amount of money she had, producing $70,000 a year from stock investments would require some very risky investments, which was not appropriate for her. I put her in some safe income-oriented securities, treasury bonds, and some common stocks which pay good dividends and hedge against inflation.

AS YOU GROW OLD

I have found that older people get less ambitious about their money as they age. This is because they are frightened of losing what they have. (In the old days, this was called "going to the poorhouse.") Those of us who lived through the Depression fear losing everything — and never recovering, because we saw it happen to some of our friends and family. As an older person myself, I have the same fears. But I have learned that I can't let my emotions completely control me when it comes to my money.

People who aren't comfortable in the stock market shouldn't be in it. Intellectually, they may know that most stock drops are temporary, not permanent, and that, in general, stocks grow in value. But if they see something bad happen, and immediately translate it into a catastrophe, and panic, they probably shouldn't be in stocks.

If you use my 120 formula, it is quite hard to lose all the money you have invested. At the very least, money invested in bonds and other fixed income investments will be safe and you won't be left empty-handed. As I say again and again, your own emotions are the best "reverse indicator" of what you should be doing in the market. When the market is bad, clients call to complain, "Why have you given me so many stocks?" Then, when the market is good, they ask, "Why don't I have a greater percentage of my portfolio in stocks?" Second guessing, especially at the last minute, is often the worst thing you can do — in investing as in other aspects of life.

I have a personal example of a mistake I made partly because of my emotions. When Hillary Clinton was developing her health reform package in 1993, I grew very concerned. I foresaw a lot of new government regulation of drug prices. So I sold some of my stock in Merck, which is one of the finest drug companies in the world, figuring it would be badly hurt by passage of the proposed legislation. But I got too emotional. When I sharply cut my holdings in Merck, I hadn't considered the possibility that Mrs. Clinton's reform package might not pass. It didn't, and I lost a lot of gain because Merck just went sailing along. Not thinking through that decision, which I made at a weak moment right after my open-heart surgery, was a painful experience, and still is.

One thing elderly people can do to protect themselves from their emotions is to delegate their investment power to someone they trust. If you are a child of elderly parents, it might be your responsibility to take care of their investment decisions. While your parents are in good health, they should give general power of attorney to you, or to whomever they want to manage their money and financial affairs.

A lawyer can explain in greater detail, but, for all intents and purposes, having general power of attorney means you can do anything you want — within reason — with the elderly person's possessions. When your parents begin to lose their discerning faculties, it is tough not having power of attorney. If they can't act, or if they act irrationally, no one can prevent them from giving away all their money, or worse. Con artists can and do take advantage of vulnerable elderly people just by being friendly and presenting a deal that looks good. Unscrupulous telemarketers can trick elderly people into making stock transactions that bring very high commissions. If you have general power of attorney, none of this can be done without your consent.

As you get older, you should give power of attorney to someone who can buy and sell securities for you, make your charitable donations, and do things that you can't or just don't want to do for yourself anymore. I have seen too many elderly people who have not delegated authority. Their stock certificates get lost. Their dividend checks are not cashed or deposited.

When you get old, you can act irresponsibly. You can be stricken. You can have a stroke. You can have a heart attack. You can have an undiagnosed case of Alzheimer's. You can lose important items. You can indiscriminately give valuable possessions away to people who prey on you. The one best way to keep all that from happening is also very simple: Give power of attorney to somebody who will truly look out for you, who will go to bat for you when you need it.

CHAPTER SUMMARY:
SAVINGS AND EARNINGS FOR YOUR FUTURE

1. *Plan for a long, healthy life. The worst thing that can happen is to live longer than you expected and not have any money left to support yourself.*

2. *Put as much money as you can into any retirement program offered you, even if you don't have a lot of money to invest. Plan early if you can, but know that it is never too late to start planning for the future.*

3. *Be as generous to your children as you can afford. Begin planning for college by giving your children money even at a very early age, and continue to give them money as they grow older. This lowers your estate tax and also allows you to watch your children enjoy the money. Remember, though: Your first obligation is to support yourself. The best gift you can give your children is your own financial security (so they don't have to support you).*

4. *Non-profit companies have to be more careful about managing their investments. They can't lose their nest egg, because they can't simply go out and earn more. An investment committee for a non-profit group should be composed of sophisticated investors: bankers, brokers, and investment managers.*

5. *If your spouse is the "investor of the family," make sure you have all the pertinent information about the family finances.*

6. *If you aren't comfortable in the stock market, don't be in it. However, if you follow my formula of 120, it will be all but impossible to lose all the money you invest.*

7. *As you get older, give power of attorney to someone you trust so they can make your investments, charitable donations, and other money decisions for you.*

For every type of person at every time and place in life, there is a different way to save and invest. You must act based on your own situation and your own aspirations. You must make decisions based not only on where you are in life, but where you hope and plan to be in 20, 40, or 60 years.

This book has been a sampler of the different places you could be and the different kinds of investment decisions you may need to make.

Wherever you are in life, wherever you want to get, I wish you good fortune. As for me, I hope to be here a long time to do what I've enjoyed doing for so many years: "Answering your money and investment questions."

Julius Westheimer

Appendix

60 REASONS WHY PEOPLE DID <u>NOT</u> INVEST IN THE STOCK MARKET

1934	Depression	1964	Gulf of Tonkin
1935	Spanish Civil War	1965	Civil Rights Marches
1936	Economy Still Struggling	1966	Vietnam War Escalates
1937	Recession	1967	Newark Race Riots
1938	War Clouds Gather	1968	USS Pueblo Seized
1939	War In Europe	1969	Money Tightens — Markets Fall
1940	France Falls	1970	Cambodia Invaded
1941	Pearl Harbor		— Vietnam War Spreads
1942	Wartime Price Controls	1971	Wage Price Freeze
1943	Industry Mobilizes	1972	Largest US Trade Deficit Ever
1944	Consumer Goods Shortages	1973	Energy Crisis
1945	Post-War Recession Predicted	1974	Watergate
1946	Dow Tops 200	1975	Resource Shortages
	— Market Too High	1976	Limit to Long-term Growth
1947	Cold War Begins	1977	Inflation Increases
1948	Berlin Blockade	1978	Interest Rates Rise
1949	Russia Explodes A-Bomb	1979	Oil Prices Skyrocket
1950	Korean War	1980	Interest Rates at All-Time Highs
1951	Excess Profits Tax	1981	Steep Recession Begins
1952	U.S. Seizes Steel Mills	1982	Worst Recession in 40 Years
1953	Russia Explodes H-Bomb	1983	Market Hits New Highs
1954	Dow Tops 360	1984	Record Federal Deficits
	— Market Too High	1985	Economic Growth Slows
1955	Eisenhower Illness	1986	Dow Nears 2000
1956	Suez Crisis		— Market Too High
1957	Russia Launches Sputnik	1987	Market Declines 20% in One Day
1958	Recession	1988	Savings & Loan Crisis
1959	Castro Seizes Power in Cuba	1989	Bank Failures Increase
1960	Russia Downs U-2 Plane	1990	Persian Gulf Crisis
1961	Berlin Wall Erected	1991	Dow Tops 3000
1962	Cuban Missile Crisis		— Market Too High
1963	Kennedy Assassinated	1992	Global Recession
		1993	Health Care Reform

AND ONE GOOD REASON YOU SHOULD INVEST:

$10,000 invested in the Stock Market (S&P 500) in January 1934 would have been worth nearly **$6,627,000** in 1993.

49-YEAR-OLDS AND THEIR IMPACT ON INVESTING

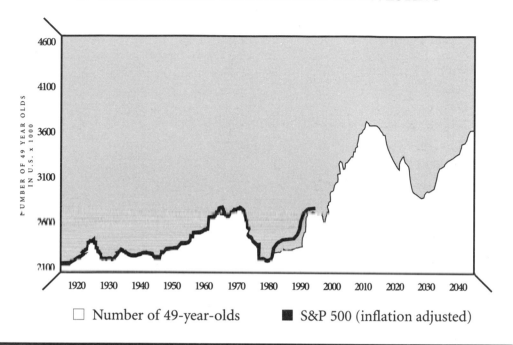

☐ Number of 49-year-olds   ■ S&P 500 (inflation adjusted)

WHY BUY STOCKS THAT PAY INCREASING DIVIDENDS

	1987	1989	1991	1993	1995	1997	Increase Since '87
BG&E	1.25	1.39	1.40	1.47	1.56	1.60	28%
Bell Atlantic	1.92	2.20	2.52	2.68	2.80	2.96	54%
Exxon	1.90	2.30	2.68	2.88	3.00	3.16	66%
Bristol Meyers	1.40	2.00	2.40	2.88	2.96	3.04	117%
Proctor & Gamble	0.68	0.75	0.98	1.10	1.40	1.80	164%

LONG-TERM EQUITY PERFORMANCE
VS. OTHER ASSETS

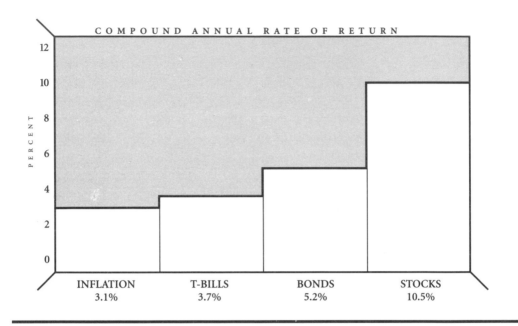

COMPOUND ANNUAL RATE OF RETURN

	INFLATION	T-BILLS	BONDS	STOCKS
	3.1%	3.7%	5.2%	10.5%

A 200-YEAR HISTORY OF LONG-TERM BOND RATES
30-year U.S. Government Bonds, 1790-1993

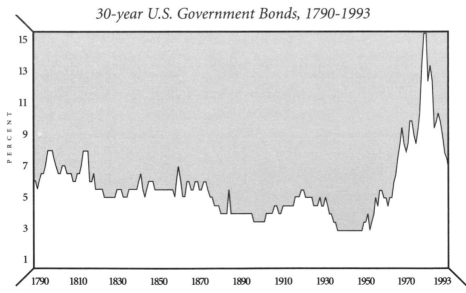

Index

120-Formula: 134, 135, 139, 209, 210, 222, 226

401(k): 8, 10, 18, 108, 122, 123, 156, 180, 192, 210, 215, 220

403(b): 8, 180, 195

Annual report: 85, 90, 92, 93, 98, 110, 207

Annuities: 156-58, 161

Barron's: 80, 83, 84, 86, 104-5, 109, 127, 128, 150, 162

Bonds: 19, 20, 27, 28, 31, 37-39, 45-46, 88-92, 96, 106, 123-26, 130, 133-51

Bearer bonds: 88

Bond funds: 130-31

"Bonds-only" investors: 135

Corporate bonds: 142-45

County bonds: 145

Coupon bonds: 147-48

Government bonds: 27, 28, 38, 131-38, 144-46, 150, 151, 161, 218, 232

Junk bonds: 39, 143-44

Registered bonds: 89

State bonds: 146-47, 161

Tax-free bonds: 5, 38, 46, 90, 137, 147, 218

Treasury bills, notes, and bonds: 137-38, 217

U.S. Savings Bonds: 138

Zero coupon bonds: 147-48

And interest rates: 80, 95-6, 100, 129, 131, 138-42, 147-48, 157, 161

And money market accounts: 148-51 (see also Money Market Accounts)

And staggered maturities: 139-42

Capital gains taxes: 79, 96, 192-93

Certificates of Deposit (CDs): 21, 80, 95, 106, 151-53, 162, 199, 216-17

Commissions: 35, 40, 41, 66, 71, 83, 86, 122, 129, 132, 177, 183, 225

Corporate reports: 92-94

Dow Jones Industrial Average: 180, 184

Dow Five theory: 3, 5, 19, 39, 180-85, 187

Dow Ten theory: 3, 5, 180-85

Earnings Per Share: 80, 201, 203

Fixed Income investing: 133, 216

Forbes: 52, 107, 113, 114, 128

Fortune: 107, 114

Individual Retirement Accounts (IRAs): 20, 36, 110, 142, 213, 156, 158, 192, 213-15

Initial Public Offerings (IPOs): 176-78, 202

Investment clubs: 67-70, 219

Investment counseling firms: 35, 44

Investment managers: 24, 55, 129, 220, 226 (see also Stockbrokers)

Kiplinger's Personal Finance: 106, 107, 124, 151, 162

Money Magazine: 106, 110, 123, 151, 160

Money Market Accounts: 14, 28, 45, 148-51, 161

Moody's: 82, 139, 144, 146

Morningstar: 125, 126, 129

Mutual Funds: 19, 32, 56, 67, 70, 83, 84, 86, 94, 103, 113, 119-32, 157, 158, 164, 184, 195, 207, 211, 215, 216

Bond Mutual Funds: 130-31, 132

For savings: 122

Index funds: 128, 132

In your 401(k): 123-25

International funds: 122, 124, 130

Load funds: 86, 130

No-load funds: 83, 86, 119, 123, 129, 132

Ratings for: 125-26

Sector funds: 129

NASDAQ: 75, 76, 81, 105

New York Stock Exchange (NYSE): 44, 63, 78, 119, 132, 183

New York Times: 104, 108, 109, 142

Portfolio shaping and advice: 5, 16, 20, 24, 25, 27, 37, 40, 42, 44, 58-59, 62, 64, 68, 97, 121-22, 134, 137-39, 148, 156, 161, 172, 176, 180, 189209, 217

Precious metals: 159-60, 162

Price/earnings (P/E) Ratio: 76, 81, 82, 86, 106, 199, 200-2, 205, 209

Proxy Statements: 94

Real Estate Investment Trusts (REITs): 153-56

Research reports, from a brokerage firm: 206-8

Risk Tolerance: 19-20, 24, 26-29, 55

Rule of 72: 157, 215

Securities: 4, 54, 71, 73, 90, 114, 143, 150, 223, 225

Standard & Poor's: 52, 81, 112, 139, 144

Stockbrokers, initial interview: 36-7, 40

Occasional negligence of: 71

Qualities of good: 56-65, 115

When to Stay and When to Leave: 58-65

Value Line: 82, 175, 201

bancroft
press

For discounted bulk purchases of this book,
please contact Bancroft Press at 800 . 637 . 7377

PRAISE FOR JULIUS WESTHEIMER

JULIUS WESTHEIMER'S new book delivers! Some fascinating insights from a real "pro" on how to make money in stocks and bonds and, more importantly, how to keep it!

> — FRANK CAPPIELLO, Chairman, Cappiello-Rushmore Mutual Funds
> and President, McCullough, Andrews & Cappiello, Inc., Investment Advisors

JULIUS WESTHEIMER brings to the business of investing not just the experience and insights of an octogenarian sage but the warmth and candor that have so endeared him to our television audience. In a business where juveniles claim infallibility after a couple of years of getting lucky, Westy reminds us that nobody's perfect (even your friendly neighborhood stockbroker) but that patience and common sense are two of the most effective weapons in anyone's portfolio.

> — LOUIS RUKEYSER, host *Wall $treet Week With Louis Rukeyser*
> and editor in chief *Louis Rukeyser's Wall Street*
> and *Louis Rukeyser's Mutual Funds*

JUST THE KIND OF LUCID, articulate, and sensible book I'd expect from Julius Westheimer.

> — SUSAN LAUBACH, investment counselor and author of
> *The Whole Kitt & Caboodle: A Painless Journey to Investment Enlightenment*

AUTHORITATIVE, FACT-FILLED, and easy to read, *Generation of Wealth* is a valuable and useful guide for all investors, especially novices. By digesting the book's contents, investors not only benefit from Julius Westheimer's wisdom and years of experience in the complex world of finance. They practically gain their own private broker.

> — DR. CARLA HAYDEN, Director, Enoch Pratt Free Library
> and *Library Journal* "Librarian of the Year 1995"